The Workshop Approach:
A Framework for Literacy

The Workshop Approach: A Framework for Literacy

Elinor Parry Ross

Christopher-Gordon Publishers, Inc.
Norwood, Massachusetts

CREDITS

Every effort has been made to contact copyright holders for permission to reproduce borrowed material where necessary. We apologize for nay oversights and would be happy to rectify them in future printings.

The Author would like to thank the following students whose work appears in the following pages:

David Allen	Bailey Garrett	Julie Longhurst
Kendra Apple	Luis Hernández Gil	Shannon McCawley
Kristen Berk	Amber Griggs	Erin Phillips
Jill Birdwell	Charles Hancock	Ben Smith
John Brady	Heather Hubbard	Clayton Smith
Meghan Breeden	James Humphreys	Kristin Stamps
Hannah Brown	Colyn C. Hunt	Rachel Strong
Rusty Burt	Matthew Johnston	Cara Treadway
Jaima Del Monaco	Misty Julian	Trudy Walker
Philip Dixon	Raushan Kharif	Jill Willis
Sacha Duke	Sun-Hee Kim	Anna Winfree
Christen Fulk	Michael Koffas	Stephanie Wingert

Christopher-Gordon Publishers, Inc.
480 Washington Street
Norwood, MA 02062

Printed in the United States of America

10 9 8 7 6 5 4 3 2 1   00 99 98 97 96

ISBN: 0-926842-50-52-8

SHORT CONTENTS

Contents

ACKNOWLEDGMENTS

This book has been a pleasure to write because of my enthusiasm for the subject and the cooperation of so many individuals. From the time I first met Hiram Howard at IRA, the people at Christopher-Gordon trusted me to create this book on a topic they knew little about. Since then Beth Cronin and Sue Canavan guided me through the publishing procedures, and the reviewers, Suzanne Fiebig, Dr. Lorraine Gerhart, Ronnie Lee, and Dr. Carol M. Santa provided helpful suggestions.

The students whose work is included throughout this handbook and their teachers deserve much credit for supplying me with ideas and materials. When I visited classrooms, I sometimes spoke directly with students, asking them if I could listen in on their conferences or if they would explain to me how they get their ideas for writing. Teachers were very cooperative in arranging times for me to visit, making copies of students' work, and helping me obtain parental permissions.

Although I had many teachers who helped along the way, I'd like to mention a few in particular. Holly Martin was the first to show me how to run a workshop when I visited her class several years ago, and on my return visit this year she shared new insights about conferring and conducting mini-lessons. Arlee Freeman convinced me just how successful writing workshops can be at the second grade level as I watched her children conduct themselves like little professionals as they wrote, conferred, and used the author's chair. Thanks also to Jill Ramsey, who always kept handy a folder of children's work that she though might interest me, and to Joy McCaleb who demonstrated her way of running a workshop with seventh graders. For the past few years I have learned much about workshops by watching my daughter-in-law, Stacy Ross, who invites her kindergartners to write with invented spelling, confer with her and with their peers, and read independently.

I also want to mention my Australian teacher friends from whom I learned so much about whole language. Dr. Marie Emmitt devoted several days to taking me to visit teachers in schools in the Melbourne area, of whom Lesley Wing Jan was an exemplary model of teaching for literacy. I also gained much understanding of how whole language works in small, rural schools when I visited several of those near Sale, Victoria. On a later visit, I met Debbie Sukarna, who not only let us visit exciting whole language classrooms at Ivanhoe Boys' Grammar School, but also spent time sharing ideas and materials with us.

I want to thank my husband Jim, who was always there when I called for help with the computer or printer, and who patiently tolerated my spending all night on the computer *again*. Thanks also to my colleagues at Tennessee Technological University who supported and encouraged my efforts.

PREFACE

In this book you will find a framework for teaching reading and writing through the workshop approach. The book is primarily for teachers in kindergarten through eighth grade, although I have used some examples from higher grades. Beginning teachers will find it helpful, as well as those who have been teaching for many years and are seeking new and better ways to help students acquire literacy. The book is for teachers who are new to the concept of the reading/writing workshop, as well as for those who already know about it but want to understand it better.

This book is a practical handbook with many reproducible pages and samples of student work. The first chapter deals with the very important theoretical base—the *why* comes before the *how.* The remaining chapters demonstrate ways to implement the workshop approach by dealing with general procedures, reading and writing workshop activities and mini-lessons, conferences, management and organization, and evaluation.

I'm using vignettes about two classroom teachers, Amy and Kevin, to open each chapter so that you can trace their progress as they set up workshops in their classrooms. The introduction gives key points to notice as you read the chapter, and the summary recalls the main ideas. Since I believe that true change occurs only through reflection, I have ended each chapter with a section that asks you to examine your beliefs.

During my visits to dozens of classrooms in Australia and the United States, I observed belief systems and practices that are compatible with the workshop approach. I visited schools in rural and urban areas, in special education and English-as-a-Second-Language classrooms, and in grades K through 8. I will use examples from these classrooms and from my own experiences. I have taught mini-lessons in the public schools and modeled the workshop approach in my college classes. Teachers have taught me a lot; most of them find workshops to be very effective ways to teach, but many are faced with problems to work through. Ideas also come from wide reading in professional journals and books and from conference presentations.

Nancie Atwell's classic *In the Middle* introduced many of us to the reading/writing workshop. Since then we have taken her ideas and adapted them for our own classes. Her workshop approach is a model, an ideal, and we must each find our own ways to make it work for us. Other writers who have mad significant contributions to the concepts in this book include Jane Hansen, Donald Graves, Carol Avery, Lucy Calkins, Linda Rief, and Shelley Harwayne.

This handbook provides suggestions and guidelines for creating your own reading/writing workshop. Workshop teachers tell me that they modify their procedures each year, depending on responses from their students and their deepening understanding of the theoretical base. Keep in mind the underlying principles, experiment with ways to implement them, and discover an exciting way to teach!

CHAPTER 1

CONSTRUCTING A FOUNDATION

September 17

Amy and Kevin approached the soft drink machine by the faculty lounge at the same time. As they inserted their coins and made their selections, they began discussing last summer's conference that had introduced them to new ways to teach reading and writing.

Amy: I was really fired up last summer to try some of those great ideas about using a reading/writing workshop approach with my second graders, but now I'm not so sure. I would have to do a lot of planning and reorganizing—and suppose it didn't work!

Kevin: I really want to do something different with my fifth grade language arts classes, and I think the reading/writing workshop might be just the answer. Maybe we should both give it a try.

Amy: I have a lot of notes and I've started thinking about ways I could begin. I'm not sure enough about how it would work to plunge right in, but I might use basal lessons Mondays, Wednesdays, and Fridays and do workshops on Tuesdays and Thursdays.

Kevin: That sounds reasonable to me—I know you've always used the basal so I suppose that would make you feel more comfortable in the beginning. I might begin gradually too, perhaps with just one class.

Amy: I really believe what the presenters told us last summer about how children learn—that they need time to read and write and that they need some sense of ownership of their work. All of that makes sense, and the workshop approach supports these beliefs.

Kevin: After the presenters recommended Nancie Atwell's *In the Middle* so strongly, I bought a copy and read it. For her, it worked really well. I'm not sure I can ever be that successful, but I believe there are some things I can do that will make reading and writing more absorbing for my students—and more interesting for me!

Amy: You've convinced me. I'm going to get started. I think my students will benefit, and I believe I'll be more effective as a teacher.

Introduction

Amy and Kevin are typical of many teachers these days who are searching for more effective ways to teach reading and writing. They are aware of innovative teaching strategies based on research about how children acquire literacy, but they are somewhat reluctant to abandon the strategies they have been using. Once they make the commitment to a new concept and have someone else's support, however, teachers like Amy and Kevin often discover a new approach to be immensely rewarding.

By providing a theoretical basis for the reading/writing workshop, this chapter lays the groundwork for the rest of the book. The following points will be made:

- Growth in literacy proceeds along a developmental continuum.
- The learner is at the center of the learning process.
- To acquire literacy children should be immersed in reading and writing.
- Learning is most effective when the curriculum is integrated.
- Literature serves as a basis for instruction.
- Children learn through social interactions.

Overview of the Reading/Writing Workshop

The reading/writing workshop is a framework for organizing reading and writing activities without resorting to workbook pages and skill sheets. It engages students in the actual processes of reading and writing during most of the class period. Although the approach varies considerably at different grade levels and as used by different teachers, the workshop generally consists of four phases: minilesson, status-of-the-class report, workshop (the major part of the class period), and group share. Each of these stages is discussed in Chapter 2.

Although the framework for reading and writing workshops is the same, I will be treating each one separately. Both reading and writing, along with oral language, occur in each, but there is clearly a difference in focus. The reading workshop focuses on learning how to read and appreciating fine literature, whereas the writing workshop stresses building proficiency in writing. Some teachers prefer the term *language lab* or *language workshop*, which perhaps represents the concept more accurately because of the interactive nature of the language arts in any workshop situation.

This approach is truly a workshop: a place where students are reading and writing according to individual needs, purposes, and interests. The order and structure of a traditional classroom are lacking, and the teacher models and facilitates rather than directs. Although there is indeed a framework and teachers rightfully hold expectations for student work, students are much more in control

of their learning than in traditional classes. Although most valida-
tion of the workshop approach comes from the testimony of teachers who have used it, there is limited research to support its use.
Second graders participating in an independent reading and writing
program in a collaborative setting improved their writing ability,
sense of story structure, vocabulary, comprehension, and language
complexity (Morrow, Sharkey, and Firestone, 1993). Kathleen Swift
(1993) reported that, as a result of participation in the reading
workshop, her sixth graders' attitudes toward reading improved
and their Gates-MacGinitie Reading Test scores increased significantly. Also, Paula Sissel found that her seventh and eighth graders, one third of whom were eligible for Chapter 1 services,
responded to the reading workshop enthusiastically by choosing
good books and reading more. They also increased their achievement
scores in language arts on the Comprehensive Tests of Basic Skills.

In an address to the National Council of Teachers of English,
Donald Graves (1994) stressed the importance of creating a literate environment. He said you don't *get* kids to do things, but you
invite them to learn. By enthusiasm and example, the teacher creates an atmosphere for the student to appreciate the value of reading and writing. In order to issue the invitation, the teacher must be
a model of literacy, then be prepared to listen and remain open to
possibilities. The reading/writing workshop is just the sort of place
where a literate environment can flourish.

What an exciting place for students to learn! Freedom to make
choices, student-centered learning, collaboration with peers, and
immersion in reading and writing—all are essential for the workshop. As you understand the theory on which the workshop is based
and as you learn ways to implement that theory, I believe that you
will discover the workshop approach to be an effective way to teach
students to love to read and write.

The Theoretical Base

Without a knowledge of theory and research, a teacher's use of an
approach to literacy is incomplete. Understanding how children
learn and why some techniques are more suitable than others provides a foundation. The workshop is more than a set of procedures; it is a method of implementing current views of how children
learn to read and write. The developmental continuum is the foundation, and research-based concepts about language learning are
the building blocks on which the workshop approach rests. (See
Figure 1.1.)

Developmental Continuum

Each child's learning unfolds naturally and proceeds continuously,
moving in an orderly sequence, with considerable differences from

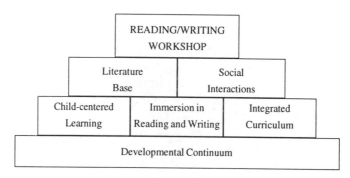

Figure 1.1:   Foundation and Building Blocks for the Reading/
Writing Workshop

individual to individual. From infancy, children respond to conditions in their environment that enable them to acquire the skills and knowledge they need to use. Schools, therefore, should provide a nurturing environment that enables students to proceed with their intellectual and social growth along the developmental continuum.

Teachers who understand this concept realize that children build on what they already know. Children learn what interests them and has meaning for them, and they emulate the practices of others whose skills they want to use (Holdaway, 1979). For instance, if they see someone reading a book that they would like to read for themselves, they watch carefully and absorb all they can about reading that book.

In actual practice, this means that teachers should be aware of the developmental levels of their students in choosing their goals and methods. They should consider children's experiential backgrounds, attention spans, levels of literacy, and readiness for learning new concepts. Thus, there will be considerable variation in the way teachers implement the reading/writing workshop as they recognize the needs and abilities of students at various stages of development.

Child-centered Learning

In keeping with the developmental continuum, the child should be at the center of the learning process. The child's readiness for learning, interests, and purposes should determine the curriculum, not the other way around.

Children should feel a sense of ownership, or empowerment, that allows them to make choices about much of their learning, within reasonable guidelines. Brian Cambourne (1988) believes that students should make decisions about when, how, and what pieces of information to learn in any task. For example, they might be able to choose what books to read, where to read them, how to respond to them, and with whom to share them. They could make decisions about their writing—what topics to choose, how to develop their pieces, and appropriate forms for publication. In a study of second graders involved in independent reading and writing, the freedom to choose was as important to them as many of the other features of the program (Morrow, Sharkey, and Firestone, 1993).

For many of us, one of the most difficult things to do is to share control. It's so easy to be in charge, to decide from our vast experience and continuing education what's best for our students. But they learn by making their own decisions whenever possible, and in so doing they develop a sense of responsibility and ownership.

Immersion in Reading and Writing

As we so often hear, children learn to read by reading and to write by writing. This makes sense. If we want to play the piano, we learn by playing it, not by completing worksheets on music theory.

Support for this belief comes from many sources. In *Becoming a Nation of Readers* Richard Anderson and colleagues (1985) state that independent reading is related positively to gains made in reading achievement. In his model of literacy learning, Brian Cambourne (1988) recommends immersion in all kinds of text and provision for time and opportunities for learners to use their literacy skills in meaningful ways. Citing a number of studies, Lesley Morrow and colleagues (1993) found gains in reading achievement and attitudes toward reading among students who do a substantial amount of independent reading. Similarly, Nancie Atwell (1987) insists that sufficient time to read and write is essential for growth in literacy. When writing, students need plenty of "think" time; when reading, they need time to become absorbed in fine books.

Finding this time for reading and writing becomes difficult when we, as teachers, feel that we must *teach* all of the skills mandated for our grade levels, or when we are pressured into having our students perform well on skill-based achievement tests. What we come to realize, however, is that through participation in workshops, students *learn* for themselves most of these skills by figuring them out on their own as they read and write, from the mini-lessons we plan in response to their needs, and through conferences with us or their peers.

Integrated Curriculum

Ken Goodman (1986, p. 30) says that "integration is a key principle for language development and learning through language." Goodman believes that language is learned easiest and best when it is learned naturally as part of a meaningful context. This holistic view of language learning is supported in the reading/writing workshop which enables students to connect reading and writing with oral language and with learning in the content areas.

In a prototypical Australian school, literacy instruction is interwoven with all other curricular activities. Students may be working on the same project, but they are reading different texts and reacting to them differently in keeping with their objectives (van Kraayenoord and Paris, 1994).

Teachers in self-contained classrooms, such as Amy in the vignette, find it easier to integrate content area studies with the reading/writing workshop than do teachers in departmentalized schools, such as Kevin. In order for Kevin to connect workshop activities with studies in other areas of the curriculum, he must become familiar with what other teachers are teaching in science, math, and social studies. Then, by providing related materials and encouraging students to apply their knowledge from these areas, he, too, can correlate language learning with content area instruction.

Literature-based Instruction

Because of its wide appeal and availability in any subject area, literature can enrich language learning. A report from the National Reading Research Center (Morrow, Sharkey, and Firestone, 1993) cites several studies to support this belief. Carol Chomsky's early research showed that young children exposed to literature learn to use sophisticated vocabulary and syntax, and D. A. Cohen found that exposure to children's literature improves both language development and success in reading. When children become acquainted with literature, Dolores Durkin found that they learn a great deal of background knowledge about content and also learn how language works.

Literature is an essential component of both reading and writing workshops. Of course, we realize that literature is the backbone of the reading workshop, but good books also inspire and serve as models for writers. By examining the styles and language patterns of favorite authors, students improve their own writing.

Providing the class with a wide variety of high-quality literature can be a problem for some teachers. Librarians can help, and so can parents. Ways of selecting and acquiring good books are discussed in Chapter 9.

Social Interactions

Social cooperation in language learning occurs as children communicate with each other about their reading, writing, and ordinary events. From the feedback they receive, they adjust their understanding of how language works. Without social interaction, children would have far fewer opportunities to observe and experiment with language in action.

Some classes become communities of learners where students feel comfortable enough to take risks with their oral and written language. Because they aren't afraid of ridicule or the teacher's red pen, they openly express their thoughts and feelings with language they find appropriate for each situation. In such an environment, trust and respect flourish, thus enabling growth in literacy.

For some of us who have been traditional teachers, the social interactions that occur in workshops may at first be overwhelming. We are no longer front and center, but instead we move quietly about the room as facilitators, conferring with students, helping them find materials, and enabling them to put forth their best efforts. Although the classroom is organized, it is not orderly. Students are reading and writing wherever they are comfortable; some are conferring with their peers; others are moving about the room searching for words, ideas, or books. Gone are the passive students sitting quietly in straight rows; in their place are active students busily engaged in purposeful, self-selected reading and writing activities.

Getting Started

If you want to make the transition to the workshop approach, you may wish to take the survey in Figure 1.2. Read the statements carefully and check the spaces that most closely match your beliefs. If you find that you agree with most of these statements, you are ready to learn more about how the workshop operates. If you disagree with most of the statements, you may prefer a traditional classroom.

Assuming you agree with most of the statements, we're ready to move on—but first a few words of caution. Making a change in methodology can be a frustrating experience. In the beginning you are not sure if you and your students will ever make it work. There will be setbacks and times when you wish you had never started. Read the ambivalent feelings that Barbara Lee, a fifth grade teacher, expressed in her journal as she began a workshop with her two language arts classes.

> Asked students to share with a peer. Peer should "critique"—talked about *constructive* critiquing. Then writer's choice to accept any criticism for changes. (Peer might say that an idea sounds unclear to them, etc., up to writer to correct.) Students observed seemed to take this seriously today in both classes. I observed some students "thinking" several minutes before writing. Some students just jump right in with pencil and paper. We discussed how both ways are OK.
>
> This whole plan worked beautifully with my first class. They seem to do well when activities are quiet and they know the whole plan. On days when small groups are working there's more goofing off. My second class tends to be more productive in small groups than the first one.

I'm beginning to see that maturity is needed to handle the flexibility. Both classes have students who can really make progress and seem happy with the responsibility and flexibility. But even as I write, two boys are wasting time. One problem I'm having is trying to work with an individual or few students and overseeing the rest of the class—but that seems to be a problem in other activities as well!

Figure 1.2:   Assessing Your Beliefs about Language Learning
Directions: Check the column that most closely represents your beliefs.

	Agree	Not Sure	Disagree
1. Students should be allowed to talk purposefully during workshop time.			
2. Students should be able to choose the topics they write about and the books they read.			
3. The teacher should share control of the class with students.			
4. Teachers adjust instruction as children progress through a natural developmental continuum.			
5. Literature can enhance any subject area.			
6. Students learn to read by reading.			
7. Students learn to write by writing.			
8. Students learn best when the curriculum is integrated.			
9. The child should be at the center of the learning process.			
10. Teachers should create a literate environment.			
11. Students need time to read and write.			
12. Changing teaching methods can be difficult and frustrating.			
13. Making research-based changes in instructional procedures can be rewarding.			
14. It's acceptable for students to progress at different rates.			

In an article for teachers "who are at different points along a continuum of thoughtful change," Dorothy Strickland (1994/1995, p. 301), offers some common-sense advice.

- Don't try to change everything at once.
- Know your belief system; it is the rock on which you build your instructional program—but be open to new ideas.
- It's okay to question new ideas, but do so sincerely.
- Learn to live with ambiguity; there are always more questions than answers.
- Collaborate with staff members to set goals and take steps to accomplish them.

Laurie Hoff (1994) relates the changes she made as she moved from traditional instruction to the workshop approach. Although she had attended conferences and read materials about new ways to teach based on educational research, she put off making changes. The burden of her work load and the lack of support from colleagues made restructuring her classroom seem impossible. Laurie noticed, however, that her students were failing to respond and were drifting away from learning. She realized that the time had come to initiate change.

Because the workshop approach appealed to her, Laurie began creating a studio in her classroom for reading and writing. Transforming the physical environment into an enticing, user-friendly workshop was a start, but Laurie found that the real secrets to a successful program were mutual respect and trust, daily personal choice, exposure to many kinds of print, and on-going self-assessment. Abandoning her standard lecture format, Laurie turned instead to short mini-lessons, then let students read and write. Students, dubious at first, soon caught her enthusiasm and responded by learning to love reading and writing.

Summary

Becoming aware of your philosophical beliefs is a first step in implementing a new program. The workshop approach to reading and writing is consistent with recent research on learning language. It acknowledges the value of learning along a developmental continuum. Embedded in the reading/writing workshop are such practices as child-centered learning, immersion in reading and writing, an integrated curriculum, literature-based learning, and social interaction. Accepting these beliefs means that you may be ready for the workshop approach, but be warned that the transition will require careful planning, restructuring, and commitment to the program.

Like Amy and Kevin who introduced our chapter, many of us are looking for new, more effective ways to teach. Such terms as *whole language, literature response groups,* and *workshops* bombard us as we attend conferences and read professional journals. What impact does this have on our teaching? Do we ignore it, excusing ourselves because of our excessive teaching loads? Do we continue as we have always done, because that's the way we were taught and it seems to work okay? Or should we seriously consider adopting a new approach that promises great rewards? As the Aussies say, "Let's have a go!"

Reflections

Seriously consider the following questions. Some answers may be found by reflecting on the chapter; others may come from your own beliefs and experiences.

1. How can I build on what I already know about how children learn to read and write? How can I use this knowledge to develop a reading/writing workshop?
2. With sensitivity for their developmental levels, how can I help my students find ways to expand their already existing store of knowledge about literacy through the workshop approach?
3. Who will work with me? Is there someone who will be my sounding board, encourage me, share my triumphs, and be patient with me when I have setbacks?

Bibliography

Atwell, N. (1987). *In the middle*. Portsmouth, NH: Heinemann.

Anderson, R., Hiebert, E., Scott, J., & Wilkinson, I. (1985). *Becoming a nation of readers*. Washington, D.C.: National Institute of Education.

Cambourne, B. (1988). *The whole story: Natural learning and the acquisition of literacy in the classroom*. Richmond Hill, Ontario, Canada: Scholastic.

Goodman, Ken. (1986). *What's whole in whole language?* Portsmouth, NH: Heinemann.

Graves, D. (1994). Let's take another look at writing. Presentation at National Council of Teachers of English, Orlando, FL.

Hoff, L. (1994). From omnipotent   teacher-in-charge to co-conspirator in the classroom: Developing lifelong readers and writers. *English Journal, 83* (6), 42–50.

Holdaway, D. (1979). *The foundations of literacy*. Portsmouth, NH: Heinemann.

Morrow, L. M., Sharkey, E., & Firestone, W. (1993). *Promoting independent reading and writing through self-directed literacy activities in a collaborative setting*. Reading Research Report No. 2. National Reading Research Center, Universities of Georgia and Maryland.

Sissel, P. (1994). Enhancing reading performance through Reader's Workshop. Presentation at the National Council of Teachers of English, Orlando, FL.

Strickland, D. (1994/1995). Reinventing our literacy programs: Books, basics, balance. *The Reading Teacher, 48* (4), 294–302.

Swift, Kathleen. (1993). Try reading workshop in your classroom. *The Reading Teacher, 46* (5), 366–371.

van Kraayenoord, C. & Paris, S. (1994). Literacy instruction in Australian primary schools. *The Reading Teacher, 48* (3), 218–228.

Chapter 2

Workshop Procedures

Kevin and Amy arrive early at a faculty meeting and take a few minutes to catch up on their reading/writing workshops.

Kevin: Well, I've started. I'm not sure how well it's going yet, but I chose my most mature and resourceful class to introduce the idea. They seem to like being able to spend more time reading and writing, and are glad not to have to use the old grammar books any more.

Amy: I think I'm still floundering. My little second graders just don't seem to be able to work independently very well. Their attention spans are so short, and they've never had a chance before to choose their own books and just sit and read or look at them. I'm giving them about ten minutes to do this each day though, and they seem to enjoy it.

Kevin: I'll bet they'll come along. I've done all the workshop steps now, but I started out slowly, too. We spent a lot of time just learning the procedures and discussing how to act—I told them I was a learner too! They liked that idea.

Amy: I believe I'll add a sharing time soon. They all seem to want to talk about their books. Sometimes they point and giggle as they read, and some can't resist looking at other children's books.

Kevin: I like the idea of the mini-lessons, but I haven't been able to cut them down to five or ten minutes yet. I'm afraid they won't learn enough if I don't spend more time teaching.

Amy: I know what you mean. There are those terrible year-end achievement tests, and we're accountable for teaching our students so many skills.

Kevin: I guess I'll have to trust them to learn most of the skills as they work on their own and with each other during the workshop part, and I'll try to fill in the rest with mini-lessons.

Amy: Well, good luck and keep me informed. I'm really interested in how it's going.

Introduction

In this chapter you will be able to learn the procedures for operating a workshop. The basic framework consists of mini-lessons, status-of-the-class report, workshop, and group sharing time. Within this framework there can be a great deal of flexibility. Much of the variation depends on the developmental levels of the students, the experience of the teacher, the time available, and the goals of the program. Figure 2.1 shows the basic model for either the reading or writing workshop approach.

Mini-lesson
Status-of-the-Class Report
Reading/Writing/Conferring during Workshop
Group Sharing Time

Figure 2.1: Reading/Writing Workshop Model

The Workshop Framework

This section describes each of the four steps in the reading/writing workshop, but gives little attention to mini-lessons and workshop activities. These are covered fully in Chapters 3 through 7.

Mini-lessons

In many traditional classrooms teachers introduce reading and writing skills with directed instruction and then have the students practice the skills in workbooks or the equivalent for the rest of the class period. I know—I used to do it myself! With mini-lessons, you simply select a skill that students need to know and find a quick and effective way to teach it. In some cases, students have a chance to use the skill immediately, but other times they may not need it for a few days or longer. By presenting your skill quickly and letting the students get on with their reading and writing, you are increasing their opportunities to apply the skill in meaningful context.

Laurie Hoff (1994) justifies the use of mini-lessons from personal experiences with her students. After only a month of using them, she realized that they had been tuning her out after the first ten minutes anyway. They were learning and retaining more from a ten-minute mini-lesson than from an hour-long lecture!

How do you know which skills to teach in mini-lessons? They come basically from two sources: your observations of what the students need to know and your grade-level curriculum guide. Ideally, you base all of your mini-lessons on what students want or need to know because that will be what they are interested in learning. However, the reality is that you are likely to be held account-

> ## TEACHING TIP
>
> To decide what skills to teach in mini-lessons
>
> a.   Jot down words that students frequently misspell, teach related spelling rules, and include the words on weekly spelling lists.
>
> b.   Observe the most frequent types of mechanical errors students are making in their journals and teach the skills they need to learn.
>
> c.   Listen to your students read and tell you about what they have read. Then decide what reading skills to teach.

able for your students' scores on achievement tests, so you need to incorporate grade-level skills also. It's important to teach only one skill per lesson so that the students can focus their attention on that skill and not become confused by being taught multiple skills at the same time.

When you first introduce the workshop approach to your students, you will probably want to devote several mini-lessons to procedures. If they understand thoroughly what to do and what you expect of them from the start, they will be able to get right to work without a lot of questions and confusion. In the reading workshop, most mini-lessons will center around literature and on the word recognition and comprehension skills and strategies students need to become competent readers. Mini-lessons in writing workshops may focus on the writing process, writing skills, and literary techniques.

Status of the Class

The status-of-the-class report is a record of what each student does each day of the workshop (Atwell, 1987). As the teacher calls the students' names, he or she quickly records a code that represents one or more of the acceptable tasks for the workshop. Students may participate in more than one activity during a single workshop period. Figure 2.2 is a sample status-of-the-class record form for a reading workshop, and Figure 2.3 is a sample form for a writing workshop. You may want to use some of the codes I've listed, but you should add others that you and your students want to include. Here are the codes and what they represent.

Reading Workshop:
- SSR Sustained Silent Reading. Students select books and read them.
- LRG Literature Response Group. Students participate in literature response groups (explained in Chapter 3).
- RK   Record Keeping. Students update record forms for the books they are reading and for related projects.

- SB Select Book. Students select books by browsing and by reading recommendations and reviews about books.
- PC Peer Conference. Students meet with one or more classmates to discuss books and authors.
- TC Teacher Conference. Students schedule conferences with the teacher.
- LL Literature Log. Students write their reflections on the books they are reading.
- PR Project Response. Students respond with projects related to what they are reading.
- DJ Dialogue Journal. Students react to their books by writing in their journals and getting responses.

Writing Workshop

- DJ Dialogue Journal. Students write about their ideas in journals and get responses.
- TS Topic Search. Students may investigate several sources to select topics for their writing.
- D1 First Draft. Students write rough drafts.
- D2 Second Draft. Students revise their rough drafts.
- D3 Third Draft. Students make additional revisions.
- RV Revision. Students complete the revision process.
- ED Editing. Students proofread and edit their work.
- PC Peer Conference. Students confer with one or more peers to get suggestions for revising and editing.
- TC Teacher Conference. Students schedule conferences with the teacher.
- PB Publish. Students put their pieces in final forms.

TEACHING TIP

When making copies of the forms for the Status-of-the-Class record,

a. Enter the students' names first so that you won't have to recopy them on the blank forms.
b. Make enough copies at one time to last all year.

Some workshops omit status-of-the-class reports, but these reports serve two vital functions. First, they help students focus on what they will be doing during the workshop. Without this focus, children may spend a great deal of time wandering around aimlessly, not being able to choose what to do. I watched pre-first graders in Tina De Stephen's class respond when their names were called by telling her what they planned to do. Tina made sure that each child selected an activity for the language workshop before she let them go, then watched to see that they remained on their chosen tasks.

Name	Date	Date	Date	Date	Date

Figure 2.2:   Reading Workshop Status of the Class

SSR	Sustained Silent Reading	PC	Peer Conference
		TC	Teacher Conference
LRG	Literature Response Group	LL	Literature Log
		PR	Project Response
RK	Record Keeping	DJ	Dialogue Journal
SB	Select Book		

Name	Date	Date	Date	Date	Date

Figure 2.3:   Writing Workshop Status of the Class

DJ	Dialogue Journal	RV	Revision
TS	Topic Search	ED	Editing
D1	First Draft	PC	Peer Conference
D2	Second Draft	TC	Teacher Conference
D3	Third Draft	PB	Publish

The second purpose of the status-of-the-class report is to enable you to keep records of what each student is doing each day. Since after the first day every student in your class is working on something different, it's the only sane thing to do! It also makes you aware of students who may need a little nudging. For example, if Dinah is still on topic search after three days, perhaps you need to give her a little help in selecting a topic so that she can move on. If Terry has been reading the same book for three weeks, you may need to check his progress. Also, the records are useful for computing grades and for sharing with parents who want to know what their children are doing during reading and writing classes.

If we check back with Kevin, we can see how he is already benefiting from using the Status-of-the-Class Report.

As he finished the mini-lesson on using quotation marks, Kevin reached for his clipboard to begin recording student activities on the Status-of-the-Class chart. He hadn't been sure about using this at first, but now realized how helpful it was. As he called the roll, the students quickly told him what they would be doing during the writing workshop. He realized that this procedure was helping them to make decisions and to focus their attention on the tasks they had selected. At first the students had been slow to respond and the process had taken too much class time, but now they knew he expected a quick answer so they planned ahead. His coding system moved the process along quickly, too, and told him at a glance what the children would be doing.

Kevin: Kim

Kim: First draft

Kevin, recording **D1** and thinking: Good. She's finally beginning to write. She had to do a lot of reading, conferring, and searching for a topic before she could get started.

Kevin: Burt

Burt: Poetry booklet

Kevin, writing Poems and thinking: I'm really glad Burt's decided to do a poetry booklet. He's so creative and this will be a good opportunity for him to use some of his wonderful ideas.

Kevin: Angela

Angela: First draft

Kevin, entering **D1** and thinking: Uh-oh. This is her fourth day to be on her first draft. I may need to visit with Angela to see if I can help her move on.

Kevin: Joshua

Joshua: Edit and teacher conference

Kevin, recording **ED** and **TC** and thinking: Good. Joshua's been working on a story about his dad for two weeks. I'm glad he's about to finish up. This story means a lot to him.

As he continued down the roll, Kevin realized that the process now only took about three or four minutes, yet it gave him a record of the children's daily work so that he could keep track of their progress. As he put the clipboard down, he looked up and noticed that most of the students had already begun working on the tasks they'd chosen for that day. Three of them had requested teacher conferences, and he needed to see a few others as well. Kevin knew that this would be another busy workshop for them all!

Reading/Writing Workshop

It's misleading to refer to a reading *or* writing workshop, because reading is very much a part of the writing workshop and the reverse is also true. Students read in order to write. They read to get ideas, to observe how authors lead into their stories, to see how to use dialogue, to find out how to write reports on factual subjects, and for so many other reasons. *Literature is a model for writers.* Also, students write as they read. They write book recommendations for books to read; variations on themes, settings, or characters; in dialogue journals; to authors of favorite books; and in literature logs to share during literature response groups. The two workshops overlap in almost every way, yet the focus *is* different.

Teachers want to know what to do while students are engaged in independent workshop activities. There are so many choices! Nancie Atwell (1987) spends the first ten minutes of her reading workshop circulating among her students, checking to see if anyone needs help, then settles down to read her own book. Occasionally she writes responses in dialogue journals during the workshop. In contrast, she starts her writing workshop by writing herself, by becoming so absorbed in her own writing that she doesn't even look up for the first ten minutes. When she finally glances around, she sees all of the students following her model. They are busily writing as well! I'm not sure if you can trust your class to do as hers did, but it works for her. She then begins circulating, conferring with students who may need help or encouragement. In Figure 2.4 you will find some suggestions for how teachers can spend workshop time.

Modeling reading or writing
Circulating among the students, offering help and encouragement
Holding conferences with students
Helping students locate resources
Recording observations
Extending the mini-lesson for students who need further instruction by giving one-on-one or small group instruction
Replying in dialogue journals

Figure 2.4:   Teacher Use of Workshop Time

Group Share

When we read a fine book, we can hardly wait to share it with someone else. If we write a poem or short story, we want someone to read it and react to it. Sharing lets us communicate our deepest thoughts and feelings with someone we trust to respond honestly and thoughtfully. It fills a basic need within ourselves.

Children are like that, too. They need an audience for their reading and writing, so group share becomes an important way to conclude each workshop. If an atmosphere of trust and respect exists and the class is truly a community of learners, this sharing session will benefit everyone and no one will be offended by any remarks.

Establishing a community of learners doesn't just happen; it takes time and effort. Patricia Hagerty (1992) tells of a class, including the teacher, that developed this feeling of community by spending time sharing who they were, what they liked to eat, what they did in their spare time, and so forth. I can sense when this feeling is beginning to develop in my college classes. The students realize they can trust me to help them learn what they need to know to be good teachers, and I show that I trust them by letting them take the lead in discussions and say what they honestly feel.

Generally, at the beginning of group-share sessions, you call the class together and two or three children read what they have written or share their reactions to books they are reading. The one who has something to share manages the discussion, calling on other students for comments and responding to their questions. You may occasionally want to intervene by redirecting comments or modeling pertinent questions if their remarks become trite or routine, but this session really belongs to the students. Specific questions are usually more helpful than general ones. For example, "Could you make Anna and Mark come to life by adding dialogue?" is more helpful than "What else could you say about your characters?"

TEACHING TIP

For a successful group share session,

a.   Give a five-minute warning near the end of the workshop so that students can complete their work and prepare for the sharing session.

b.   Make this time relaxed and informal, perhaps by inviting students to sit on the floor in a circle or gather in a special area, with the one who is sharing seated in an "author's chair."

Group-share sessions may not always follow the same format. Lucy Calkins (1986) suggests that listeners could sometimes write comments on 3 x 5 index cards to give to the author. This method provides feedback from everyone but lacks the interaction of oral responses that build on one another. Another way to conduct a group-share session is to ask listeners to focus their attention on specific ideas. Lesley Wing Jan, year five teacher, told me she believed that each group share should have a specific focus, such as how to develop the ending to a composition. When students were writing poetry, Georgia Heard conducted a focused group-share session by asking the class to listen for three things (Calkins, 1986, p. 305):

- Is the overall image clear?
- Did you get a strong feeling? If so, what is it?
- What strategies are used in the poem?

As with any of the procedures in workshops, you and the children will need to establish a set of guidelines. This short, precious time cannot be wasted. Although you will eventually form your own rules to share by, Figure 2.5 gives some starters.

1. **Don't humiliate, embarrass, or ridicule anyone.**
2. **Ask constructive questions or make helpful comments.**
3. **Wait to be called on before you speak.**
4. **Listen courteously and respond if you think you can help.**
5. **Stick to the point; don't get off the subject.**
6. **Don't monopolize the discussion.**
7. **If you are sharing, be sure you have a purpose.**
8. **Treat everyone with respect.**

Figure 2.5:   Guidelines for Group Share

A practical problem to face in conducting group share sessions is deciding who gets to share, and the ten-minute time period is far too short for everyone to have a chance for in-depth sharing. Your extroverts will want to talk whether they need help or not, and the quiet ones who may need help are reluctant to speak in front of the whole class. Here are some solutions, and you may find others.

- Limit the number of students who can share to two. If a third student has a desperate need to share, there may still be enough time for a quick-share.
- Let students sign up in advance, and when the two spots are filled, they will have to find another day.
- Occasionally let all students share by having each one tell in one sentence what he or she is working on.
- Encourage a shy child to share by inviting him or her to sign up for a time.
- When a large number of children want to share at the same time, divide the class into groups so that each child who requests an audience can share within a group.
- As you move about the room during workshop time, give out numbered (1-5) cards to students who need to share and call on them to share (Hagerty, 1992).
- Increase the amount of time for group share and hence the number of students who can share if you have at least an hour or more for the entire workshop.

Group-share sessions can also help teachers. As observers and sometime-participants, teachers have opportunities to subtly instruct by interjecting questions and comments and to evaluate students' thinking and interactions. Jotting down a few notes at this time can be helpful in identifying topics for mini-lessons or conferences and for evaluating progress.

Flexibility within a Framework

A number of factors affect the design of your workshop. No two teachers will do workshops exactly the same way, and you may change your procedures somewhat as you go. Keeping the workshop flexible is the way it should be. The one essential component is a block of time for students to engage in independent, self-selected reading or writing.

Developmental Levels

The developmental levels of your students make a difference in your organization, resources, and expectations. As Amy realized, her children needed to begin gradually with short periods of time for independent work before moving into more complex activities. With some preliminary instruction on procedures, Kevin's students, on the other hand, were ready to move into the full workshop program. An example from an Australian school (van Kraayenoord and Paris, 1994) illustrates how teachers observe developmental levels (see Figure 2.6).

Year	Activities and Materials
1	Reading and writing at emerging levels with peers Taking books home at night to read with parents Drawing with storytelling Using wordless story books, big books, journals, and scrapbooks
2-3	Maintaining personal reading and spelling logs Keeping writing or response journals Learning cursive writing, grammar, and spelling in the context of composition Doing process writing and publishing books Selecting and reading books, writing reactions and composing creative stories
4-7	Applying reading and writing across the curriculum Using computers for word processing of final copies Discussing progress with teacher and receiving help in overcoming any difficulties
	Note: Year 1 students are mostly five year olds.

Figure 2.6:   Developmentally Appropriate Reading and Writing Activities in Australian Primary Schools

Examples of workshops from a first grade classroom and a twelfth grade classroom provide two extremes in developmental differences. The sequence for reading/writing workshops that Christine Duthie and Ellie Zimet (1992) use with their first graders adds several features to the typical workshop format.

- Journal writing
- Calendar time, including classroom news
- Shared big book reading with related skill instruction (a mini-lesson)
- Read-aloud story by teacher to illustrate a literary element (a mini-lesson)
- Response by children to the teacher's oral reading
- Independent reading or writing time (30 minutes) when children can work together and the teacher circulates
- Shared reading or writing by two children followed by responses during group share time

In contrast, Mitch Cox and Christine Firpo (1993) had three goals in mind as they created their workshops for high school seniors: to get students hooked on novels, to help them discover real-world purposes for writing, and to make them self-directed learners. Some students confessed that this was the first time they had ever read a book all the way through, and many became hooked on westerns and detective fiction. Mini-lessons prepared students for revising and editing, and they selected such topics for writing as consumer complaint letters, job and college application essays, stories and poems for the school's literary magazine, and letters to the editor. They accepted responsibility for selecting, starting, and completing their work, so the teachers felt that the workshop had enabled the students to meet the goals that teachers had set.

The Teacher

If you are a beginning teacher or this approach is new to you, be sure to go slowly and spend plenty of time preparing the students for what you want them to do. You may want to start out by allowing students a block of time to do self-selected reading and writing, gradually increasing the time until they are able to sustain their attention for longer periods. You will need to spend a great deal of time, perhaps through mini-lessons, establishing independent work habits and rules of behavior. Chapter 9 provides more information about classroom management. Since you may still be reluctant to trust your students to master skills without your direct instruction, you may spend more time teaching mini-lessons than you will later.

Because of differences in developmental levels and experiences with managing workshops, your distribution of time will vary. Figure 2.7 illustrates how this may happen. Of course, the amount of time allotted for language arts may vary considerably—I've heard of as many as 110 minutes in some schools and as few as 45 minutes in others—so I'm not specifying any time amounts. When a workshop is in full swing, mini-lessons usually take about five to ten minutes, status-of-the-class reports three to five minutes, group share ten minutes, and the remainder of the time is spent on workshop activities.

Mini-lesson	SoC	Workshop	Group Share
For younger children and/or less experienced teachers			
Mini-lesson	SoC	Workshop	Group Share
For more mature students and/or more experienced teachers			
(SoC stands for Status of the Class.)			

Figure 2.7:   Distribution of Time for Workshops

Your goals for helping students continue their growth in literacy will affect the way you operate your workshops also. For me, the overriding goal is to enable students to enjoy reading and writing and to have the strategies necessary to do so. Because of the emphasis placed on skill mastery in some districts, you may place that at the top of your list. Other possibilities include appreciation of literature, reading comprehension, ability to write a composition, and so forth. What you set as your priorities will make a difference in how your students learn.

Class Populations

The composition of your class will also affect the way you manage your workshop. Through the reading/writing workshop, sixth graders in Holly Martin's ESL class were given a great deal of independence in selecting books and writing topics that reflected their cultures and helped them gain proficiency in English. In a multiethnic year one class in inner city Melbourne, Australia, I saw a bilingual (English and Vietnamese) child translating for a monolingual Vietnamese child during workshop time. The freedom to interact and translate while learning to read and write was helping both children become more proficient in English.

Special education classes have an advantage—and a disadvantage. Since the number of students is smaller than in regular classrooms, the teacher can respond more easily to individual needs. On the other hand, the time period is short and it is difficult to fit all of the steps into a 25 or 30 minute time span. Teachers of these classes should experiment with different formats, perhaps spreading a workshop over two days.

Workshops are ideal for multiage classes. Students with similar goals but differing age and ability levels have the freedom to confer and learn with others, select appropriate activities, and move at their own paces. In a three-room rural school, I observed Chris McClendon working with students in years four through six. For several weeks the students had been investigating Graeme Base's *The Eleventh Hour*, a challenging and fascinating book by an Australian author. Chris had a list of about 25 activities for the children to choose, and students were working in groups or individually wherever they could find space in the crowded room. Naturally, boys were working with boys and girls with girls! Chris circulated among them, responding to questions and making suggestions. The students had written to Graeme Base, and Mr. Base had mentioned each of their names in a two-page letter he wrote that told them how he had written the book. Chris's list of activities extended across the curriculum and included such projects as:

- Investigating the clues and identifying the culprit
- Brainstorming banquet ideas
- Writing stories or poems about unusual foods
- Making a grid to relate animals, costumes, and names
- Researching animals mentioned in the book
- Developing secret codes and anagrams
- Looking through magazines to find recipes and write menus

The children's enthusiasm for their study was evident—even after several weeks—and the walls filled with posters and charts reflected their interest.

Summary

The framework for the reading/writing workshop consists of four procedures. The mini-lesson is a five-to-ten-minute directed teaching lesson that relates to what students need to know. The status-of-the-class report is a chart for recording what work each student plans to do during the workshop session. During the actual workshop, which represents the largest portion of time, children are working on self-selected reading or writing projects. At the concluding group-share session the class gathers to listen and respond to students who want reactions to their projects.

Within this framework is room for a great deal of flexibility. Teachers' own personalities, goals, and teaching styles affect the format and operation of the workshop, but so do students' developmental levels, the teacher's experience and confidence, and the classroom composition. This flexibility means that the teacher, with student input, can continually monitor and adjust each workshop according to what works best.

Reflections

Seriously consider the following questions. Some answers may be found by reflecting on the chapter; others may come from your own beliefs and experiences.

1. What are my personal goals for using the workshop approach? What do I hope to accomplish through this approach that I am not able to accomplish with the way I am teaching now?
2. How do I feel about gradually relinquishing some control of the classroom and letting students make more decisions and choices? Will I be able to step back at times and help them to learn for themselves?
3. How will I know if I'm giving them too much independence too quickly? What are some things that will tell me if this is so?
4. At the grade level(s) I am teaching, what types of mini-lessons and workshops would be meaningful and developmentally appropriate?
5. How will I decide which students will read during the group-share session? What are some priorities I could set? Can I involve students in setting guidelines for selecting those who share? If so, how?

Bibliography

Atwell, N. (1987). *In the middle*. Portsmouth, NH: Heinemann.

Calkins, L. M. (1986). *The art of teaching writing*. Portsmouth, NH: Heinemann.

Cox, M., & Firpo, C. (1993). What would they be doing if we gave them worksheets? *English Journal, 82* (3), 42–45.

Duthie, C., & Zimet, E. (1992). "Poetry is like directions for your imagination!" *The Reading Teacher, 46* (1), 14–24.

Hagerty, P. (1992). *Reader's workshop*. Richmond Hill, Ontario, Canada: Scholastic Canada.

Hoff, L. (1994). From omnipotent teacher-in-charge to co-conspirator in the classroom: Developing lifelong readers and writers. *English Journal, 83* (6), 42–50.

Reutzel, D. R., & Cooter, R. (1991). Organizing for effective instruction: The reading workshop. *The Reading Teacher, 44* (8), 548–554.

van Kraayenoord, C., & Paris, S. (1994). Literary instruction in Australian primary schools. *The Reading Teacher, 48* (3), 218–228.

CHAPTER 3

THE READING WORKSHOP

October 27

Kevin, spying Amy in the hall with an armload of books: Let me help, Amy. There's no need for you to stagger under that load of books. What are you doing with so many anyway?

Amy, laughing: I could use some help! I've just been to the library to pick up these books for my little ones. Beth helped me pick them out and she checked them out to me for a month. That should keep my children interested for awhile. They're turning into eager readers, and I can hardly keep enough books on hand.

Kevin, sharing Amy's load and walking with her to her class-room: I'm glad they're so interested. You must be making reading exciting for them.

Amy: I'm really trying. I read **to** them and **with** them and I'm giving them more time to read for themselves and with part-ners. They usually read for about 20 minutes on their own now, and we've started sharing after that. They love to talk about their books. How are things going with your class?

Kevin, putting the books on the table in Amy's room: The workshop is running okay I guess, but I'm really disappointed in the students' responses to what they read. When I ask them to write in literature logs, they mostly just write summaries or very boring reviews. Sometimes I don't believe they know how to **think.**

Amy: Maybe you're right. Probably nobody ever taught them how to think. Can you do it?

Kevin: That's quite a challenge. I'll see what I can do. I believe I read something about dialogue journals—maybe that's a way to model thinking. I'd better go now—they'll be coming in any minute from the playground.

Amy: Thanks for helping with the books. See you later.

Introduction

As Amy realized, one secret to a successful reading workshop is a large supply of quality books. Once her children discovered the joy of selecting their own reading material and having free time to read, Amy could not disappoint them.

In this chapter you will see the value of using literature instead of workbooks and skill sheets for teaching reading. You will learn about the three essential components of a workshop: *time* for reading, *ownership* through self-selection, and *response* through dialogue journals and literature-related activities. I will share literature response groups with you, one of my favorite ways for students to discover the pleasure of reading, as one of several variations on the workshop theme.

Literature in the Reading Workshop

For decades teachers felt bound to basals and their hierarchies of skills; there seemed to be no alternatives! During skills lessons I've seen children yawn, wiggle, squirm, look around the room, and ask to get a drink of water or go to the bathroom. Now, with the ever-expanding influence of whole language, teachers are discovering many ways to use literature and children are fascinated with their books. Figure 3.1 shows some reasons why teachers can and should use literature.

Use of Quality Literature

Most of us would agree that we should choose fine quality books so that children can benefit fully from their exposure to literature.

Under the right conditions, literature can . . .

- help students develop a sense of story
- motivate children to read
- be a model for writing
- stretch the imagination
- help students under- stand themselves
- enable students to relate to those who are different from them
- provide children with a cultural heritage
- be a source of pleasure
- inform students of other places, people, and ideas
- promote language development
- connect learning across the curriculum
- provide vicarious experiences
- help students form their values
- increase vocabulary
- promote problem solving and higher- order thinking skills
- help children learn how to read

Figure 3.1:   Reasons for Using Literature

Quality books are those whose rich illustrations inspire us, whose language lingers on our tongues, whose characters become part of our lives, and whose themes remain with us long after we've finished reading. It is important for us to read these books aloud and to have them available for children to read. From the first day of school Linda Fernandez shares fine big books with her kindergarten class, pointing out authors and illustrators and making children aware of their styles. When the parents of one of her children brought home a new book in October, he took a careful look at it and said, "That's an Ezra Jack Keats book!" Already this kindergartner could recognize an author/illustrator's style because of his daily interactions with good books.

I also believe, however, that children may not always choose books considered by authorities to be fine quality literature. When they are young, their ability to analyze literary elements and select fine literature is limited. As a former avid Nancy Drew reader, I remember resenting anyone who interfered with my pursuit of reading *all* of her books, and even today I sometimes choose less than the highest quality books for pleasure reading. For young people, the freedom to choose overrides the necessity for always reading the best books in terms of literary merit. As children get older, the likelihood of maturing tastes that lead to more discriminating selections is a high probability. A science fiction comic book reader may later turn into a Roy Bradbury or Carl Sagan fan.

TEACHING TIP
In addition to allowing children to choose their own books, introduce them to quality literature as you
a.   Read aloud to them.
b.   Order books for the whole class to read.
c.   Choose books for your classroom library.

Genres

Fiction is a good starting place for getting acquainted with literature, but children need to know about other genres as well. Most of them come to school knowing nursery rhymes, so poetry is a logical extension of what they already know and like. Children are naturally curious, so they can enjoy nonfiction books that give information about specific topics and stimulate them to further investigation. I knew a second grader whose favorite kind of book to read was a biography "because it was about someone who *really* lived." Many children have heard folktales, i.e., "Little Red Riding Hood" and "The Three Little Pigs" since their early years, so they can easily build on this familiarity as they read other versions, including Ed Young's beautifully illustrated *Lon Po Po*, a Chinese Red Riding Hood tale, or Jon Scieszka's tongue-in-cheek *The True Story of the Three Little Pigs*.

Jill Ramsey, teacher of a grades two-three multiage class-room, says, "I'd rather teach science with Joanna Cole's Magic School Bus series than with science textbooks." With 15 copies of these humorous informational-fantasy books to choose from, many of Jill's children select them to read and respond to during workshop time. In fact, "Mrs. Frizzle" and her magic school bus are so much a part of their classroom that the children called Jill Mrs. Frizzle one day when she accidentally wore a mis-matched pair of earrings. Figure 3.2 lists some genres for chil-dren to explore.

- Alphabet and counting books
- Concept books
- Picture story books
- Science fiction
- Detective/mystery stories
- Wordless picture books
- Traditional folktales
- Fables
- Hero/heroine stories
- Poetry
- Modern fantasy
- Contemporary realistic fiction
- Biography
- Informational books
- Multiethnic books
- Legends
- Tall tales
- How-to books

Figure 3.2:   Genres for Reading Workshop

A well-balanced selection of genres for children to read dur-ing workshop time serves many purposes. Students who have read nothing but fiction become aware of other forms of literature that they can enjoy. Those with hobbies or special interests discover informational books, and those with a flair for poetry can savor the works of favorite poets. The various genres also serve as models for writers. During the writing workshop, students who have ex-amined the features of various types of books can pattern their own writing on them. After reading several fables to her class, Jill Ramsey invited the children to create their own fables. Example 3.1 is Sacha's story of "The Deer and the Owl," complete with moral.

The Deer and the Owl

"I'm very, very hungry," said the deer to the owl. "Well, go get some food," said the owl.
"I can't," said deer, "Why can't you?" said owl. "Because the hunters are there," said the deer.
"Oh!" said owl. "Well I can go attack them and you can get the food," said owl. "Ok," said deer.
The owl attacked them and deer got his food. The deer hugged the owl.

The End

Always think of a friend before yourself.

WONDERFUL!

Example 3.1

Approaching fables from an analytic view, Joy McCaleb asked her seventh graders to respond to the fable "The Fox and the Grapes." She discussed the moral of the fable and asked students to suggest an analogy to real life. They agreed on this analogy: If you're from a family in which no one graduated from high school, you believe it's out of reach, or impossible, for you to do so, so you don't try hard. Then students wrote individual responses in their reading journals, and Example 3.2 shows what Kristin wrote.

> In the story "The Fox and the Grapes" the fox tries in vain to reach a bunch of grapes. The fox tries several times, but gives up easily. There are lots of people I know who think something is out of reach like the fox. They give up without even really trying. How can they tell if they don't even try? People sometimes tell me they know they can't do something, so why try? I'll tell you why. How do you know you can't? It's better to have tried and failed than not to have tried at all.
>
> I can't say I've never said that I couldn't do something. I catch myself saying it often. I have a friend who likes to live on the wild side, and try new and sometimes dangerous things. She has a way of talking me into them. After I have tried, I always feel great. Even if I can't do whatever it is, I still feel great. Now, I try more. I've tried to be the best in things like giving my reading project. We need to be careful what we try and be sure it's something we need to do and want to do.

Example 3.2

Christine Duthie and Ellie Zimet (1992), first grade teachers, collaborated on a poetry unit to use with their reading/writing workshops. They prepared the children by reading a wide variety of poems to them, collecting poetry anthologies, and designing bulletin boards for children's poetry writing that featured three headings: *feelings, images,* and *things around us.* At the beginning of each workshop teachers used mini-lessons to present some aspect of poetry, such as repetition, alliteration, or refrain, based on what they found the children needed to know. The children created personal anthologies of their favorite poems, then assembled a class anthology of the poems they wrote—complete with author index.

Choosing another genre, Christine Duthie (1994) introduced her first graders to nonfiction during the reading/writing workshop. Although she usually gives children choices of genre, books, and topics, she finds that focusing on a particular genre for a period of time results in more productive whole-group sharing sessions and conferences. Also, mini-lessons—in this case dealing with such topics as organizing material and comparing books on the same topic—are immediately relevant for all of the children. By the end of the unit, children were able to identify characteristics of nonfiction, publish their own nonfiction, and analyze different types of informational books.

Terri Wilkerson asked her fifth graders to read informational stories and to respond to them from different points of view. Benjamin chose "Reynard: The Story of a Fox Returned to the Wild" by Alice Mills Leighmer and wrote first from the fox's point of view, then from Dana's (the caretaker's) point of view (see Example 3.3).

Implementing the Reading Workshop

You are already familiar with the general procedures for reading/writing workshops, so here we will be looking at some ways to implement the reading workshop and at some variations in its format. The workshop structure basically offers a small amount of direct instruction, a large block of time for reading with opportunities to respond, and a group-share session. Students in a workshop generally experience a sense of community, a bond that holds them together so that they can freely exchange thoughts and ideas.

Guidelines

For a workshop to operate efficiently, students need to observe guidelines. The teacher should be responsible for setting and enforcing these guidelines, but students also need to contribute their ideas so that they will feel responsible for following them. Each workshop operates somewhat differently, but Figure 3.3 gives a working list of procedures.

From Reynard's point of view

> have got lost in New York, man thought I
> was a dog, and now I am being cared
> for in this big place. What makes that woman
> think that I am going to bite? She
> doesn't need gloves. This is one wild adventure.
> I do not know if I have had a
> wilder journey than this, or maybe it was
> when the time I was born. I wonder if
> these guys are going to hurt me.
> So far they have been nice. I wonder
> If I will ever see the wild again?

So far I (insertion)

From Dana's point of view

> I let Reynard is having a
> good time with the new cage It will
> be hard to let that fox go. He will
> never guess what his next surprise is.
> His next surprise is a female fox called
> a vixen. The orphan is acting like it
> should if it was in the wild, and that is
> a good sign because we have to
> release him. We do not want to
> nurse him to were he needs us all
> the time. Just to where we help him but
> he is still wild.

Example 3.3

Participate in the mini-lesson by taking notes and applying what you learn.

Be ready to give a response when you are called on during
the status-of-the-class check.

When it is time to read, have your book, your dialogue journal, a pen or pencil, and any other supplies you need.

Spend your time reading your book, not doing homework
or other activities.

If you need to schedule a conference with me or with another student, sign up in advance.

If you give your book a fair try and still don't like it, give it
up and choose another one. You may want to read it later.

When you need to choose a new book, consider reviews on
file, other books by a favorite author, or a new genre.

Be prepared to read for the entire period.

If you want to share during group-share time, sign up in
advance and be prepared.

Figure 3.3: Guidelines for Implementing a Reading Workshop

Organizing Reading Workshops

The way that teachers use reading time varies, depending on their goals, the ages and reading levels of their students, and other factors. Patricia Hagerty (1992) recommends letting primary students read by themselves for a period of time, then with partners for the remaining time. Kindergartners in Robin Gutkin's (1990) class look at and talk about books during what she calls "SLR"—Sustained LOUD Reading time. They often choose familiar books that she has read to them, but later in the year begin to experiment with whatever books appear interesting. At the secondary level, Sharon Kletzien and Barbara Hushion (1992) hold reading workshop only one day a week, using the remaining days for other types of English instruction.

With five language arts classes of fifty minutes each, Linda Rief (1992) has to make careful choices about how to spend her workshop time. Because she expects her students to read at least a half an hour at home each night, she spends most of her time in class on writing. She does, however, spend one entire day on reading so that students can see the value she places on it. Reading time is divided among reading aloud, silent reading, and whole class sharing. In addition to having her students read at home, she expects them to keep a list of books read and to respond in their logs with several pages of written responses each week.

Two of my teacher friends like to spend a large chunk of workshop time in group work. Relating each workshop to a theme, Pam Petty places her second graders in groups by subjects. When I observed her, the class was studying patriotism, and the groups were investigating such topics as the Bald Eagle, national monuments, the White House, the Statue of Liberty, and the Lincoln Memorial. They searched through books, encyclopedias, and pamphlets to find important information that they wanted to include in their own class book.

During her workshop period, Leigh Jones' students were reading their own copies of Theodore Taylor's *The Cay* and then sharing their ideas. Leigh divided her fourth graders into groups of four, with each student choosing the role of leader, materials handler, recorder, or reporter. The students were to brainstorm ways for elderly Timothy, a black West Indian, and blind Phillip, a white boy, to get coconuts from a tall tree. This activity caused students to become aware of the interdependence of these two characters and required them to use problem solving skills.

In most cases workshops allow students the freedom to choose their own books. In some cases, however, all children may be reading or listening to the same book, as in Leigh Jones' class discussed above. In some primary grades many children are unable to read good books themselves, so the teacher reads to the class. Sometimes a beginning teacher isn't yet comfortable with having all of the students reading different books, so the students read and discuss their copies of a preselected junior novel. In Linda Rief's room (1992) students sometimes choose their own books, but at other times all of the students read the same book. By studying the same book together, they can explore themes and appreciate different points of view. Bruce Anderson found this to be true when he guided his eighth grade honors English class through *The Once and Future King*, a lengthy and complex novel. In her response to the book, Sharon McCawley points out the relevance of this book to life in the twentieth century. (See Example 3.4.)

The novel, The Once and Future King, offers a host of ideas and wisdom that I find to be very significant to the life of the modern twentieth century reader. These ideas and this wisdom can clearly be seen through each of the novel's characters.

First of all, we can see an example of the idea that "what goes around comes around." In the first book, the Sword and the Stone, we find that Kay is undoubtedly Sir Ector's son. In this book, Kay is portrayed as superior and, in many ways, selfish. He usually gets his way, and he is treated in a respectful manner. On the other hand, "Wart's" inferiority is distinctly presented early on by the fact that he is not even addressed by his proper name. It seems as if all through Wart's childhood, he is constantly having to cater to Kay. Because of this, we as the audience can find sympathy for Wart, and he comes across as kind, docile, and patient. Later on, he pulls the sword out of the stone and, as if by magic, transforms from Wart to King Arthur.

This novel also gives us wisdom and advice on subjects such as change and violence. Through the novel, we can appreciate and accept change. The novel also expresses ideas on war and violence. It lets us know that just because someone is bigger, better, or has more material possessions than another person, he or she is not automatically right. It is what is in the heart that counts.

I have greatly enjoyed reading the novel, The Once and Future King. It is a very good book, and I hope everyone has a chance to experience its contents.

Example 3.4

TEACHING TIP

In order to meet the needs and interests of each student, provide a variety of experiences such as

a.   Whole class reading of a core book.
b.   Individualized reading of self-selected books.
c.   Group reading with thematic topics or literature response groups (explained later in this chapter).

Using Basal Readers

Perhaps you are thinking as you read this chapter:

> "What am I to do? My principal insists that I teach with basals. We don't have any multiple copies of trade books, but we do have basal readers for each child."

Don't despair! It's possible to use basal readers within the workshop structure, but teachers need to supplement the stories with trade books and use basals in a different way. For some teachers and administrators who are reluctant to give them up, basal readers provide a sense of comfort and security, especially during a transitional period when teachers may be moving toward whole language or literature-based reading. Basal readers are becoming much more literature-based, but many of the stories are poor adaptations of the original versions (Routman, 1991). If you must use basal readers, try these suggestions:

- Don't use skill-and-drill pages from workbooks.
- Choose only the best stories.
- Let students read and respond to these stories as they would to trade books—with authentic questions, differing points of view, and comments about related personal experiences.
- Be selective about what you use from the teacher's manual. (Some enrichment activities may be very beneficial!)
- Allow time for reading and discussing whole books and authentic literature in addition to basal stories.
- Develop your own meaningful guide for interpreting the story and incorporating reading strategies.

Components of a Workshop: Time, Ownership, and Response

The personal, social, and knowledge-based potential for literature shown in Figure 3.1 doesn't just happen. Teachers can abuse literature by skilling and drilling it, by failing to give children the time they need to read and share it, and by not allowing students to have some choices in the books they read and the ways they respond. Three important elements of a reading/writing workshop that contribute to quality experiences with literature are time, ownership, and response.

Time

Over the past years many of us have been appalled by statistics that show how little time children spend reading in school. John Goodlad (1984) pointed out that children in grades K–6 spend only six percent of their school day reading, and students in junior high read only three percent of their time in school. The *Becoming a Nation of Readers* report (Anderson et al., 1985) confirms that little time is actually spent reading independently in school—as little as seven to eight minutes a day for primary level children and only 15 minutes a day for intermediate grade children. Also, students spend up to 70 percent of their reading instructional time on independent practice, such as workbook pages and skill sheets which are unrelated to yearly gains in reading and have questionable value for transferring skills to reading (Anderson et al., 1985; Lamme, 1987; Weaver, 1990). Yet we know that the amount of time students spend reading contributes significantly to their gains in reading achievement (Taylor, Frye, and Maruyama, 1990).

If our aim is to invite students to learn to love to read, then we must give them time to do so—a significant, uninterrupted amount of time to browse, select books, read and reflect, and respond. If we truly value reading, we need to show our own commitment to it by reading as they read, at least part of the time. We should encourage children to take books home to read, but we can't rely on all students to read at home, so we must make time during the school day to read. When there is time to read and little or no pressure to meet deadlines and complete related worksheets, children will have the opportunity to discover the pleasure of reading for themselves.

Ownership

Ownership is achieved primarily through self-selection—of books, response activities, and literacy goals. As children make choices about what to read and how to respond, they assume responsibility for their reading. When they get to choose their reading material, they feel a deeper commitment to it than when the teacher chooses it for them. Giving students the freedom to choose lets them find books that meet their interests and needs, as well as those that are comfortable for them to read in terms of difficulty. Although some students may naturally choose the good literature that the teacher models, others may seem to be stuck in a mire of mediocrity. No one knows better than they do, however, when they are ready to move on to more rigorous and better quality literature.

Making the right choice is not always easy. I believe that's one reason why students like series books, such as the Goosebumps and Baby Sitter series; they know what to expect. Sometimes students make the wrong choices. I've seen first and second graders pick out books because of their colorful jackets or their sizes and shapes. If a student starts a book and finds it to be a poor choice, the student should be allowed to abandon the book and begin another. A mini-lesson on selecting books would be helpful in giving students the guidance they need for making wise selections.

To enable students to gain ownership of literacy, teachers can encourage them to set their own goals or purposes for reading and writing (Carroll and Christenson, 1995). Charlene, a fifth grade teacher, introduced her students to goal setting by discussing students' concepts of reading and writing, their perceptions of themselves as readers and writers, and goals in general. She then invited them to set goals for themselves. Although their initial goals dealt primarily with such superficial tasks as "read faster" and "read harder books," they eventually chose more appropriate goals, such as "make a little more sense in my head when I read" (p. 45). Charlene guided them toward setting more valid goals with her mini-lessons and by allowing students time to reflect on their goals and set new ones if they wanted to do so. During workshop they also had time to pursue their goals as they began to accept responsibility for their learning. Group-share sessions often consisted of student discussions about the progress they were making toward achieving their goals.

Response

Just as you are eager to share a good book, so are children. When we talk about a favorite book we tell how it makes us feel, the way we relate it to our personal experiences, or why it is so special—a far cry from the traditional book report! Although I believe in Sustained Silent Reading (SSR), I feel that something is missing. There is usually no opportunity for readers to respond to the literature and share their ideas with others. Children need to share as all good readers do, perhaps through oral discussions or written dialogues.

The Dialogue Journal. One of the most effective ways to encourage children to respond to literature is through the dialogue journal. Students write their responses to what they read, and someone replies—usually the teacher but sometimes another student or adult. Dialogue journals shouldn't be summaries or retellings; they should be a place for students to express their reflections, emotional involvement, and thoughtful reactions. Three simple guidelines for students to follow when writing in dialogue journals are:

- Be specific.
- Share your feelings.
- Relate to your experiences.

Although you can adapt dialogue journals to meet your own needs, Figure 3.4, based on Nancie Atwell's ideas (1987, pp. 193–194), gives some basic procedures for using them.

Get your own spiral or three-ring notebook.
Keep all of your responses in order and number the pages.
Write your thoughts, feelings, questions, and wonderings.
Write as often as you wish, but at least once a week.
Keep your log in the place provided for it when you are
    not writing in it.
Write in your log during or outside of reading workshop.
Date your entries in the upper right corner.
Capitalize and underline book titles.
Keep a log of titles, authors, and date completed for each
    book you read.

Figure 3.4:   Procedures for Using Dialogue Journals

Preparing students to give thoughtful responses. A major
challenge in using literature dialogue journals is getting students to
write *responses* instead of *summaries.* It is far easier for them to
simply retell what has happened than to respond thoughtfully. Although some teachers may also want students to give brief plot
summaries, they should emphasize critical reactions to what students read. Three ways to teach students how to make thoughtful
responses are guided discussions, modeling, and dialogue journals.

When each student is reading the same book, the teacher has
an opportunity to guide the discussion so that students will need to
use higher-order thinking skills in order to respond. Sara Angeletti
(1991) begins teaching her students how to respond by asking them
to state their opinions orally about a book that she is reading aloud
to them. During her reading she stops occasionally, inviting comments and asking the kinds of questions that she wants her students
to use later as prompts for their written responses. Sara asks not
only for opinions, but for reasons why they feel or believe as they do.

Mini-lessons in which you model the type of response you
want help students understand how to respond also. Using a book
that is familiar to the class such as Phyllis Naylor's *Shiloh*, write
your reflections on the board or on a transparency. You might write
something like this:

Near the beginning of the book I suspected the dog had been
abused. I thought this because of words the author used to
describe him: *slinking, head down, tail between legs, cringe,
like he's hardly got the right to breathe, slinks off.* I can identify with Marty because I love dogs and would hate to know
that someone was kicking or beating a dog. This reminds me
of my next door neighbor who has a springer spaniel that is
scared of people because he was mistreated when he was a
puppy.

Point out that you referred to specific examples from the text,
expressed your feelings, and related the episode to a personal
experience.

Another way to show students how to respond is by giving them some prompts that will cause them to think deeply about the book. Figure 3.5 gives some examples of prompts that can apply to most stories.

Choose a character from the story. What feelings do you have about him or her?

What do you think might happen next? What makes you think so?

What questions do you have about the story so far?

Which character do you like best? Why?

How does this story remind you of your own experiences?

How has this story affected the way you feel about people?

How would this story be different if it happened in your own neighborhood?

What do you like or dislike about the book?

How well does the author describe the setting? What are some descriptive words or phrases that help you visualize it?

How effectively does the author write?

If you could change something about the story, what would it be?

Was the ending satisfying? Why or why not?

Figure 3.5:   Prompts for Dialogue Journals

TEACHING TIP

When using prompts,

a.   Don't give too many at once or you will simply confuse the students.

b.   Encourage students to make thoughtful responses without relying on prompts as soon as they are able to do so.

Replying to journal entries. When replying to a journal entry, affirm what the writer has said and extend her or his thinking by asking a question or making a comment that may cause the student to think more deeply. Be honest and sincere in your reply, showing genuine curiosity or interest; avoid letting the correspondence become a typical teacher-student, question-answer situation. Your replies may sometimes be serious and thoughtful, sometimes light and humorous, and sometimes related to your personal experiences. Journals are informal, first-draft writings, so this is not the time to make corrections, but you should expect the writing to be legible. Example 3.5 shows how John, a sixth grader, shares his reactions to Julia Sauer's *Fog Magic* with his teacher in a dialogue journal. (The teacher's replies are in brackets.)

Example 3.5

Through your replies, you can individually guide students' developing reading strategies and appreciation of literature (Wollman-Bonilla, 1991). Your replies can

- model ways to respond to literature.
- encourage children to be aware of literary elements (for example, plot, characters, theme, setting, author's style).
- point out helpful reading strategies (for example, making and confirming or modifying predictions, noting sequence of events, making inferences).
- provide background information to make meanings clearer.
- show how to relate personal experiences to the reading.
- present a different perspective.
- challenge students to examine their assumptions and viewpoints for possible alternatives.

Corresponding with your students should be an anticipated pleasure—a time to get to know them, to understand what they think, and to visit with them on an informal basis. Writing replies can become a frustration and a burden, however, if you feel compelled to reply so often that you have no time for anything else. If you begin to dread spending hours writing replies, perhaps you are writing too frequently.

During her first year of teaching, Katy Humphrey began using dialogue journals while teaching several sections of reading at a middle school. She explained to me that her students don't write in their journals every day because they do other types of response activities as well. She also admitted it is difficult for her to find the time to respond to each of her 145 students, so she usually writes to each one only once every three weeks.

Katy wanted to teach a novel to the whole class and chose Mildred Taylor's *Roll of Thunder, Hear My Cry.* She engaged her students in a discussion of racial prejudice and desegregation before introducing the book, so the students had background knowledge and feelings to draw from as they read. She found that by offering questions or prompts about the story, the seventh graders were likely to think more critically about what was happening. Example 3.6 is an entry from Meghan's journal. She is responding to a purpose-setting question, and Katy is replying to her response.

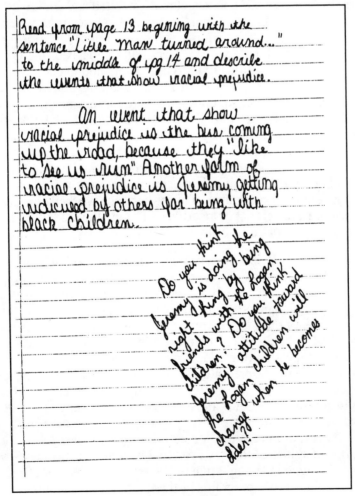

Example 3.6

Peer dialogue journals. Teacher replies undoubtedly offer many benefits, but peer and other adult replies also serve valid purposes. Nancie Atwell (1987) observed that students write to one another differently than they do to their teachers. They are less careful with mechanics, but more emotional and more playful with their peers, more trusting of each other's advice, more descriptive of their feelings, and more likely to write longer and more frequent notes.

Nivia Ayers (1994) explained to us how she invites her secondary students to choose reading partners with similar tastes and reading rates when they use peer dialogue journals. Together the partners choose a book and each reads a copy of it during the same period of time. She gives her students time to read, to write in their journals, and to get together for discussions. Book selections, often historical fiction or nonfiction, are tied to historical themes, such as the holocaust or the cold war, in order to correlate English and history. When corresponding with their peers through dialogue journals, Nivia says, students get really excited and tend to be more careful, serious, and analytical in their responses than when they read for themselves. Nivia looks at their journals twice during each nine-week period and evaluates them on the basis of the depth of their emotional reactions toward characters and events.

Also supporting the use of partner reading, Joanne Gillespie (1993) introduced her seventh graders to partner reading by sending them to the library in pairs to select a book. Both students had a personal copy to read and respond to through buddy journals, which they enjoyed writing because of the interaction with their classmates. Later in the year, each student asked an adult to be a buddy book partner, typically a parent but sometimes an older sibling or a college companion. This experience worked equally well but offered a different perspective and found the student often taking the lead in making comments about the book.

Other Types of Responses. In many literature and activity books you will find dozens of ways to respond to literature: puppetry, readers' theater, art, time lines, sewing, music, drama, story maps, cooking, crafts, and so forth. Some teachers post a list or keep a source book of literature response options for students to use when they finish a book. Many of these ideas are useful for enriching students' understanding of a period in history or for helping a kinesthetic learner appreciate a story. Such activities also help to connect areas of the curriculum. Although these ideas seem clever and intriguing, they may do little to advance understanding and appreciation of literature if they get too big. Be careful that the benefits of literature extension activities justify the time and effort in terms of students' literary growth. I have seen many cases where "the tail wagged the dog"; that is, the related project, not the literature, dominated the program. In these situations students had little opportunity to extend their knowledge and appreciation of literature.

Many teachers find effective alternatives to dialogue journals for encouraging students to respond to literature. Joy McCaleb asks her seventh graders to keep reader response journals to record their reactions to books they read. Example 3.7 shows Misty's feelings about a favorite author, R. L. Stine, and her plans to cooperate with friends during a group share.

Patricia Kelly (1990) involved her third graders in a variety of responses, such as flannel board retellings, dioramas, collages, illustrations for their own books, and book sharing groups. Her main thrust, however, was to get the students to think about what they noticed in the book, their feelings about the book, and the way the book related to their own experiences. Since her students ranged in reading levels from grades one through four, Patricia decided to read a variety of literature aloud to them rather than asking students to read silently. In the first phase of her literature response program, she recorded students' oral responses on a large sheet of paper. During the second phase the students wrote their responses and later shared them in groups.

> Dear journal
>
> I am already on my second book. The first book I read was "The Secret" by R. L. Stine. It was kind of gross but it was an easy book and I enjoyed it. Now I am reading "The Wrong Number" it is also by R. L. Stine. I enjoy R. L. Stines Books he will get you at a point and you just can't stop reading and I like that.
>
> Misty Mayberry, Amy Smith, and I all liked the thrill of his books. I think our group will do a commercial act for our presentation.

Example 3.7

I believe that Patricia Kelly's idea of reading aloud to her students is particularly effective at lower grade levels when many students must struggle to read for themselves. As the students contributed their varying responses, they learned that it is acceptable to have different points of view. Their oral responses helped them to understand what they were expected to write during the second phase of the program.

In another reader response program, Sara Angeletti (1991) created sets of opinion-question cards for her first and second graders. They dealt with such ideas as analyzing characters, determining the truth of a story, and evaluating the ending. Sara modeled ways to respond to the questions, and students used these cards in oral discussions and during peer conferences. Each workshop began with modeling responses to questions; continued with letting students read silently, then meet in groups to respond to the questions; and concluded with students writing individual responses. Students could choose their own questions, or combinations of questions, as they wrote their responses.

Teachers encourage students to respond to literature in a variety of ways. When Sacha read the informational story "An Oak Tree Dies and a Journey Begins" in Jill Ramsey's class, she wrote a response that told how the oak tree felt about getting swept away in a storm (see Example 3.8). Stacy Ross read her kindergartners Jan Brett's *The Mitten,* which tells how small and big animals accumulate in a handknit mitten. Then she asked her children to think of the animals that might get into their own mittens, and Cara wrote and illustrated the story shown in Example 3.9.

Some children, of course, cannot read and respond as well as others. In her resource room, Joanne White read *White Horse,* an easy-to-read book, to her little group of fourth graders and then encouraged them to read it for themselves. She asked them to write how they thought the horse felt, and Charles, a certified learning disabled child, wrote the response shown in Example 3.10.

James, one of Ellen Wolfe's fourth graders, could barely read. One day during workshop time, Ellen sat with him and listened to him tell her what was happening in the wordless picture book *Anno's Journey.* As he told her each sentence, she recorded it for him. Ellen then encouraged him to read it back to her, which he was able to do with much help. James's first dictated paragraph reads as follows:

> He took the boat on the shore and walked on the trail. He bought a horse. He rode it down the trail. There were a lot of trees. He saw a lot of deer on the way to the house. He crossed the bridge in his wagon.

Stephanie   about an oak tree
Charecters

MY Bad Dream
Boy
Girl

"Hi. My name is skippy, I'm skippy
a old oak tree. I live on a river
bank all by my self. Once I
had a journey. There was a
huge storm on April 29, 1846.
It blew all my leavs away.
I got torn out of the ground.
It was awful. My branches were
broken off. Oh! I shouted HELP!
But nobody heard me. I got
Bnocked in to the ocean.
I road the waves, got stuck in
sand, (and got chopped in to fire
wood. One day the tide puled
up one last very twisted root.
A boy came and picked it up
but took it to his sister.
She loved it. The root looked
like it was a shiny gold.
I had woke up right as the
good part happend. Well, it was
all a dream. The date is
1998."
                The End

Example 3.8

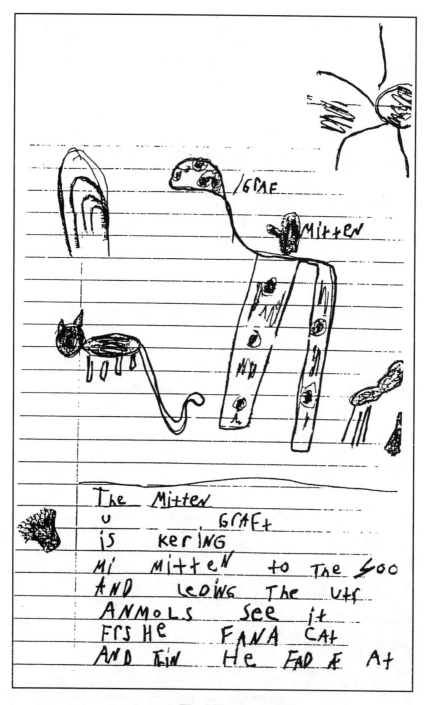

The child's drawing and writing reads:

/GPAE

Mitten

The Mitten
U   GrAFt
is   ker ING
Mi Mitten   to The ZOO
AND   LeDiNG The   utr
ANMoLS   see   it
Frs He   FaNA   CAt
AND TiN   He   FAD Æ At

The Mitten

A giraffe is carrying my mitten to the zoo and letting the other animals see
it. First he found a cat and then he found an ant.

Example 3.9

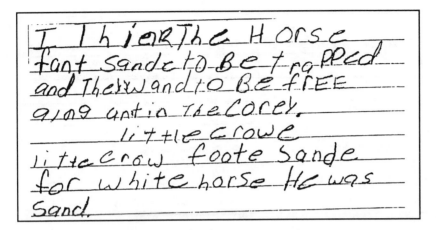

I think the horse felt sad to be trapped and they wanted to be free
again and in the country.

Little Crow felt sad for white horse. He was sad.

Example 3.10

Group-Share Sessions

At the conclusion of each reading workshop, students have opportunities to share what they have been reading. For many children this is the icing on the cake—the time that they get to talk about and listen to favorite books. (Refer to Chapter 2 for more information on conducting group-share sessions.)

The types of materials children share come from literature and children's responses to it. Children at every age level can participate, with kindergartners telling about picture books and older students reading or giving in-depth responses to books they have read. Some topics for sharing in reading workshops are:

- Reading a paragraph or two from a favorite book and explaining why this book is special
- Presenting a literature response project in progress
- Giving a book talk to recommend a book
- Dramatizing a scene from a story that students are converting into a play
- Reading passages from books by the same author to show characteristics of an author's style

When children read selections from favorite books during group-share sessions, members of the audience may become interested in reading these books themselves. In fact, sharing time is an excellent opportunity for students to recommend books. Because of this, you may want to post a form such as the one shown in Figure 3.6 so that students can refer to this list of recommended books when they are making their selections.

Reader's Name	Date Shared	Title	Author	Comments

Figure 3.6:   Group-Share Recommendations

Before students share books, they need to rehearse their oral reading with a partner. The listening partner should be able to advise the reader on ways to improve oral reading so that the selection will be well received by the audience. You might want to post a list of criteria for good oral reading, with contributions from the students as well as yourself. The following list offers some questions to consider before students sign up to share.

- Have I chosen a book that the audience will enjoy?
- Can I read with fluency and expression?
- Do I know the passage well enough to look at the audience sometimes while I am reading?
- Have I estimated the amount of time it takes (no more than five minutes)?
- Do I hold my book so that the audience can see my face?
- Do I read loudly enough for everyone to hear me?
- Do I know all the words and can I pronounce them clearly?
- If I am reading dialogue, can I show with my voice that different people are speaking?
- Do I avoid distracting gestures and mannerisms?

Of course, students may share in other ways as well, but in any case they should be well prepared in order to use this time effectively. Whenever time permits, students should be able to react to presentations by their classmates by asking probing questions or making insightful comments. You might want to claim some of that time yourself to share something you've read, to show a new type of response, or to allow a child to share who didn't sign up in advance but has something timely and worthwhile to contribute.

Joy McCaleb's seventh and eighth graders recommend books to their classmates during sharing time by presenting well-prepared book talks, often with visual aids. Ricky used a diorama to illustrate *White Fang;* Clint used a model of where the characters lived as he discussed *Tuck Everlasting;* and Melody dressed as a bag lady as she told about *December Stillness.*

An alternative to whole class sharing sessions is to allow students to share in groups. Both arrangements are useful, so you may want to use each some of the time. Divide the class into groups according to the books they are reading, such as by genres, books by the same author, theme-related books, or some other reason. Even a random grouping can be helpful by allowing children to share books of different types. The main advantages of small group sharing are that students have more opportunities to share and settings are more intimate.

Sometimes groups of students who read the same book can share it with the rest of the class, as in the case of a group of fourth graders in Sue Thompson's room who had read Katherine Paterson's *Bridge to Terabithia.* The students became intrigued with the similarities and differences between Jess and Leslie, the two main characters, so they shared ways that the two were alike and different. A shortened form of their list looks like this:

Alike	Different
Rulers of Terabithia	Jess hates school; Leslie likes it
Like to run	Jess has TV; Leslie has no TV
Live on farms	Jess is average, Leslie is rich
Use their imaginations	Jess has 4 sisters; Leslie is an
In same class at school	only child

Literature Response Groups

An activity that can work comfortably within the workshop framework is literature response groups, sometimes called literature circles. Here we have the three components of a workshop: time to read, ownership by self-selection, and response through group discussion and entries written in literature logs.

In order to use literature response groups, you need several sets of five or six popular, good quality books. Introduce the books to your class by giving brief book blurbs. For instance, if you are introducing Gary Paulsen's *Hatchet,* you might show the book and say the following:

> This is an exciting survival story about Brian who was in a plane that crashed in the Canadian wilderness. As the only survivor, he had to find ways to keep himself alive. At first, he had few skills, but by drawing on his experiences and with the help of his hatchet, he solved many problems and managed to cope successfully with his surroundings.

After your children have heard about each of the books, ask them to fill out slips of paper on which they write their first two or three choices of books they want to read. Place students in groups by preferences (not by achievement level), so that you have several groups of four to six children.

To prepare students for working in literature response groups, you should establish expectations. Students must know what to bring with them to group, how to interact with each other, and how to conduct themselves during discussions and silent reading. You may want to introduce this procedure to one group of students at a time, making sure that they can handle the responsibility before involving the whole class.

TEACHING TIP
When placing children in groups,
a.   Keep a record of which children get their first choices.
b.   Place children who don't get their first choices in their favorite selections the next time.

Children usually meet in groups two or three times a week for about three weeks. As they read their books, they write in literature logs, which may be spiral notebooks or a few sheets of paper in manila folders. Good topics for literature logs are:

- Reflections on what they are reading
- Questions about unfamiliar vocabulary words
- Confusions about what is really happening in the story
- Predictions about what will happen next
- Ways that they can personally relate to the characters
- Issues they want to discuss with the group

TEACHING TIP
On the first day that children meet in groups before they have read any of the book, ask them to use their logs
a.   To tell why they chose the book.
b.   To make predictions about what will happen.

When children meet in groups, one child generally assumes the leadership role. Teachers tell me this can work several ways. Sometimes children take turns being the group leader; sometimes they vote for a leader who retains that role while the group reads a whole book; and sometimes leadership just emerges naturally. The leader usually begins by asking students how far they want to read next time and the students determine for themselves how many pages or chapters to read. The students then read from their literature logs, and their entries become the basis for discussing the novel. When the children have shared their entries and participated in the discussion (usually about ten minutes), they spend the rest of the workshop time reading their books.

TEACHING TIP
When students are writing in logs, ask them to put the page number of each question or comment they make. Otherwise many minutes may be wasted as students search through chapters saying, "I know it's in here somewhere."

While the children are conducting their group discussions, what are you doing as the teacher? Essentially, you have two roles: participant and evaluator. You may join a table as participant by entering into the discussion as a group member, not as leader or questioner. You may model higher-order responses and questions, or you may just wish to give your own thoughts about the book being read. This is a time for students to engage in *grand conversations,* sharing ideas and opinions, expanding and extending their understanding, and reconstructing meaning (Weaver, 1990). Joining a group also lets you observe and evaluate student participation. (Chapter 10 gives information on evaluating literature response groups.)

You may find that some groups do not finish as quickly as others. Those who finish early may create a literature extension activity, but this activity is much less important than reading, responding to, and sharing the books. Examples of extension activities are:

- Find information about the author and write a report.
- Respond to the book through music, art, or drama.
- Choose a character from the book and write a story about having the character visit your school.
- Compare this book to others by the same author.
- Discuss or write how this book would have been different if the setting had been at your school.

Allow the students to brainstorm their own ideas for extension activities, but they may ask you for some suggestions.

Most of the teachers I know who use literature response groups organize them once every six weeks. They spend the rest of the time on other types of reading instruction, such as individualized reading or thematic reading-writing activities. If groups meet too often, students' enthusiasm dims for this type of activity, you may not have enough sets of books to use all year, and students miss opportunities to do other types of reading. Figure 3.7 is a summary of the procedures for using literature response groups.

One of my former college students, Trena Farmer, used literature response groups with her sixth graders in Alaska. She wrote:

> "My students and I *love* the literature response groups! It is so successful! I bought a classroom set of *Number the Stars.* I caught a child today sneaking and trying to read ahead!"

Preparatory Activities

Teacher shows books and gives brief book talks about each one.

Students write their choices on slips of paper and the teacher forms groups based on student preferences.

Teacher sets expectations for behaviors during group sessions in order to prepare students for working in groups.

Group Reading Procedures

Students meet in groups according to assignments based on their selections.

They decide how far to read each time.

Students read from their literature logs and discuss their ideas about the book.

Students spend most of their time reading their books and writing comments in their logs.

Follow-up Activities

Students do extension activities if time is available.

Students evaluate themselves.

Figure 3.7:   Procedures for Literature Response Groups

Later, Trena stopped by and told me that her students' favorite book was Jerry Spinelli's *Maniac Magee*. She also offered some advice based on her experiences with literature response groups:

- Give students one minute to get into groups.
- Guide them in dividing the book into chapters so that all groups will finish about the same time.
- Have them decide how far to read in the first two minutes.
- Give a generic prompt at first for writing in logs, such as
  - ♦ Make predictions.
  - ♦ Identify your favorite character and tell why.
  - ♦ Describe the setting and tell how it makes you feel.
  - ♦ Give the problem that is developing.
  - ♦ Write a critique of the book (when finished).

Some classroom teachers are unfamiliar with literature response groups, but I use them in my combined children's literature/reading methods class and the college students enjoy this approach. When they do the practicum portion of the class, they sometimes introduce these groups to the children, as well as to their cooperating teachers. Ronnie Manis used them during practicum with his fourth grade students, who definitely preferred literature response groups to their traditional basal reader approach (see Example 3.11).

I really like the book I am reading. The Real Thief. I like it because it captures my mind more than any other book I have ever read. I got hooked at the very beggining - pages 9-16. The beggining made me want to learn about Gawan and what happened to him. The King is unfair to Gawan in this book. I like this project because I get out of that stupid reading book that only talks about summarizing. It also gets me out of boring old charts. I wish we could do this everyday while Mr. Ronnie Mantis - or something like that - is still here.

Thank-You,
Christen

Example 3.11

Some alternatives for conducting literature response groups are as follows (Burke, Strand, and McCord, 1995; Routman, 1991):

- Follow the same procedure with the whole class instead of with groups.
- Select group members yourself so you can place students according to those who work well together.
- Select one book for the whole class to read and you assign the number of chapters to read each day.
- Pair those who have difficulty reading the text with better readers or provide them with a tape of the book.
- Let students spend Mondays and Tuesdays reading and responding to logs, Wednesdays and Thursdays in group discussions, and Fridays catching up.

Summary

Reading workshops offer students large blocks of time to read whole books, a sense of ownership by choosing their own reading materials and setting personal goals, and opportunities to respond. Response is likely to occur through dialogue journals, in which readers share their reflections with their teacher or with a peer or other adult. Many other types of responses are possible, but in any case teachers should urge students to respond thoughtfully in order to deepen their appreciation and understanding of literature. Literature response groups can operate within the reading workshop format, and they consist of groups of students who read and share insights about the same book.

Reflections

Seriously consider the following questions. Some answers may be found by reflecting on the chapter; others may come from your own beliefs and experiences.

1. How important do I believe it is for students to think about and reflect on the books they read? What are some ways I could encourage them to do this?

2. How well acquainted am I with good quality children's and adolescent literature? Will I be able to select good books and recommend them to my class? How can I keep updated on new books in a variety of genres?

3. How do I feel about giving children complete freedom to choose their reading materials? Should I place any limitations or restrictions on their choices? I should keep in mind my goals—and the students' goals—for reading as I consider these questions.

4. Is there a teacher who is using reading workshop whom I can observe? What are some things that I should look for to get ideas for my own workshop? If I don't know anyone who is using this approach, is there someone in my school with whom I could make plans to implement it?

5. Are there some procedures that I am already using that are consistent with the workshop approach? How could I build on these ideas that I am already using or planning to use to create a workshop?

Bibliography

Anderson, R. C., Hiebert, E. H., Scott, J. A. & Wilkinson, I. A. (1985). *Becoming a nation of readers.* Champaign, Ill.: Center for the Study of Reading.

Angeletti, S. (1991). Encouraging students to think about what they read. *The Reading Teacher, 45* (4), 288–295.

Atwell, N. (1987). *In the middle.* Portsmouth, NH: Heinemann.

Ayers, N. (1994). Integrating world literature and world history. Presentation at the National Council of Teachers of English, Orlando, FL.

Bell, B. (1990). Literature response groups. Presentation at Richard C. Owen Workshop *Whole Language in the Classroom.* Oak Ridge, TN.

Burke, L., Strand, B., & McCord, S. (1995). Literature study groups. Paper presented at the International Reading Association Convention, Anaheim.

Carroll, J., & Christenson, C. (1995). Teaching and learning about student goal setting in a fifth-grade classroom. *Language Arts, 72* (1), 42–49.

Duthie, C. (1994). Nonfiction: A genre study for the primary classroom. *Language Arts, 71* (8), 588–595.

Duthie, C., & Zimet, E. (1992). Poetry is like directions for your imagination. *The Reading Teacher, 46* (1), 14–24.

Five, C. L. (1988). From workbooks to workshop: Increasing children's involvement in the reading process. *The New Advocate, 1* (2), 103–113.

Gillespie, J. (1993). Buddy book journals: Responding to literature. *English Journal, 82* (6), 64–68.

Goodlad, J. (1984). *A place called school.* New York: McGraw-Hill.

Gutkin, R. (1990). Sustained _____ reading. *The Reading Teacher, 67* (1), 490–491.

Hagerty, P. (1992). *Readers' workshop.* Richmond Hill, Ontario, Canada: Scholastic Canada.

Hansen, J. (1987). *When writers read.* Portsmouth, NH: Heinemann.

Kelly, P. (1990). Guiding young students' response to literature. *The Reading Teacher, 43* (7), 464–470.

Kletzien, S., & Hushion, B. (1992). Reading workshop: Reading, writing, thinking. *Journal of Reading, 35* (6), 444–451.

Lamme, L. L. (1987). Children's literature: The natural way to learn to read. In B. Cullinan (Ed.) *Children's literature in the reading program.* Newark, DE: International Reading Association, pp. 41–53.

McWhirter, A. (1990). Whole language in the middle school. *The Reading Teacher, 43* (8), 562–565.

Norton, D. (1994). *Through the eyes of a child.* Englewood Cliffs, NJ: Merrill, an imprint of Prentice Hall.

Parsons, L. (1990). *Response journals.* Portsmouth, NH: Heinemann.

Peterson, R. & Eeds, M. *Grand conversations: Literature groups in action.* Richmond Hill, Ontario, Canada: Scholastic.

Reutzel, D. R., & Cooter, R. B. (1991). Organizing for effective instruction: The reading workshop. *The Reading Teacher, 44* (8), 548–554.

Rief, L. (1992). *Seeking diversity.* Portsmouth, NH: Heinemann.

Routman, R. (1991). *Invitations.* Portsmouth, NH: Heinemann.

Strickland, D., Dillon, R., Funkhouser, L., Glick, M., & Rogers, C. (1989). Research currents: Classroom dialogue during literature response groups. *Language Arts, 66* (2), 192–205.

Taylor, B., Frye, B., & Maruyama, G. Time spent reading and reading growth. (1990). *American Educational Research Journal, 27* (2), 351–362.

Weaver, C. (1990). *Understanding whole language.* Portsmouth, NH: Heinemann.

Wollman-Bonilla, J. (1991). *Response journals.* New York: Scholastic.

Zogby, G. (1990). Literature groups: Empowering the reader. Presentation at Whole Language Umbrella Conference, St. Louis, MO.

CHAPTER 4

MINI-LESSONS FOR READING WORKSHOP

Amy, seeing Kevin approaching: Hey there, Kevin! Tell me if you've found a way yet to get your students to think.

Kevin, smiling and nodding his head: Oh, yes. We were talking about that earlier. I believe I've made some progress with some students, but we still have a long way to go. I'm not sure why, but they can't seem to break away from writing summaries. Maybe that's what their other teachers asked them to do.

Amy: I suppose so—that's what I always did in school. You said you might try using dialogue journals. Did you—and did they work?

Kevin: I'm spending a great deal of time with their dialogue journals. I'm convinced they help, but it takes a lot of my time to write in them. I have to be so careful to write something that will cause them to reflect on what they read. We're learning together though, and I think we'll all get better at it. Are you still checking out all those books?

Amy: I have a room full of books and my kids are reading up a storm! In order to read as much as they do, they must be learning how to read, but I worry about whether they're getting the skills. I used to do so many worksheets, and now I feel a little insecure just letting them read.

Kevin: You need to use mini-lessons. They're a great idea for some direct teaching. I've got mine down to eight or ten minutes now, and I find that's all the time I need to get the point across to most of the students. Have you tried mini-lessons?

Amy: I've done a few, but I'm not doing them on a regular basis yet. Is there some list or sequence to go by? I hardly know where to start.

Kevin: I get some ideas for mini-lessons from the fifth grade curriculum guide. Most of the time though I just get an intuitive feel of what they need to know by observing them as they read and by conferencing with them. Then I try to think of a meaningful way to teach those skills.

Amy, pondering what Kevin said: I have some ideas for teaching with big books that I've been trying. They seem to work pretty well. . . . Anyway, thanks for the encouragement, Kevin. I'll keep at it and report back in a week or two. Bye, now.

Introduction

The mini-lesson is the first component of the reading workshop, and in this chapter we will consider some sample lesson ideas. These will be divided into four parts: workshop procedures, literary appreciation, word recognition skills and strategies, and comprehension skills and strategies. The lesson ideas are simply models and are not meant to prescribe what and how you teach—that will depend on your own goals and your students' needs.

Mini-lessons

Mini-lessons are brief, directed-teaching lessons that focus on one specific skill only. They generally take five to ten minutes at the beginning of the workshop. When this amount of time is insufficient, the teacher may want to return to the same concept another day to reinforce the mini-lesson or present it in a different way.

Teachers decide which skills or strategies to teach by observing students' needs during conferences and informal observations. In her book *When Writers Read*, Jane Hansen (1987, p. 163), citing Donald Graves, says that teachers "teach what the students need, when they need it, in the context of their own reading or writing, wherever the problem arises." Sometimes students will ask us to teach them something they need to know in order to be better readers and writers. Thus, because mini-lessons are responsive rather than directive, teachers cannot plan them far ahead. One day's observation of students' needs may become the next day's mini-lesson.

Ideally, this is how we as teachers should plan our mini-lessons, but reality also forces us to consider mandated grade-level skills. Principals and parents hold us accountable for students' scores on achievement tests that measure mastery of specific skills, so we must be sure to teach them. Many skills are of doubtful value in learning to read; for instance, of what value is it to the reader to be able to recognize a schwa? A teacher at a nearby whole language school told me of her frustration with achievement tests by saying, "Our students didn't do well on skill mastery, but they did great on comprehension." If they can comprehend—the goal of reading, does it matter if they can answer questions about discrete skills? Nevertheless, when teachers and school systems are judged by test scores—an unfortunate, but realistic situation in many places, teachers must consider curriculum guides and achievement tests, as well as students' needs.

When teaching mini-lessons, we need to make sure the students understand what they are learning and how it will help them be better readers and writers. We begin by saying something like, "I've noticed several of you are having trouble identifying themes in your stories, so today I'll help you find themes in some of the stories we've been reading together."

We use literature as a basis for mini-lessons because we want students to see immediately how they can apply the strategy we are teaching to the books they are reading. In other words, we want them to understand the value of the strategy for helping them read better. Using literature makes the connection to their personal reading much clearer than does completing worksheets about the skill or strategy.

Modeling is one of the most effective ways for students to learn, so teachers often model the skills they want students to know. They do this by saying their thoughts aloud as they demonstrate how to use a skill or strategy. For instance, a teacher might copy a selection from a story on the chalkboard or a transparency and say, "When I come to a word I don't know, such as the word *pilfer* in the middle of this sentence, I try to figure it out by thinking about what would make sense. . . ." The teacher continues with other useful strategies, then shows how she/he eventually figures out the meaning of the word. The teacher asks students for questions, comments, and other strategies they have found useful in identifying words they don't know. She/he then reminds them to use these strategies in their reading.

Although they serve widely varying purposes, most mini-lessons follow the procedures outlined in Figure 4.1.

1. Give the students a purpose for what they will be learning.
2. If possible, relate the lesson to a selection from literature.
3. Model ways to apply the strategy or skill.
4. Ask for questions and comments.
5. Remind the students to use the new information in their reading.

Figure 4.1:   Procedures for Mini-lessons

Big books are useful for teaching mini-lessons because all of the students can see them easily. When using big books to teach skills or strategies, however, you should first simply read the book with your class for pleasure. Using big books for pleasure reading is primary; using them as sources for teaching skills is secondary.

The remainder of this chapter deals with samples of mini-lessons that I have taught myself, observed teachers using, or developed as samples for teachers to follow. I've divided them into the following categories: procedural, literary appreciation, word recognition skills and strategies, and comprehension skills and strategies.

Procedural Mini-lessons

Nancie Atwell (1987) stresses the importance of establishing procedures for using reading workshops so that all students will understand what to do. She does this with a series of mini-lessons, each of which is designed to help students understand how the workshop operates and why it is a useful framework for learning to read. Figure 4.2 lists some of the procedures that students need to know.

- Materials students need to bring with them to the workshop each day
- What homework, if any, is required (you may want students to read or respond at home)
- Guidelines to follow (see Chapter 3 for a suggested list)
- Why it's important for students to choose their own books and have lots of time for reading
- How to use dialogue journals
- Where to find and replace books and supplies
- What check-out system to use when borrowing books from the classroom library

---

Figure 4.2:   Topics for Procedural Mini-lessons

Following are two procedural lessons that Amy and Kevin might use as they introduce the reading workshop.

Procedural Lesson
Explaining the Workshop

Amy, sitting in a rocking chair and gathering her children around her on the story rug: Today we're going to learn about a new way to read books that I think you'll enjoy. How many of you like to choose your own books to read?

Amy, as the children's hands shoot up: That's what I thought, so we are going to do a reading workshop that will let you each choose a book and spend lots of time reading it. Do you know where to find the books in our room?

Tony: There are some books on those shelves under the windows.

Anne: I've been looking at the ones in the milk crate near the nature center. They're mostly about animals and plants and outdoors.

Jimmy: Can we look at magazines too? There are some of those on the table by the writing center.

Amy: Of course you may read magazines, too. Don't forget about the books in our library corner behind where I'm sitting. We also can read the library books we check out each week. When it's time for our reading workshop, I'll expect you to have a book or magazine ready to read. Do you think you can do that?

Amy, waiting for the children to agree that they could be ready: When you have your books and it's time to read, where would you like to go to read?

Clarissa: I like to sit on the floor in a corner all by myself.

Amy: Fine, and Bobby, how about you?

Bobby: Is it okay if I read with Tommy? He and I like to read the same kinds of books.

Amy: You may try it and we'll see how it works.

Cheryl: I like to sit on a pillow near the window to read.

Amy: I know many of you have different ideas about where you want to read, and I want you to read where you're comfortable. Can you think of anything we have to remember while we're reading?

Joyce: I don't want anybody to bother me while I'm reading. Should we have a rule about interrupting?

Amy: That's a good idea—maybe we should. Let's get started though before we make any rules. Then we'll decide what rules we need and make a list. I think we're ready to start now, so let's take the library books we checked out this morning and start by reading them. If you finish your library book early, you may choose another book or magazine to read.

Procedural Lesson
Introducing Dialogue Journals

Kevin: Yesterday we talked about some guidelines for our reading workshop, and today I'd like to tell you about using dialogue journals. A dialogue journal is a place where you can write your thoughts, feelings, and reactions to what you read. It's important for you to understand what the author is saying, but you also need to think about what you're getting out of your reading. Your dialogue journal will be a place to write your thoughts. You will need to have some sort of spiral notebook or composition book by Monday, but today as you read you may write your responses in your writing notebooks.

Trudy: If it's a dialogue journal, does someone write back to us?

Kevin: Exactly. I'll be writing to you about once a week, but I'd like you to write an entry each time we have the workshop. It doesn't have to be long, but be sure you put the date for each entry. Later, perhaps you'll be writing and responding to each other.

Steve: What do you mean when you say we have to write our thoughts and feelings? Can't we just write what happened?

Kevin: No, that's not what I'm looking for. I want you to *reflect* on what you read. You remember how we discussed *Tuck Everlasting* and wondered if we would like to live forever. That's the kind of thing I want you to write in your journals. I've just started reading *Dicey's Song* to you, so let me show you the kind of entry you might write about what we've read so far.

> I wonder what Dicey meant when she said she "couldn't let it get her down." I wonder what she was feeling down about, and I wonder what had happened to her mother that she didn't want to have happen to her. A little later Gram seems to be doing things. Are the children living with their grandmother now? Is Dicey's mother unable to care for the family? I want to find out more about this family!

Kevin: What have I done here? Can you see what I mean by reflecting on what you read?

Trina: You're wondering about what's going to happen. You're trying to make sense out of how the story begins.

Kevin: Right. That's the idea. Sometimes you might relate the story to your personal experiences, and other times you might just think about what the story means to you. Does anyone have any questions?

Beth: How long does it have to be?

Kevin: No special length. Just write as much as you want to say about it and then continue reading. I want you to *think* about what you're reading, so try to do this as you read your books today.

Mini-lessons for Literary Appreciation

By their very nature, mini-lessons on literary appreciation use literature as a basis for instruction. In many cases, the teacher refers to books that the class has shared at an earlier time, but in some cases the teacher reads entire books or passages from books during the lesson. A mini-lesson is likely to exceed the normal amount of time if a teacher includes the reading of an entire book, no matter how short, as part of the lesson.

You may wish to survey your children's existing knowledge of literature and their attitudes toward pleasure reading before you begin teaching these lessons. The knowledge you get from students' answers may guide you in planning appropriate lessons and in selecting books on which to base them. For instance, if students can name no authors or illustrators, you know you will need to make them aware of who writes and illustrates books. If they have no knowledge of poetry or informational books, you may want to direct them toward these genres. Figure 4.3 is a survey that you could give to your class.

1. Name your three favorite books. _____

_____

2. Name your three favorite authors. _____

_____

3. What kinds of books do you like to read best?____

_____

4. Where do you get most of the books you read?____

_____

5. Name your three favorite poems or poets. _____

_____

6. Do you ever read books for information? If so, what kinds? _____

_____

7. How do you select the books you read?_____

_____

8. Do you like to read books? If so, why? If not, why not? _____

_____

9. What would you like to learn during reading workshop about how to read books? _____

_____

_____

10. What are your goals for yourself as a reader?_____

_____

_____

Figure 4.3:   Survey of Literary Interests

A golden rule for selecting books and poems to read aloud is to choose those books that you feel passionate about yourself. There are thousands of books available, but some will not grab you or stir your emotions. When you are enthralled or captivated by a book, the students sense your commitment and are eager to adopt it as their own. Your enthusiasm shows in the way you introduce the book, in your body language as you put yourself into the story, and by the expression in your voice.

The following mini-lessons deal with various aspects of literary appreciation. Those intended primarily for lower grades are labeled (L); those for upper grades are marked (U); and those that can apply to any grade are labeled (A). Additional resource possibilities are listed at the end of each lesson.

(A) Literary Appreciation Mini-lesson
Characterization

Tell the students to listen for the way Jerry Spinelli develops his main character in *Maniac Magee*. Read the first two pages which describe Maniac Magee through a series of legendary incidents and unusual comparisons. Ask the students to recall key phrases that Spinelli used to create his image of Maniac and list them on a chart. The students tell you: stomach like a cereal box, heart like a sofa spring, rats guarding him as he sleeps, an eight-inch pet cockroach. Ask the students to watch for figurative language and descriptive phrases that authors use to build their characters. Tell them that they can use these same techniques as they create characters for their own stories. Source book and other books for strong characterization:

(U) Jerry Spinelli. *Maniac Magee*. Scholastic, 1990.
(L) H. A. Rey. Curious George books.
(U) Barbara Robinson. *The Best Christmas Pageant Ever*. Avon Camelot, 1972.
(A) Astrid Lindgren. *Pippi Longstocking*. Viking, 1950.
(U) Katherine Paterson. *The Great Gilly Hopkins*. Crowell, 1978.

(A) Literary Appreciation Mini-lesson
Styles of Poetry

Tell the students that you will read poems by two poets who have very different styles. Ask them to listen for each poet's style. Read one or two poems by Shel Silverstein and ask the students to tell you what they notice about his style of writing poetry. They tell you: the poems are funny; they rhyme; he understands how

I feel about things; his illustrations are silly. Then read a poem from Mary O'Neill's *Hailstones and Halibut Bones* and ask them to tell you what they notice about her poems. They tell you: her poems make pictures in my head; I like the images; I can see the colors in my mind; sometimes her words are soft; she makes my mind dreamy. Point out that poets use different styles of writing and convey different moods. Ask them to watch for poet's styles when they read poetry and to try using different styles when they write their own poetry.

Source books and other poets whom children enjoy:

(A) Mary O'Neill. *Hailstones and Halibut Bones.* Doubleday, 1989.

(A) Shel Silverstein. *Light in the Attic.* Harper & Row, 1981.

(A) Shel Silverstein. *Where the Sidewalk Ends.* Harper & Row, 1974.

Robert Frost

Jack Prelutsky

Langston Hughes

Aileen Fisher

Myra Cohn Livingston

(A) Literary Appreciation Mini-lesson
Fables

Tell the students that you are going to introduce them to a different type, or genre, of literature: fables. Ask them to listen for characteristics of fables as you read Aesop's "The Hare and the Tortoise." Point out the moral and ask the students what else they noticed about this fable. They tell you that it's about animals that talk like people and it's short. Then read "The Town Mouse and the Country Mouse" and ask if it has the same features. Ask them to identify the moral, and they tell you it's better to be poor and free than to be rich and live in fear. Ask them to try to write a fable of their own during writing workshop.

Source book and other sources of fables:

(A) Aesop. *Aesop's Fables.* Illustrated by Heidi Holder. Viking, 1981. (A) Many other versions of Aesop's fables.

(A) Lionni, Leo. *Frederick's Fables.* Pantheon, 1985.

(A) Lobel, Arnold. *Fables.* HarperCollins, 1980.

(A) Literary Appreciation Mini-lesson
Making Connections

Remind students of two books they have discussed recently: *Brother Eagle, Sister Sky* and *Where the Forest Meets the Sea*. Ask students to compare and contrast the two books as you record their comments on a Venn Diagram (see Figure 4.4). Point out that they should be aware of ways that books connect with each other as they read. Encourage them to find other pairs of books with similar themes.

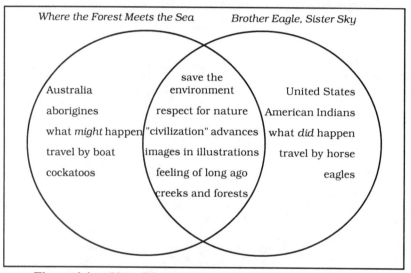

Figure 4.4:   Venn Diagram

Source books and other pairs with similar themes:
- (A) Susan Jeffers. *Brother Eagle, Sister Sky*. Dial, 1991, and Jeannie Baker. *Where the Forest Meets the Sea*. William Morrow, 1987. (Theme: save the environment)
- (L) Judith Viorst. *Alexander and the Terrible, Horrible, No Good, Very Bad Day*. Atheneum, 1972, and Patricia Reilly Giff. *Today Was a Terrible Day*. Puffin, 1987. (Theme: having a bad day)
- (L) Nancy White Carlstrom. *Northern Lullaby*. Philomel, 1992, and Mem Fox. *Time for Bed*. Gulliver, 1993. (Theme: getting ready to sleep)
- (U) Virginia Hamilton. *The People Could Fly*. Knopf, 1985, and Patricia McKissack. *The Dark-Thirty*. Scholastic, 1992. (Theme: African-American folktales)
- (A) Lloyd Alexander. *The King's Fountain*. Unicorn, 1989, and Katherine Paterson. *The King's Equal*. HarperCollins, 1992. (Theme: the courage of simple folk to stand up to the King)
- (A) Comparisons of folktales from different lands are good sources for making connections.

(A) Literary Appreciation Mini-lesson
Story Structure

Show *Mirette on the High Wire,* a book that you read to the class earlier in the week. Tell the students that when authors create stories they generally follow a structure that consists of a problem and its solution. Ask them to think about the problem in the story. They tell you that the great high-wire walker Bellini has lost his courage—he is afraid. Then ask them for the solution, and they tell you that Mirette's appearance on the high wire gives him the courage to overcome his fear. Ask the students to give you another example of a story that has a problem with a solution, and they tell you King Bidgood's in the Bathtub. The king wouldn't get out of the tub until the boy pulled the plug.

Source books and other problem-solution books:

(A) Emily Arnold McCully. *Mirette on the High Wire.* G. P. Putnam's Sons, 1992.

(L) Audrey Wood. *King Bidgood's in the Bathtub.* Harcourt Brace Jovanovich, 1985.

(A) Patricia MacLachlan. *Sarah, Plain and Tall.* Harper & Row, 1985.

(L) Libba Moore Gray. *Miss Tizzy.* Simon and Schuster, 1993.

(U) Gary Paulsen. *Hatchet.* Bradbury, 1987.

(A) Literary Appreciation Mini-lesson
Reader Response

Tell the students that some books help us gain information and also make us feel deeply about things. Remind them of the book *On the Day You Were Born* that you have already shared with them. Ask them to listen to it again, first for the information, and tell you what they can learn about the earth. They respond with comments about gravity, the pull of the tides, the spinning earth, and leaves making oxygen. Then you ask them to listen again for the feelings they get from the words and pictures. They tell you that the words sound like poetry, that they get a feeling of being part of a vast universe, that it makes them think of the connections among the earth and all living things, that they feel small, but somehow important. Ask them as they read their books today to see if they can find information and also feel deeply about the book they are reading.

Source book and other books that can create both efferent (knowledge) and aesthetic (feelings) responses follows on page 72:

(A) Debra Frasier. *On the Day You Were Born*. Harcourt Brace, 1991.
(A) Ehlert, Lois. *Red Leaf, Yellow Leaf*. Harcourt Brace Jovanovich, 1991.
(A) Jeffers, Susan. *Brother Eagle, Sister Sky*. Dial, 1991.
(A) Patricia Polacco. *Pink and Say*. Philomel, 1994.
(A) Sherry Garland. *The Lotus Seed*. Harcourt Brace Jovanovich, 1993.
(U) Russell Freedman. *Lincoln: A Photobiography*. Clarion, 1987.

Note: Although most of these are picture books, the content is appropriate for middle grade as well as primary students.

(A) Literary Appreciation Mini-lesson
Author/Illustrator Study

Remind the children that you have been sharing several books by Chris Van Allsburg, including *The Wretched Stone, The Widow's Broom, Jumanji,* and *The Polar Express.* Ask the students to tell you what they notice about the way Chris Van Allsburg writes. They say he usually begins as if the story is real, then moves his characters into fantasy. They comment on the feeling of mystery and magic, such as the bell in *The Polar Express,* the strange game that comes to life in *Jumanji,* and the glowing rock in *The Wretched Stone.* Point out that the author is indeed able to write in such a way that he carries you into a world of fantasy so that you are not sure where reality ends and fantasy begins.

Next you question the children about Chris Van Allsburg's illustrations. They observe that sometimes he uses color as in *The Polar Express* and *The Wretched Stone,* but that his black and white drawings in *Jumanji* and *The Widow's Broom* are very intriguing also because of the details in his pictures. Help the students realize that his illustrations complement the text, that they add to the feelings he creates with his words. Then introduce them to another of his books, *The Wreck of the Zephyr,* and tell them that they will also find mystery and detailed illustrations in this book.

Source books by Chris Van Allsburg:

(A) *Jumanji*. Houghton Mifflin, 1981.
(A) *The Polar Express*. Houghton Mifflin, 1985.
(A) *The Widow's Broom*. Houghton Mifflin, 1992.
(A) *The Wreck of the Zephyr*. Houghton Mifflin, 1983.
(A) *The Wretched Stone*. Houghton Mifflin, 1991.

Other authors and author/illustrators to study:

(L) Eric Carle   (U) Katherine Paterson
(L) Tomie de Paola   (U) Lois Lowry
(L) Ezra Jack Keats   (U) Gary Paulsen

Mini-lessons for Word Recognition Skills and Strategies

Most educators distinguish between skills and strategies in this way. A skill is an isolated bit of knowledge, such as knowing the short sound of a vowel as it occurs before a consonant. A strategy is a selective combination of skills that a reader uses to reach an answer, such as using context, phonics, and structural analysis to identify a word. A discrete skill is often of little use, but in combination with other skills may be quite helpful. In this section and the next we will look at ways to teach both skills and strategies with mini-lessons.

Word recognition skills consist of sight words, phonics, structural analysis (such as compound words, affixes, and contractions), context, and dictionary skills. According to Anderson et al. (1985), teachers should complete phonics instruction by the end of second grade, so all of the phonics lessons are for lower grades. Context and dictionary skills can be used for comprehension as well as for word recognition.

(L) Word Recognition Mini-lesson
Concept of Word

Realizing that many of your children are confused by such concepts as *letter, sound,* and *word,* you decide to teach them how to recognize what a word is. Point to the language experience chart that they dictated yesterday, and ask them if they can read the first sentence with you. As you move your hand under the words, read "We made vegetable soup." Tell them that this sentence has four words in it and ask if anyone can find the four words. When Carlos volunteers, ask him to come to the chart and point to each word. After he is able to do this successfully, ask him how he knows that these are words. He tells you "because there is space on both sides." You agree that words have spaces on both sides of them, and you tell the children that they use the same words when they talk as they use when they write. Continue through the chart, reading the sentences and asking the children to point to individual words on each line. Then ask the children to read the whole chart together.

Sources:

You may use most language experience charts and big books to help children identify what a word is.

(L) Word Recognition Mini-lesson
Sight Words

Realizing that prepositions can be difficult words for children to recognize because they have no concrete referents, you decide to use *Rosie's Walk* to help them learn some prepositions as sight words. Earlier this morning you read them the big book version of the story, helping them to predict what might happen to the fox on the next page and enjoying Rosie's safe return to the barnyard. Now you return to the book, asking the children to help you read the words that tell where Rosie went: *across* the yard, *around* the pond, and so forth. Record these phrases on a chart page, underline the prepositions, and put a little reminder picture beside each phrase.

You have prepared cards with phrases on them that use the prepositions from the story, but you have adapted them for the classroom. Some of them say: *over* the trashcan, *past* the teacher's desk, and *across* the room. Select a child to take a card, read the card to the class, and follow the directions on it. Continue until the children have taken all of the cards. As you finish your lesson, remind them to look at the chart when they come to one of these words in their reading and remember what Rosie did.

Source book and other books for teaching sight words:

(L) Pat Hutchins. *Rosie's Walk*. Macmillan, 1968.
(L) Bill Martin, Jr. *Brown Bear, Brown Bear, What Do You See?* Holt, Rinehart and Winston of Canada, 1982.
(L) *At the Zoo*. Harcourt Brace Jovanovich, 1990.
(L) Joanne Nelson. *Peanut Butter and Jelly*. Modern Curriculum Press, 1989.
(L) Lois Ehlert. *Color Farm*. Lippincott, 1990.

(L) Word Recognition Mini-lesson
Phonics, Initial Sounds

Having already shared *The Very Hungry Caterpillar* with the class, you return to it for a mini-lesson. Point out that both the title and the author's name have words that begin with the letter *C*. You ask the children to read these words with you, and they say "Caterpillar" and "Carle." Ask them to notice that the words begin with the same letter and the same sound. Write the letter *c* at the top of one side of the chart and put these words under the letter. Then ask them to look through the book with you to find other words that begin with the letter *c* to see if they sound like *Carle* and *Caterpillar* at the beginning. As you search together, the children find words which you add to your list of words beginning with *c*. When the children see the words *cheese* and *chocolate*, they notice that even though they start with *c*, they begin with a different sound.

Start another list beside the first one for the new words and ask the children if they have any idea why these words sound different. They notice that *cheese* and *chocolate* both start with *ch*, not just *c*, so you put *ch* at the top of the second column. When the children have found all of the *c* and *ch* words, ask them if they can think of any other words to add to their lists, and they suggest additional words, including *collie* and *catalog* for the *c* list and *church* for the *ch* list. When you finish the chart, it looks like this:

<u>c</u>	<u>ch</u>
Carle	chocolate
Caterpillar	cheese
came	cherry
cake	church
cone	
cupcake	
collie	
catalog	

Ask them to watch for other words that begin the same ways so that you can add them to the chart.

Source book and other books that teach initial sounds:

Eric Carle. *The Very Hungry Caterpillar*. Crowell, 1971. (initial consonant *c* and digraph *ch*)

Ellen Appleby (illustrator). *Three Billy Goats Gruff*. Scholastic, 1984. (initial consonant blends *br, tr, cr,* and *gr*)

Janet and Allan Ahlberg. *Each Peach Pear Plum*. Scholastic, 1978. (initial consonants *p, b,* and *w*)

Gene Baer. *THUMP, THUMP, Rat-a-Tat-Tat*. Harper & Row, 1989. (initial digraph *th* and consonants *p, f,* and *s*)

(L) Word Recognition Mini-lesson
Compound Words

You have been reading Eric Carle's books as part of an author/illustrator study, and you read *The Grouchy Ladybug* to the class earlier this morning. Tell the class that the story they just heard has an unusual word in the title: *Ladybug*. After discussing what a ladybug is, point out that it is one word but it is made of two words, so we call it a compound word. Can they find the two words? They answer *lady* and *bug*. Explain that many of our words are like this and that one way to recognize a long word is to see if it has two words in it. Tell them that the book has another compound word in it, *firefly*. Then say that you will make a chart of compound words. After writing *Compound Words* at the top, write *ladybug* and *firefly*. Using two different colors of felt-tipped pens, underline each part of each word. Ask the children to watch for other compound words as they read their books so that you can add them to the list.

Source book and other books with compound words:

(L) Eric Carle. *The Grouchy Ladybug.* Harper & Row, 1977.
(L) Lois Ehlert. *Planting a Rainbow.* Harcourt Brace Jovanovich, 1988.
(L) Margaret Wise Brown. *Goodnight Moon.* Scholastic, 1975.
(L) Audrey Wood. *King Bidgood's in the Bathtub.* Harcourt, Brace, Jovanovich, 1985.
(L) Bruce Degen. *Jamberry.* Scholastic, 1983.

(L) Word Recognition Mini-lesson
Phonics, Rhyming Words

Begin by telling the children about rhyming words—that they are words that sound alike at the end. Say two or three Mother Goose rhymes together that use rhyming words, such as "Little Jack Horner" and "Mary Had a Little Lamb." Then remind the children of the big book story *Across the Stream* that you read them earlier and tell them that it has some rhyming words in it. Read it to them again and ask them to listen for the rhyming words. Have a chart tablet ready to record the rhyming words as the children come to them. They soon discover rhyming pairs and triplets, including *dream* and *stream*, and *luck, duck,* and *cluck*. Write these down as they say them, then call their attention to how the words that rhyme are spelled alike at the end of the words. Suggest that when they write their stories and want to know how to spell a word that rhymes with a word they already know, they can end it with the same letters.

Source book and other books with rhyming words:

(L) Mirra Ginsburg. *Across the Stream* Scholastic, 1989.
(L) Bill Martin, Jr. and John Archambault. *Chicka Chicka Boom Boom.* Simon & Schuster, 1989.
(L) Dr. Seuss. *The Cat in the Hat.* Random House, 1957. (Most Dr. Seuss books use rhyming words.)
(L) Deborah Guarino. *Is Your Mama a Llama?* Scholastic, 1989.
(L) Paul Rogers. *What Will the Weather Be Like Today?* Scholastic, 1989.

(L) Word Recognition Mini-lesson
Context

Wanting to stress the importance of having children
think about what word would make sense when they
come to a word they don't recognize, you decide to
use the cloze procedure with a familiar story, *The Three
Billy Goats Gruff*. The children have acted out this story
and it is one of their favorites. Today you present them
with a big book of the story, but you have used sticky
tags to cover up some of the key words. You begin
reading, with the children following along, and you
come to a word that has been covered up with the
sticky tag. The sentence reads: "Who's that trip-trap-
ping over my _____?" Ask the students what
word would make sense here and remind them to look
at the picture for clues also. They quickly say "bridge"
for the answer. Ask if it could be anything else, and they
say "path" and "road." Then say, "Let's check by
peeking at the first two letters to see if they'll help us
know what the word is." Carefully peeling back the
sticky tab, let the children see the letters *br* and ask
them if that helps them know what the word must be.
They chorus "bridge!", and you continue uncovering
the word so that they can see that the word is indeed
bridge. Continue through the story, stopping each time
the children need to figure out a covered word. At the
end of the lesson ask them, "What do we need to think
about first when we come to a word we don't recognize?" They answer, "Think of a word that makes sense
and then check to see if it begins with the right letters."

Source book and other books appropriate for teaching
context:

(L) Ellen Appleby. *The Three Billy Goats Gruff*. Scholas-
tic, 1984.
(L) H. A. Rey. *Curious George*. Scholastic, 1941.
(L) Don Freeman. *A Pocket for Corduroy*. Scholastic,
1978.
(L) Mercer Mayer. *Me Too*. Houghton Mifflin, 1993.
(L) Joy Cowley. *Greedy Cat*. Richard Owen, 1983.

(U) Word Recognition Mini-lesson
Dictionary Skills

You've asked students to make lists of vocabulary
words that they have trouble figuring out from context
as they read their books. Students in a literature response group who are reading *Jacob Have I Loved* are
trying to identify the meaning of the word *progging* in

the phrase *progging for crab*. In this case context isn't much help, so they ask you to tell them what the word means. Instead, tell them you will talk about it in tomorrow's mini-lesson. Make an enlargement of the dictionary entry, make a transparency of the enlargement, and show it on the overhead projector. Help the students use the diacritical marks to get the correct pronunciation, then direct their attention to the definition, which is prowling or foraging for something. Ask them how they can apply this definition to their reading and they say it must mean that Louise was digging or searching for crabs. You point out that they will need to refer to the dictionary when they are unable to figure out a word any other way.

Source book:

Katherine Paterson. *Jacob Have I Loved*. Harper & Row, 1980.

Students may need to refer occasionally to the dictionary for words in many adolescent novels.

Mini-lessons for Comprehension Skills and Strategies

Comprehension is the very heart of the reading process, so learning to understand at literal and higher levels of thinking is crucial. Sometimes teachers settle for literal comprehension, but students need to *think* about what they read—to analyze, evaluate, and make connections to what other writers say and to their own lives. In so doing, teachers are not only teaching them to be thoughtful readers, but to be critical decision makers as adults.

(L) Comprehension Mini-lesson Cause and Effect	
Refer to a big book that the children read with you, *If You Give a Mouse a Cookie*, and tell them that you would like to discuss it with them. As you discuss the story, ask them to think about what caused the mouse to want the next thing and put their ideas on a piece of chart paper. Turning the pages of the big book, they tell you what they remember from the story and you make a chart like this:	
Cause	**Effect**
Give a mouse a cookie	Wants a drink of milk
Has a drink of milk	Wants a napkin
Looks in the mirror	Notices his hair needs a trim
His hair needs a trim	He needs a pair of scissors

Your chart continues like this until the children finish going through the book. Ask them to look for causes and effects in the stories they read for themselves.

Source book and other cause-effect books:

(L) Laura Joffe Numeroff. *If You Give a Mouse a Cookie.* Scholastic, 1985.

(L) Ellen Stoll Walsh. *Mouse Paint.* Harcourt Brace Jovanovich, 1989.

(L) Pat Hutchins. *Rosie's Walk.* Macmillan, 1968.

(L) Judi Barrett. *Animals Should Definitely Not Wear Clothing.* Aladdin, 1970.

(L) Eve Merriam. *That Noodle-head Epaminondas.* Scholastic, 1974.

(A) Comprehension Mini-lesson
Making Inferences

Tell the students that authors often expect readers to "read between the lines," or to make inferences as they read. Authors don't say everything, but readers are supposed to figure out some things on their own from the clues authors give in the story. As you introduce *Sarah, Plain and Tall*, ask the students to read the first page with you and see what inferences they can make from the clues. Sean says he thinks it's winter because Caleb is sitting close to the fire. Cora thinks that Caleb was talking to his brother or sister because they're both referring to Mama and Papa. Seth thinks that their parents are dead because they don't sing any more. Christie thinks whoever *I* is may be losing patience with Caleb because he asks the same questions over and over again. Tell them that they are making good use of the clues and that some of what they think is probably true. When they make inferences, they can't always be sure if they're right so they need to read on to see if the author clarifies or confirms their inferences.

Source book and other books for making inferences:

(A) Patricia MacLachlan. *Sarah, Plain and Tall.* Harper & Row, 1985.
(U) Doris Gates. *Blue Willow.* Scholastic, 1940.
(U) Wilson Rawls. *Where the Red Fern Grows.* Curtis, 1961.
(L) Harry Allard. *Miss Nelson Is Missing.* Houghton Mifflin, 1977.

(A) Comprehension Mini-lesson
Point of View

Explain to the children that each of us has a point of view, that we often look at things differently because of our experiences. Tell them that you know they are already familiar with the story of the "Three Little Pigs," and today you are going to read them a story told from a different point of view—the wolf's side of the story. Introduce *The True Story of the 3 Little Pigs!* and ask them to listen to how the wolf feels. When you finish, ask the children which version they believe and why. Then ask them to contrast the viewpoints of a pig and the wolf when the wolf eats the pig. From a pig's view, this is a savage and cruel thing to do, but from the wolf's view, it makes sense to eat something he likes if it would just go to waste otherwise. Ask the children to look for characters' points of view as they read their books and see if they think there could be another way of looking at things.

Source book and other books that show point of view:

(A) Jon Scieszka. *The True Story of the 3 Little Pigs!* Viking, 1989.
(A) Jon Scieszka. *The Stinky Cheese Man and Other Fairly Stupid Tales.* Viking, 1992.
(U) Armstrong Sperry. *Call It Courage.* Macmillan, 1940.
(A) Lynne Cherry. *The Great Kapok Tree.* Gulliver, 1990.
(A) Dr. Seuss. *The Lorax.* Random House, 1971.

(A) Comprehension Mini-lesson
Predicting and Drawing Conclusions

Reading a chapter from the popular Encyclopedia Brown series, ask the children to listen carefully for clues that will lead to a solution. Tell them that they can be detectives along with Encyclopedia. Encourage them to take notes of anything that might help them predict how Encyclopedia solves the problem. When you finish reading the story, ask them to tell you their clues and make their predictions. For example, children might identify the following clues for the solution to "The Case of the Hair Driers": the hair driers muffled the voice, the deaf person could read lips, and everyone was watching the fire. They might then conclude that Mrs. O'Brien was the guilty one.

Then turn to the back of the book and read the clues that Encyclopedia Brown used to solve the mystery. Tell them that mystery stories are full of clues that readers can use to make predictions and that they should watch for clues as they read. Source book and other mystery stories:

(A) Donald J. Sobol. *Encyclopedia Brown Solves Them All.* Scholastic, 1977.
(A) Many other Encyclopedia Brown books.
(A) Graeme Base. *The Eleventh Hour.* Abrams, 1989.
(U) Ellen Raskin. *The Westing Game.* Dutton, 1978.
(A) Chris Van Allsburg. *The Mysteries of Harris Burdick.* Houghton Mifflin, 1984.

(L) Comprehension Mini-lesson
Sequence

Sequence is important for comprehending many stories, and some stories feature a sequence of events. In order to make your children more aware of sequence, read them *Seven Blind Mice.* After you read the story, ask them to look back through the book with you and tell you how to make a sequence chart of the order of the mice, the days of the week, the colors of the mice, and what the mice think the strange "Something" is. Your chart looks like this:

Sequence Chart for *Seven Blind Mice*

Number of Mouse	Day of Week	Color of Mouse	What "Something" Is
first	Monday	red	pillar
second	Tuesday	green	snake
third	Wednesday	yellow	spear
fourth	Thursday	purple	great cliff
fifth	Friday	orange	fan
sixth	Saturday	blue	rope
seventh	Sunday	white	elephant

When you complete the chart, remind the children to look for sequence in the stories they read.

Source book and other books for teaching sequence:

(L) Ed Young. *Seven Blind Mice.* Philomel, 1992.
(L) Donald Hall. *Ox-Cart Man.* Viking, 1979.
(L) Eric Carle. *The Very Quiet Cricket.* Philomel, 1990.
(L) Audrey Wood. *The Napping House.* Harcourt Brace Jovanovich, 1984.
(L) Lois Ehlert. *Planting a Rainbow.* Harcourt Brace Jovanovich, 1988.

(U) Comprehension Mini-lesson
Multiple Themes

Point out to the students that a book can have several themes, or messages from the author, and you would like them to consider the themes in *The Giving Tree*. The students already know the story, so they begin discussing it. Jon thinks the main theme is that you are happier when you give something away than when you take something. He supports this theme by saying that the tree seemed happy to be giving, but the boy never seemed happy when he took things. Most of the students agree, but you ask them to think if there are other themes. Karla says that it bothered her that the tree was cut down and not replaced. Perhaps there is an environmental theme. Again, the children agree. Tom thinks that the boy is very selfish and therefore he can never be happy, but the tree is very generous so she is happy. Therefore, it doesn't pay to be selfish. Todd thinks the tree was stupid to give so much of herself away. Could one of the themes be never to give away so much of yourself that you are no longer you? Praise the class on their insightful comments about the themes and agree that all of these are possibilities.

Tell the students that there is one more theme that occurs to you and ask them if they can find it. It deals with the relationship between the female tree and the male boy. Barb says that it might mean that women, like mothers and wives, are always giving and men are always taking. That could be a theme. You agree that indeed it could, and say that some people call this book sexist because of that theme. Tell the students that most of the books they read have major themes with underlying themes as well. They might want to discuss their books in groups or with partners who have read the same book to see if they can uncover several themes.

Source book and other books with multiple themes:

(A) Shel Silverstein. *The Giving Tree*. Harper & Row, 1964.

(A) E. B. White. *Charlotte's Web*. Harper & Row, 1952.

(U) Theodore Taylor. *The Cay*. Doubleday, 1969.

(U) Joan Blos. *A Gathering of Days*. Scribner, 1979.

(U) Cynthia Rylant. *Missing May*. Orchard, 1992.

(U) Comprehension Mini-lesson
Social Significance

You have chosen *The Giver* as a class novel for your eighth graders and want them to consider its implications for society. Lead them in a discussion of freedom versus a controlled society. When you ask them to find the advantages and disadvantages of the controlled society described in *The Giver*, they come up with the following list.

Advantages	Disadvantages
no poverty	no color
full employment	no emotions
everyone equal	no individuality
no crime	no memories from the past
no people with disabilities	dark secrets

Ask them what they would have done if they had been Jonas. Would they have stayed in this controlled society, or would they have sought a free society? Which kind of society is better for us? Do we value our freedom, or do we take it for granted? Is a "perfect" society worth giving up so much?

After her seventh graders finished reading Lois Lowry's *The Giver*, Joy McCaleb got a variety of reactions. Students had strong feelings about the artificial society described in the book and expressed concerns over the way the story ended. Erin's response is shown in Example 4.1.

Source book and other books with social significance:

(U) Lois Lowry. *The Giver*. Houghton Mifflin, 1993.

(U) Natalie Babbit. *Tuck Everlasting*. Straus & Giroux, 1975.

(U) Robert O'Brien. *Mrs. Frisby and the Rats of NIMH*. Atheneum, 1971.

(A) Susan Jeffers. *Brother Eagle, Sister Sky*. Dial, 1991.

(U) Lois Lowry. *Number the Stars*. Houghton Mifflin, 1989.

I think the book The Giver is an excellent book, although there were many parts I did not agree with. I think this is the writer's purpose, however, to make you think about what is going on in this book in comparison to what is going on in our society today. I really like how she came up with all these great ideas and the pieced them together. For example, when the book goes back and tells that Rosemary was the Giver's daughter. Once I read that, it all started to go together. It talks about the sincere love the Giver had for Rosemary and how it disappointed him the most when Rosemary asked for release.

   I thought alot about the community having climate control. Even though I wish Lowry would have told us more about that, I think it's great that she didn't. It made me think about the idea and imagine how I thought it worked. Another thing I thought was really creative was the concept of light eyes. It made me think about how the book mentioned only Jonas, Gabe, the Giver, and a female Five having the special property of light eyes. Something in the book made me think that Rosemary had light eyes, too. I think the part where the Giver said his daughter's name was Rosemary gave me this thought that maybe Jonas was really the Giver's grandson. I don't know how, but it was just a thought.

   One thing that I didn't like about the book was the ending. I think that Jonas should have gone back and helped the people and become their leader.

Example 4.1

Summary

Mini-lessons are the first component of the reading workshop. Teachers present reading skills and strategies during a five to ten minute period and demonstrate how students can apply these skills in their reading. Most mini-lessons fall into one of the following four categories: (1) procedural, which teaches students how the workshop operates; (2) literary appreciation, which makes students aware of literary elements, genres, and themes; (3) word recognition skills and strategies, which help students learn what they need to know to decode words; and (4) comprehension skills and strategies, which teach both lower and higher level thinking strategies for students to apply in their reading. This brief directed teaching activity focuses on only one skill for each lesson and allows students to spend most of their time actually reading.

Reflections

Seriously consider the following questions. Some answers may be found by reflecting on the chapter; others may come from your own beliefs and experiences.

1. How can I condense my directed instruction lessons into mini-lessons? What are the essential components of my typical lessons that I could adapt for mini-lessons?
2. From a student's viewpoint, how would I react to mini-lessons and the freeing up of time for more independent reading? Would I miss the normal amount of teacher talk and practice exercises, or would I welcome the new arrangement?
3. Using the models given in this chapter as examples, how could I plan mini-lessons to cover the skills and strategies I need to teach at my grade level? What trade books could I use for the lessons?

Bibliography

Anderson, R., Hiebert, E., Scott, J., & Wilkinson, I. (1985). *Becoming a Nation of Readers*. Washington, D.C.: The National Institute of Education.

Atwell, N. (1987). *In the middle*. Portsmouth, NH: Heinemann.

Duthie, C. (1994). Nonfiction: A genre study for the primary classroom. *Language Arts, 71* (8), 588–595.

Duthie, C., & Zimet, E. (1992). "Poetry is like directions for your imagination!" *The Reading Teacher, 46* (1), 14–24.

Hagerty, P. (1992). *Reader's workshop*. Richmond Hill, Ontario, Canada: Scholastic Canada.

Hansen, J. (1987). *When writers read*. Portsmouth, NH: Heinemann.

Jackson, N., & Pillow, P. (1992). *The reading-writing workshop: Getting started*. New York: Scholastic.

CHAPTER 5

THE WRITING PROCESS

December 7

Kevin, excited about teaching a mini-lesson: Amy—can you talk a minute? I've got to tell you about a mini-lesson that I taught on finding multiple themes. You know how I've been trying to get my students to think about their reading and writing.

Amy: Right, I remember. What did you do?

Kevin: I'd read them Paula Fox's **One-Eyed Cat**, a novel that really made them think. In the mini-lesson I asked them to each write what they thought was the theme, and they came up with so many different answers. The next day we discussed their different ideas, and some of them rather heatedly defended their points of view. Those kids were actually arguing over what they thought the author meant!

Amy: Wow! I think they're getting the idea.

Kevin: My mini-lesson on using the dictionary to look up words they can't figure out from context really bombed though. They just don't want to go to all that trouble—they'd rather skip the word.

Amy, laughing: Frankly, I don't blame them! I never want to interrupt my reading to look up a word. I just use my best guess.

Kevin: You've got something there, but I still need to teach dictionary skills and I'd like to find a way to make them seem useful—related to something they need to know. Perhaps I can work them into my communication theme.

Amy: I'm going to try to do more with the writing workshop. The reading part seems to be going well, but we haven't really done much with writing, except for their journals. Do you have any pointers?

Kevin: Since they enjoy their reading so much, you might begin by letting them respond to the books they're reading. They can write their reactions and share them in groups.

Amy: We're already doing that. They all keep literature logs now and write ideas they get while they read.

Kevin: They can write variations on the stories they read—a different point of view, a surprise ending—something like that. You could also help them find topics—that's often a problem for my students. We sometimes brainstorm ideas or get topics from our experiences.

Amy: Good ideas. Thanks. Oh, by the way, did you get a notice about our TAWL* meeting Thursday?

Kevin: That's right—I almost forgot. Guess I'll see you there.

(*Note: TAWL is Teachers Applying Whole Language.)

Introduction

Kevin's advice to Amy about using literature as a basis for writing is sound. Children's responses to good books provide a bridge to writing.

In this chapter we will consider the writing process, a procedure for guiding children from a topic or idea to a finished piece of writing. We will begin by looking at ways to choose a topic, and then we will consider prewriting which occurs in the minds of writers before they begin writing their drafts. A rough draft expresses the writer's initial ideas, and additional drafts show revisions and refinements that result from conferences, feedback, and personal analysis. The next step is proofreading for mechanical errors (i.e., spelling, grammar, and punctuation) and editing. Students publish their work by writing it in a finished form for others to read, and they begin a new writing project when they have completed one. We will see that this framework is useful for guiding students' writing, but that it can vary considerably depending on student-teacher negotiations.

The Writing Process

During writing workshops students often participate in one or more phases of the writing process (see Figure 5.1), but they may also engage in any type of authentic writing activity. We will focus here on the writing process as we look at ways writers find their topics, construct their drafts, and revise them until they are ready to publish. The amount of time required for completing the process varies considerably, so students are likely to be at different stages of writing at any given time. Conferencing occurs throughout the writing process, but I will mention it only briefly here because it is discussed fully in Chapter 8.

Although these steps provide a framework for the writing process, advocates of process writing warn that they can easily become too rigid. Teachers who adhere to them too closely, particularly those who believe topic search starts the process on Monday and publishing ends it on Friday, are missing the point. The writing process enables students to select and develop their topics at their own paces, which vary from student to student and from one piece to another. The steps within the process itself may differ when an author skips a step or two, uses steps simultaneously, or shifts the order as purposes for writing become clearer. Some would like to see the process integrated with the curriculum so that writing occurs in every subject and relates to theme studies. There is a danger that the writing process may be viewed as a subject in itself rather than as an integral part of the total curriculum.

```
┌─────────────────────────────────────┐
│ Topic Search                         │
│         Experiences                  │
│         Literature                   │
│         Prompts                      │
│         Topic Conferences            │
│ Prewriting                           │
│         Rehearsal                    │
│         Graphic Organizers           │
│         Writing Notebooks            │
│ Drafts                               │
│ Revisions                            │
│ Proofreading/Editing                 │
│ Publishing                           │
└─────────────────────────────────────┘
```

Figure 5.1:   The Writing Process

Topic Search

Writers get ideas from many sources. One group of students told me that they get ideas from a list of topics the class creates, from their interests, and from news stories on television. Finding a topic can be the most difficult and crucial part of the writing process, so we will consider four major sources for identifying topics: experiences, literature, prompts, and topic conferences.

Experiences: Most writers begin by telling about something related to their experiences, for this is what they know best. Children have much to say about their home life, which they may view as either emotion-packed encounters or familiar and comfortable daily routines. They know family stories, those oft-told tales shared around the kitchen table and at family gatherings. Shelley Harwayne (1992) believes teachers should start the school year by inviting children to bring their lives into the classrooms—their photo albums, family stories, hobbies, and collections.

Many children are experts on special topics. Writing lets them express not only what they know, but also the excitement and pride they feel about their specialty. For instance, Tom has a stamp collection and Sylvia knows all about dirt bikes. They are also likely to feel the need to read further in order to write about their favorite hobbies.

Writing personal narratives enables students to examine their inner thoughts and feelings; it helps them understand themselves and clarify their relationships with others. Raushan, a student in Mary Martin's seventh grade class, shows rare insight into the various aspects of his personality. (See Example 5.1.) Collections of such writings become personal histories.

Kaushan

My Personalities

Loud, crazy, loving, and a leader, do these words describe me? Many people think they know me, but they do not. This essay will shed more light on me.

First off, there is my quiet, mature, and respectable side. This is probably the personality with the highest impact on me. It causes me to make the right choices in life. There is nothing much to say about it except I like to be the one in charge.

Next, there is my crazy, humorous, and immature side. I often show this side because of the need to get away from maturity (and it works!). I often get in trouble because of this but it does not faze me as long as it is small trouble.

Last, but definetely not least, is my more --- outgoing and rebellious side. This side is more thuggish, unpredictable, and unreliable. It is basically the total opposite of everything I have been taught that is right. It often causes me to be unpredictable and mean, very different from the other two personalities, and it gets me in serious trouble. Sometimes I will indulge in is personality because it gives me a feeling of power and control, but it also makes me do whatever it takes to get the job done for me. It causes me to lie, steal, cheat, fight, and betray people just to make the game more exciting. And as a response, I will give a fiendish grin and leave. I know this side is wrong but it is very corruptive and addictive. The more I use it, the more I want it.

Even though it sounds as if my personalities can not be similar at all, one has to realize they make up the very essence of my being. They also have a very powerful effect on who I am. I hope that those who read this essay have learned more about me and can understand why I do what I do.

Example 5.1

Personal narratives can also be therapeutic as a way of releasing emotions or as a rehearsal for dealing with difficult situations. Mike, a seventh grader in Joy McCaleb's class, began expressing his feelings about his family's divorce with an entry in his personal journal. He returned to it several times, each time revising it, until he typed the copy shown in Example 5.2. Such writing, warns Sarah McCarthy (1994), can also place the teacher in an awkward position. If a student reveals instances of child abuse, for instance, the teacher must know what to do.

My Bad Childhood Memory

I want to talk about a bad childhood memory—my mom and dad getting a divorce. All I remember is my mom and dad arguing a lot, and I didn't like it at all. It was very bad for me, and I hated myself for the divorce, because I thought it was my fault for being bad or something.

I still remember the day my dad moved out. Everybody but mom was crying, and she wasn't doing anything but standing there looking mad. She was probably mad at dad for something.

My big brother went to live with my dad, and I missed them both very much. It was hard to realize that I had to live without them now.

Still sometimes I just break down and cry to get some of the pain out of missing my dad. My brother has come to live with us since the divorce. My mom got married, but my dad has not remarried. Now, I don't blame myself because I talked to a counselor and she helped me.

I realize the divorce was not my fault. I still have problems with the fact that people divorce and families are separated, and I hope I will never have to go through another one.

Example 5.2

Literature: Rachel, a first grader in Connie Kinnaird's class, told me she gets her ideas for writing from the books she reads and from those her teacher and parents read to her. Her favorite topic for writing is fairy tales because "you can use your imagination and you can let animals talk." She begins each day by writing stories on the computer—her favorite part of the day. Example 5.3 is a story she wrote with story elements obviously borrowed from the fairy tales she knows.

Onets upon a
time there lived a
miler who had a
byudaful dawter.
The dawter of
the miler did not
know how to spin
straw into gold.
But the miler told
the king that his
dawter could spin
the straw into
gold. The king took
the dawter of the
miler to his kasle.
The dawter of
the miler spun
three rooms and
the king was
sprised with her.
the king and the
dawter of the
miler got
married.

Example 5.3

Shelley Harwayne (1992, p. 58) calls literature a "seedbed for discovering topics." Most students can relate their own experiences to such intergenerational stories as Sharon Bell Mathis's *The Hundred Penny Box* or Karen Ackerman's *Song and Dance Man,* to such regional tales as Walter Dean Myers' *Scorpions* set in the inner city or Cynthia Rylant's *When I Was Young in the Mountains* set in the hills of Appalachia, or to multiethnic texts that weave culture into story such as Faith Ringgold's *Tar Beach* or Patricia McKissock's *The Dark-Thirty: Southern Tales of the Supernatural.*

A book that generates ideas for topics is Byrd Baylor's *I'm in Charge of Celebrations,* set in the Southwest. It is the story of a young girl who discovers and records in a notebook her own causes for celebrations: a view of a triple rainbow that she shares with a jackrabbit, a whirlwind of dust devils, and a Time of Falling Stars in mid-August. Using this book as a springboard, children can record their own celebrations in notebooks for developing into writing projects.

Prompts: Although students ideally arrive at their own topics, some teachers feel that children need prompts to help them get started. Be sure that children don't become dependent on prompts, however, and that they have the option of writing on topics of their own choice. Don't use prompts about topics that students know little or nothing about because they won't be able to draw on their experiences.

Teachers may suggest prompts to open new possibilities for students who limit their writing to the same topics. Jill Ramsey asked her second/third grade students to write persuasive pieces based on a fantasy prompt about keeping a hippopotamus as a pet and to incorporate dialogue (see Example 5.4).

Linda Rief (1992, p. 38) uses prompts at the beginning of the year to help students get to know one another. She asks students to write about what makes learning hard or easy for them, a sentence they believe is true for all of the students in the room, and a sentence they believe is true only for themselves. Nancie Atwell (1990, p. 167) uses prompts for learning log entries and finds them successful when they cause writers to think and learn. Her prompts help students use prior knowledge, find their own opinions, and envision other people's experiences. Across the curriculum, prompts invite writers to brainstorm, list, express opinions, make observations, predict, map, ask questions, or try new genres. Figure 5.2 shows some sample prompts.

Topic Conferences: Discussing possible ideas helps students discover topics and find ways to develop and expand them. During conferences with students who are struggling with their topics, Nancie Atwell (1987) suggests asking them open-ended questions

On a Tuesday afternoon
I was chewing my
bubble gum and I saw
a big mouth, flat feet
hippopotamus. I said to
it, "Come here, I won't hurt you!"
Next thing I knew it yawned right in my
face. It was amazing. I rode it home.
I said to mom, "Can we keep someone?
My mom replied, "Who is it?" I said "Well,
it's a hippopotamus!" I opened the door
and she fainted. She said "Sure. It"
eat carrots + lettus." "I'll give it a bath
with the nose. I said, "Oh
thank you, thank you and
thank you!" I also got to tell
"Can I also keep an alligator?"
                    THE END

Example 5.4

that lead them to discover significant points and reach deeper levels of meaning. Students also exchange their ideas with classmates to get reactions for topic choices and directions for expansion. For many children, talking must come before writing; small brainstorming sessions spark ideas.

Prewriting

Along with topic selection comes prewriting, the thinking about and recording of ideas that may—or may not—develop into writing projects. During this process and the writing that follows, children need to find their voices. Voice lets the individual shine through the writing; it is the "driving force" of the writing process (Graves, 1994b, p. 81). Voice is present in all phases of the process; without voice, writing is dull and lifeless. In looking at prewriting, we will consider rehearsal, graphic organizers, and writing notebooks.

Rehearsal: Rehearsal prepares us for writing (Calkins, 1986, 1994). We rehearse by lingering over a thought and by savoring a special moment. We not only observe, but we ponder and reflect. Something small and insignificant becomes important because of personal associations or experiences. Scuffling through the dry leaves early in the spring I uncover a small flower, and I recall the time my father and I discovered a pink lady slipper as we were hiking in the woods. This memory sweeps through me, and with it comes the feel of that early spring day and the loving companionship of my father. This, I think, is something that I would like to write about.

Life Experiences

What is something you do well? Explain how you do it.

What person has influenced you most? How and why?

What is one of your most important values? Why?

How can school help you become the person you want to be?

Explain what you would do in the following situations:

> You find a wallet with $50 cash and identification.
> You see someone shoplifting.
> You see a hit-and-run driver.

Curriculum

How would the United States be different if it had been settled from west to east?

Compare your neighborhood today to your neighborhood 50 years ago. Is it a safer and better place now or then?

Brainstorm a list of words that relate to the environment.

Make a word map that shows the relationships among plants and animals in a habitat.

Write a series of journal entries about living as a Native American on a reservation.

Figure 5.2: Sample Prompts

And so it is with writers. They rehearse by collecting ideas and making connections over time. When I asked first-grade Rachel how she got her ideas for writing, she told me that she thinks about them the night before. Lucy Calkins (1986) points out that writers rehearse differently at various levels: first graders may rehearse by drawing, second graders by talking, and fifth graders by mapping. In any form, rehearsal is a way of contemplating ideas that are worth preserving in print.

TEACHING TIP

If you want children to rehearse before they write,

a.   Give them a consistent time to write.

b.   Let them choose their own topics.

Graphic Organizers: Before placing words on paper, some writers create graphics to help get their thoughts in order. Karen Bromley (1991) recommends webbing instead of outlining to help children plan what to include in their writing. Outlining is linear and sequential, but webbing allows writers to place thoughts randomly, with attention to sequence coming just before writing begins. For mature writers, strands connecting different parts of the web can show rather complex relationships. Young children's webs are rather simple, however, and some may prefer to use pictures instead of words. Alice Pleming asked her third graders to create webs that centered on topics they would like to write about, and Amber made one about her cat and another about her bike wreck (see Example 5.5). Before her fifth graders began writing personal narratives, Eva Hearn asked them to construct webs that recalled sensory impressions. Example 5.6 shows Philip's sensory webs and his final copy.

Linda Rief (1992) asks her students to list the best and worst things that ever happened to them. They identify their most significant positives and negatives, then volunteer to share them. Drawing a time line across the center of graph paper to represent the median, each student plots the high and low points of his or her life. Lines point upward to indicate a skiing trip, or downward for the loss of a pet. She asks them to identify topics that are worth further investigation, and they brainstorm ideas related to each topic they select. Often these charts get students thinking and writing from their own points of view.

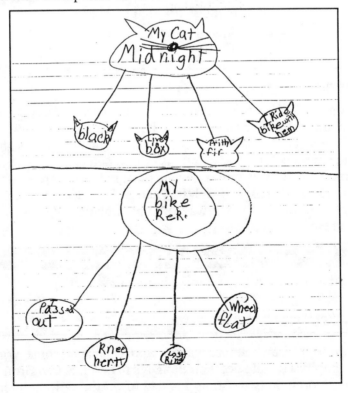

Example 5.5

Baseball Game

People   Hot Dogs   Fans Yelling   Philip

Players — See — Food   Smell   hear

empty Seats   The Field   Crack Of the Bat

Hot Sun

Hot Dogs — Taste   Touch — The Ball

Souveneers

The Braves V.S. Dodgers Game

My Vacation

The summer I was nine years old I went with my family to a baseball game in Atlanta Fulton County Stadium. We saw the Braves V.S. Dodgers game on a hot summer day in June.

When we got to the stadium on the left was a parking lot on the right was a ticket booth. We went right on into the stadium. When the game started I could smell the hot dogs and the field. I could see some empty seats, players warming up and thousands of people. I could hear the ball come off the wooden bats and the fans yelling. We could taste the hot dogs. The last part of the game the Braves hit a homer and I all most caught the ball, but it just skinmed off my finger tips and at the end of the game I got some souvenirs.

Example 5.6

Writing Notebooks: Many writers keep notebooks of random thoughts, anecdotes, ideas, musings, and reflections for later development into pieces of writing (Harwayne, 1992). They keep their notebooks handy for recording memorable phrases or insights so that they will not lose them to faulty memories. Entries come from a variety of sources: a view of the sunset, the splash of waves, a conversation, a song, a radio or television commentator, or amazement at an ordinary event. Literature can introduce the idea of recording significant events as in *I'm in Charge of Celebrations,* or it can be a continual source of inspiration for entries. Notebooks, growing as they do from the experiences and observations of the recorder, lead writers to "make surprising discoveries, find recurring themes, and follow new pathways to thinking" (Harwayne, 1992, p. 61).

Teachers can introduce students to writing notebooks with mini-lessons by brainstorming types of writing to include and demonstrating how these bits of writing can lead to fully developed works. The best way to convince students of the value of notebooks, say Lucy Calkins and Shelley Harwayne (1991), is to write in them frequently yourself. For students who are reluctant to use them, you can demonstrate ways to turn entries into writing projects. Each student may use the notebook differently, some incorporating webs and illustrations, some jotting notes randomly, and some carefully recording and embellishing their ideas. Expect and welcome such varied responses.

Any kind of notebook with plenty of blank lined pages is appropriate, and students may decorate or individualize their notebooks according to their own tastes. They should use them often, date each entry, and look through them periodically for themes, powerful language, and insightful glimpses of themselves (Fiderer, 1993). Figure 5.3 lists some types of entries.

Wordplay	Hopes, dreams, and goals
Poems	Special memories
Family stories	Interesting connections
Sensory impressions	Tantalizing words
Memorable phrases	Speculations
Story ideas	Responses to literature
Personal celebrations	Word and picture images
Random thoughts	

Figure 5.3:   Entries for Writing Notebooks

> ### TEACHING TIP
> To help students overcome writer's block, let them
> a.   Draw a picture first.
> b.   Discuss their ideas with someone else.
> c.   Choose another topic.
> d.   Ask you to help them focus.
> e.   Refer to their writers' notebooks.
> f.   Simply start writing about anything.

Drafts

Once children have identified their topics and gathered some ideas for writing, they are ready to begin their first drafts. Expect these initial drafts to be messy because they represent first attempts to put thoughts on paper; some teachers refer to them as *sloppy copy*. Quick writing helps authors nail down ideas without interrupting themselves to check standard conventions. Crossed-out words, arrows leading from one place to another, and abbreviations characterize these drafts. For some children who have spent years in classrooms where teachers valued form over content, such writing comes hard. To convince these students that you truly mean *rough* drafts, model your own first draft with its false starts, crossed-out words, misspellings, inserts, and omitted punctuation.

Developmental writing levels make a difference in the way students view drafts (Tchudi, 1994). Beginning writers, feeling confident about their writing, create only a single draft and assume their audience will understand their stories. A little later children choose their words more carefully and are aware of the need for revision, but they are easily discouraged. I've seen many youngsters unwilling to spend the time and effort on rewriting, even though they know they could improve their pieces. More mature writers organize ideas better and develop their topics more completely.

When I talked with Kelly Walker, a second grade teacher in a school with a large number of ESL (English as a Second Language) students, she told me that these students love the writing process and that their "language improves dramatically." Second grader Sun-Hee from Korea spoke no English when she began kindergarten, but is now writing her own books and speaking English quite fluently. Traces of her native language structure remain in her early second grade work (see Example 5.7), but Kelly placed Sun-Hee with two strong writers in book collaborations. By composing books with her peers, she is quickly grasping English syntax.

Example 5.7

Revisions

Revisions begin almost as soon as writing begins. Not satisfied with a lead, the writer tries again. Unable to find the right word, the author substitutes one until a better word comes to mind. Moving from one draft to another, the writer revises by changing the focus, developing a character more fully, filling in gaps of information, or providing a more logical and satisfying conclusion. Other purposes for revision include:

- Clarifying confusing passages
- Responding to suggestions from peers
- Shortening or lengthening the piece
- Shifting to a different genre (e.g., from a story to a script for a play)
- Writing for a different audience (e.g., rewriting a report for an upper grade to present to kindergartners)
- Reworking the piece to let the author's voice come through more clearly
- Focusing, in depth, on a particular incident

Teaching revision comes through conferencing and mini-lessons. Lucy Calkins (1986, p. 20) has her students ask themselves, "'What am I trying to say?' 'How does this sound?' 'Where is this leading me?'" in order to reflect on the text they are creating. Through their reflections, students not only view their writing from different perspectives, but also gain insight into understanding themselves.

Good teachers help children to think of themselves as authors and to identify with authors as they create their stories. A teacher might say, "Listen to Chris Van Allsburg's lead in *Two Bad Ants*. 'The news traveled swiftly through the tunnels of the ant world.' How does that sentence draw you into the story? Does it make you wonder what the news is? Do the `tunnels of the ant world' sound like an intriguing place to learn about? Perhaps you could draw readers into your story by writing leads that whet their appetites for reading more." Commercially published authors become models for young authors.

As they consider revisions, children might read or reread books by favorite authors to see what literary techniques the authors use to make their books appealing. The class could then identify these features and contribute them for a chart to use as a guide for their own writing. Although the list might start with just one or two techniques, it might grow into one that resembles Figure 5.4.

Good authors . . .

Use enticing leads to capture the reader's interest.

Include specific details and concrete examples.

Focus their writing by sticking to the topic.

Use active, not passive, voice with strong verbs.

Vary sentence lengths.

Experiment with various kinds of writing.

Organize their material so that readers can follow it.

Omit any unnecessary words.

Give complete information.

Figure 5.4:   Techniques Good Authors Use

TEACHING TIP

To make revisions and editing easier, have students

a.   Write on one side of the paper only.

b.   Write on every other line to leave space for making changes.

c.   Use word processors.

Proofreading/Editing

When writers are satisfied with their revisions, they are ready to proofread and edit. Of course, they have already changed some spellings and grammatical errors, but now they are ready for serious proofreading before they publish. (Figure 5.5 shows some standard proofreading symbols.) Their primary purpose should be clear: to make their writing "reader friendly" so that their work will be free of distracting errors. This is also the time, however, for the teacher to make sure that students can use writing conventions appropriately. In order to succeed in life beyond school, students must be able to use language appropriately. This means correct spellings and standard English. Recurring errors in the use of conventions call for mini-lessons or conferences to make students aware of correct usage.

Students first edit their own work, then ask classmates to proofread it, and finally turn to the teacher for the final editing. Editing standards vary by grade level, ability level, and desire for perfection. Most children lack the tolerance for rewriting until a piece is completely error free. Editors should be careful to preserve the voice of the writer when making suggestions for changes.

TEACHING TIP

To make sure both the student and classmates have proofread a piece before you see it, ask each to use a different colored marker. Then use another color when you edit it yourself (Atwell, 1987).

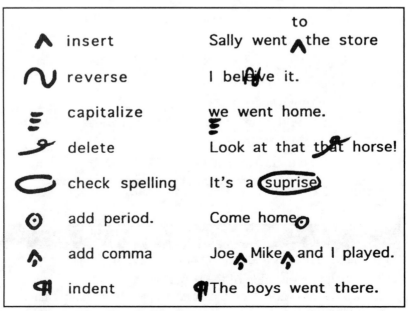

Figure 5.5:   Proofreading Marks

Editing for misspelled words is an issue that deserves special attention. Critics are quick to condemn invented spelling, but they fail to realize that even kindergartners possess tremendous composing power if allowed to approximate spellings. Five-year-old Kendra's writing in Example 5.8 shows an awareness of story, including dialogue, that results from her freedom to experiment with language. Kendra's print-rich home environment, coupled with kindergarten teacher Martha Dawson's encouragement through modeling and shared book reading, sparked her interest in writing.

Kendra's Story

Once upon a time there was a little girl named Jenny. She lived with her mother and her father. It was a calm little house. They had plenty of food. One day her mother went to buy some more food. Jenny said Can I come, too. No said her mother. Please said Jenny. Well all right said her mother. Yay said Jenny. When they got back their house was a mess and they never left the house again.

The Little Girl

Example 5.8

On the other hand, in most situations teachers should expect students to spell words correctly when students have already learned to spell them and when they can locate correct spellings easily. Students might keep a list of frequently used words for quick reference. Unless teachers hold students accountable, students may not realize the value of correct spelling and become careless with their writing.

As children grow older, teachers expect more from them. Lesley Wing Jan assigns her year five students to work in groups of three as they write third person recounts (a variation on the typical first person retelling) of a recent excursion to an art gallery. They write on large chart paper, then proofread their work, circling words that need to be checked for spelling. Groups then combine so that six members now proofread two charts. Lesley chooses one or two charts to edit with the whole class, inviting everyone to look for ways to improve the writing.

Publishing

The final step in the writing process is publishing, a way of putting a revised and edited piece into a polished form for others to read. Example 5.9 shows one of several drafts that Luis, a former ESL student, wrote, along with his published copy.

Everyone needs to publish, not just the best writers. Publishing is an essential step because writers must know they have an audience when they work hard to prepare their pieces for others to read. Not every piece of writing reaches the publication stage; writers may abandon some pieces because they lose interest, at least temporarily, or find other topics more compelling. Reasons why children need to publish include the following (partially based on Clark, 1987):

- Writers receive recognition for their work.
- The audience goes far beyond the teacher.
- Audience response provides helpful feedback for writers.
- Students get ideas by reading what others have written.
- Publication provides an incentive for multiple revisions.
- A collection of students' writings over a year represents their best achievements.
- Students experiment with different genres.
- Writers understand the value of writing by sharing their works.

Publication can take many forms from simply putting samples of student writing on a bulletin board to having pieces accepted for professional publication. A class or school newspaper provides students with the opportunity of having their work appear in print. Students in Joy McCaleb's seventh grade class created an eight-page junior version of the high school newspaper called *Upperman Times, Jr.* In it Clayton Smith, a resource student, wrote the editorial on page 105 entitled "Not in My School."

"Not in My School!"

I think Not In My School is a great program to keep drugs and weapons out of schools. We need to keep the hallways safe so that Upperman will be a good school for the future and for our children.

I think this is such a great program because my brother got mixed up in drugs. Drugs ruined his life forever, and my family was torn apart. I wonder what would have happened if my brother had known about Not In My School. If drugs had been kept out of school, would my brother still have a chance? I believe so, and that is why I am active in this organization.

There are a few students who are on this special board with each class at Upperman represented. Our main goal is to let people know that someone will listen to them. If they know there are drugs or weapons in our school, we give them the access to anonymously report those crimes.

I hope all the students support this idea of keeping our school safe. I, for one, support the Crimestopper organization for making this special organization possible at Upperman High School.

Sharon Ford's kindergartners participate in publishing by working in committees of three or four to produce big books. Nearly every week Sharon helps a group of children compose a story, format it into a big book, and illustrate it. By the end of the year each child has worked on several books, and each then chooses a book to take home and keep.

Publishing in most classrooms is fairly simple since it should occur frequently without consuming a great deal of time with the book-making process. I make my favorite kind of book by stapling together a piece of colored construction paper folded in half with several sheets of white typing paper folded inside. Children can make their own books this way, but be careful that they know how to use the stapler safely. This kind of book is not very durable, however, and you may want to let your students select special pieces occasionally to publish in a sturdier fashion, perhaps with the help of a teacher assistant or parent volunteers.

Many local, state, regional, or national organizations sponsor writing contests. In Tennessee the state council of the International Reading Association sponsors an annual Celebrate Literacy contest which invites children in grades K–12, including a category for special education students, to publish books and submit them for state awards. Thousands of students enter the contest, publishing their books according to a special format that uses matting boards covered with wallpaper and typing paper sewn with dental floss. Local council judges send their best entries on to state judges who then select the winners, but every student who enters receives recognition.

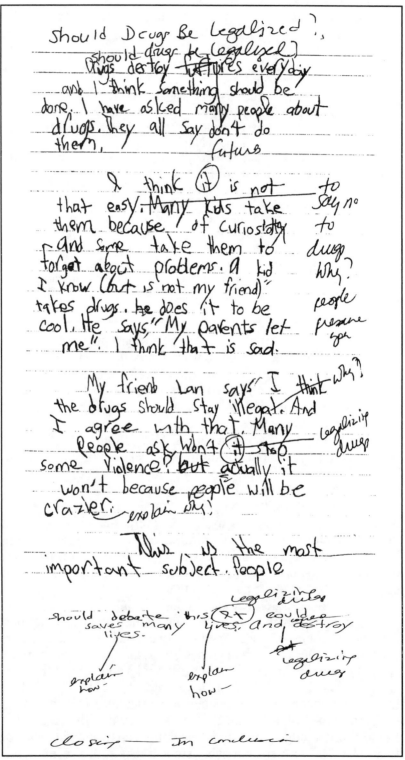

Example 5.9; continues on page 107

```
                   Writing
                                Luis

    I think drugs shouldn't be legalized
because drugs destroy futures every day.
I personally think something should be
done. I have asked many people about this
and they all say just don't do them.
    I think it is not that easy to say no.
Many kids take them becuase of peer pres-
sure. Other kids take drugs to forget
problems. A kid I know takes drugs. He
does it to be cool. He says, "My parents
let me." I think that is sad. My friend
Pat says, "I think drugs should be legal-
ized in a controlled way." Many ask,
Won't the legalizing of drugs stop some
violence? Actually it won't becuase
people would get high. And drugs would
cost money so if someone who takes drugs
wants drugs he or she would have to
steal.
    This is the subject that would affect
everybody. People could stay alive if
drugs are legalized because if a police
officer arrests you you could get shot.
And if you take drugs you could over dose
and die.
    In conclusion more people think drugs
shouldn't be legalized.  You should speak
out.
```

Example 5.9; continuation from page 106

Many commercially published children's magazines accept work from student writers, and a list of those that exclusively or regularly use readers' work appears in Appendix II. Before submitting their own writing, students should read these trade magazines carefully, looking for preferred genres, writing style, and approximate length, as well as submission requirements. Aiming for professional publication can be discouraging, however, since such magazines receive hundreds of submissions each month from all over the country and can choose only a few to publish. Local newspapers provide another option for publication, especially during Newspaper-in-Education week each March, when some newspapers actively recruit student writing. Our local newspaper prints a special section on schools every Thursday, and the editor claims he is deluged with submissions from students.

There are dozens of ways to publish students' writing, but Figure 5.6 shows some of the possibilities. You may be able to brainstorm other options.

Classmade books

Newspapers (class, school, and local area)

Yearbooks or literary journals published by the school

Writing contests

Posters, displays, diagrams, and charts

Pamphlets and brochures

Correspondence with pen pals, school sponsors, or special people

Invitations and greeting cards

Trade magazines

Big books

Figure 5.6:   Ways to Publish Students' Writing

Once a student's writing is published in one form or another, make sure that others get to read it. You can create visibility by using these ideas.

- Place writing displays on the walls outside your classroom.
- Create shelves in your classroom for student books.
- Exchange your books with books from other classrooms.
- Ask your librarian to display the books for a period of time. (Place library check-out cards in them.)
- Create themed bulletin boards of student writing.
- Have an authors' party and invite parents and school personnel.

TEACHING TIP

One way to publish is to make post cards:

a.   Take a 4 x 6 unlined file card.

b.   Draw a picture of a special place on one side.

c.   On the back draw a line that divides the card in half vertically.

d.   On the left side write a brief message about the place pictured on the front.

e.   On the right side put a stamp (real or imaginary) and the name and address of the person who will receive it.

Summary

The writing process is at the heart of the writing workshop. It consists of a series of stages, although they may sometimes occur recursively and interactively. The first stage is the search for a topic, which is followed by prewriting when students rehearse or plan what they will write. Students write drafts, beginning in a rough fashion with attention to content rather than form. They make revisions as they discover ways to improve their writing, and then they proofread and carefully edit their pieces before publishing them.

Each of these steps is important, but don't insist that students follow them rigidly and adhere to a specific time frame. Keep in mind that the primary purpose of process writing is to help students discover a way to express their ideas and communicate effectively.

Reflections

Seriously consider the following questions. Some answers may be found by reflecting on the chapter; others may come from your own beliefs and experiences.

1. What do I believe about helping students find their topics? Is there ever a time when I should give them prompts, or should I just help them discover their own topics?
2. What is the most effective way for me to model for my class? Should I talk them through various procedures, use an overhead projector to show them my writing, or find another way?
3. How will I be able to convince my students that revision is more than editing? How can I help them think through their pieces to find more effective ways to express their ideas?
4. How perfect should the published copy be? Is it acceptable to still have some mistakes? Should I have different expectations for different grade levels, different degrees of motivation and persistence among students, and different capabilities? Should I accept published forms that still contain grammatical or spelling errors?

Bibliography

Atwell, N. (1987). *In the middle.* Portsmouth, NH: Heinemann.
Atwell, N. (1990). *Coming to know.* Portsmouth, NH: Heinemann.
Au, K. (1993). *Literacy instruction in multicultural settings.* Fort Worth: Holt, Rinehart and Winston.
Avery, C. (1993) . . . . *And with a light touch.* Portsmouth, NH: Heinemann.
Calkins, L. M. (1986). *The art of teaching writing.* Portsmouth, NH: Heinemann.

Calkins, L. M. (1991). *Living between the lines.* Portsmouth, NH: Heinemann.

Calkins, L. M. (1994). *The art of teaching writing,* new edition. Portsmouth, NH: Heinemann.

Clark, R. P. (1987). *Free to write.* Portsmouth, NH: Heinemann.

Cunningham, P. M., & Allington, R. (1994). *Classrooms that work: They can all read & write.* NY: HarperCollins.

Emmitt, M., & Pollock, J. (1991). *Language and learning.* South Melbourne, Australia: Oxford University Press.

Fiderer, A. (1993). *Teaching writing: A workshop approach.* NY: Scholastic.

Graves, D. (1994a). Be a better writing teacher. *Instructor, 104* (4), 43–45, 71.

Graves, D. (1994b). *A fresh look at writing.* Portsmouth, NH: Heinemann.

Graves, D., & Hansen, J. (1983). The author's chair. *Language Arts, 60* (2), 176–183.

Graves, D., & Stuart, V. (1985). *Write from the start.* NY: E.P. Dutton.

Hansen, J., Newkirk, T., & Graves, D., eds. (1985). *Breaking ground.* Portsmouth, NH: Heinemann.

Hansen, J. (1987). *When writers read.* Portsmouth, NH: Heinemann.

Harwayne, S. (1992). *Lasting impressions: Weaving literature into the writing workshop.* Portsmouth, NH: Heinemann.

Hill, B. C., & Ruptic, C. (1994). *Practical aspects of authentic assessment: Putting the pieces together.* Norwood, MA: Christopher-Gordon.

Jackson, N., & Pillow, P. (1992). *The reading-writing workshop: Getting started.* New York: Scholastic.

Karelitz, E. B. (1993). *The author's chair and beyond.* Portsmouth, NH: Heinemann.

Kucera, C. (1995). Detours and destinations: One teacher's journey into an environmental writing workshop. *Language Arts, 72* (3), 179–187.

McCarthy, S. J. (1994). Opportunities and risks of writing from personal experience. *Language Arts, 71* (3), 182–191.

Newkirk, T., ed. (1994). *Workshop 5.* Portsmouth, NH: Heinemann.

Olshansky, B. (1994). Making writing a work of art: Image-making within the writing process. *Language Arts, 71* (5), 350–356.

Pike, K., Compain, R., & Mumper, J. (1994). *Connections: An integrated approach to literacy.* NY: HarperCollins.

Puhr, K., & Workman, G. (1992). Monitoring student progress through a conferenced writing program. *English Journal, 81* (2), 49–50.

Rief, L. (1992). *Seeking diversity.* Portsmouth, NH: Heinemann.

Rief, L. (1994). Writing for life: Language arts in the middle. *Language Arts, 71* (2), 92–100.

Routman, R. (1991). *Invitations.* Portsmouth, NH: Heinemann.

Simic, M. (1993). Publishing children's writing. *Eric Digest,* Clearinghouse on Reading, English, and Communication. EDO-CS-93-08.

Sudol, D., & Sudol, P. (1991). Another story: Putting Graves, Calkins, and Atwell into practice and perspective. *Language Arts, 68* (4), 292–300.

Sudol, D., & Sudol, P. (1995). Yet another story: Writers' workshop revisited. *Language Arts, 72* (3), 171–178.

Tchudi, Susan. (1994). *Integrated language arts in the elementary school.* Belmont, CA: Wadsworth.

Wing Jan, L. (1991). *Write ways.* Melbourne, Australia: Oxford University Press.

Yellin, D., & Blake, M. (1994). *Integrating language arts.* NY: Harper Collins.

CHAPTER 6

THE WRITING WORKSHOP

January 6

Amy, admiring the newly fallen snow as she approaches the parking lot after school and thinking to herself: I wonder if we'll have school tomorrow.

Just then a snowball strikes Amy in the back. Whirling around she sees Kevin, scooping up snow for a second hit.

Amy: Hey, no fair! I didn't even see you coming.

Kevin, laughing: Okay. I'll get the tree with this one. Did you have a good holiday?

Amy: It was great—lots of family, that kind of thing. How about you?

Kevin: Same here. But now it's back to work, and I've got a real problem with those kids. All they want to write is fiction and they do such a poor job of it!

Amy: Why is that?

Kevin: They think they're the authors of the next Saturday morning cartoons—pow, bam, blood and guts all over the place. Most of their stories are so violent!

Amy: Sounds terrible. What can you do?

Kevin: I've thought of placing some subjects off limits so that they'll have to find other topics. I hate to restrict their choices, but this kind of writing isn't getting them anywhere!

Amy: What I like most about fiction is the characters. Can you get them to work on characterization?

Kevin: That's just what I was thinking. We might look at some of the books they've enjoyed with strong characters, such as Brian in **Hatchet,** and focus on how to create realistic heroes.

Amy: Right. Then the characters take over the story in a natural way as they respond to events. Setting can affect them too—that's something else to work on.

Kevin: I've got to get them away from **Star Trek** and back to reality. I think I'll ask them to think of favorite books, discuss the characters in them, and observe ways the author created those characters. Some group discussions might be good here to get everyone involved.

Amy: Sounds good to me—hope it works. Brrrr—I'm freezing standing out here. See you tomorrow—if we have school.

Introduction

The writing workshop consists primarily of a large, flexible block of time for students to write. It follows the same basic procedures as the reading workshop—mini-lesson, status of the class, workshop, and group share. We will take a close look at writing mini-lessons in Chapter 7, and we already considered status-of-the-class reports for writing workshops in Chapter 2. Most of this chapter, therefore, focuses on what happens during the writing portion of the workshop and the concluding group-share session. Although a variety of authentic and content-related writing activities can fit nicely into the workshop framework, many teachers use this time for guiding students through the writing process. Just as we investigated different genres in reading, we'll see how teachers can help students write in different genres. The intent here is to invite students to first pursue their ideas and put their thoughts on paper, then to revise and edit so that they can publish their completed pieces.

Commenting on student writing, Donald Graves (1994b, p. 154) takes a long-term view by asking himself: "What can I do today that will help this child to use writing as a tool for thinking and learning throughout his/her life?" This question helps us focus on the child's developing awareness of the power of written language.

Implementing the Writing Workshop

After the teacher conducts the mini-lesson and the status-of-the-class reports, the students are ready to begin writing for an extended period of time. Since each student is probably working on something different, the teacher can use the status-of-the-class report to check each one's progress and decide who might benefit from a conference. During part of this time the teacher may model the importance of writing by writing herself, but most of the time she will probably confer briefly with individual students to answer questions, listen and respond, give a "nudge" to those who need it, and assess progress.

The atmosphere of the room should convey a sense of purpose. Writers are also readers and thinkers, and they need to feel that their work is important. Some children may wish to confer with others to test their ideas, but some may want to concentrate without interruptions. In order to meet each student's needs, the teacher may set off areas of the room for teacher conferences, peer conferences, or uninterrupted writing. Of course, students will make some noise as they confer and move about, but the noise level should be moderate—a nondisruptive working hum, not out-of-control chaos.

Guidelines for Writing Workshops

Workshops require a great deal of self-directed, disciplined activity, so you should make your expectations clear. Start with a few workable procedures and add others as they become necessary. If some guidelines don't seem to be working or others are needed, consult your students during a mini-lesson or discussion period. Ask them, "What can we do to keep the noise level down?" or "How can we make it easier to get the materials we need for writing?" When they are involved in setting policies, they are more likely to understand the need for them and follow them.

The guidelines in Figure 6.1 are possibilities, but begin with only a few that are essential. Don't overwhelm the students with more than they can handle.

Sharpen pencils and gather materials before the workshop starts.

Listen carefully to the mini-lesson and use the information in your writing if you can.

Be ready to report what you plan to do when I call your name.

Think about your topic in advance so that you will be able to start writing when the workshop begins.

Don't interrupt me when I am working with someone else. Raise your hand if you need help and I will come to you as soon as I can.

If you need to get additional materials, go quickly and get them; then return directly to your seat.

Label and date what you are working on each time we meet.

Write on one side of your paper only.

Keep all of your notes. You may need to refer to them later.

If you need to, you may confer quietly with another student, but be sure not to disturb other writers.

Keep your writing folder organized so that you can show me your work when I stop by.

When you are ready to publish, choose one of the blank books on the table and neatly write your final copy.

When you want to use the author's chair to share your work, sign up on the schedule sheet or ask me.

Put finished books on the library shelf. Put other finished pieces in your writing folder.

When you finish your piece, begin another one.

Figure 6.1:   Guidelines for Writing Workshop

Components of Writing Workshops

As with reading workshops, *time, choice,* and *response* are essential components of writing workshops. How different from traditional writing instruction! Figure 6.2 shows the comparison between traditional writing classes and writing workshops.

Traditional Writing Instruction	Writing Workshop
Time	
About one half hour once a week Spur-of-the-moment decisions	Minimum of four days out of five for 35-40 minute periods Ongoing thinking about writing
Choice	
Topics assigned by teacher	Free choice of topics based on purposes and interests
Response	
Corrections, primarily of mechanics, by teacher only	Continual conferring, primarily about content, with both teacher and classmates

Figure 6.2: Comparison between Traditional Writing Instruction and Writing Workshop Approaches to Time, Choice, and Response

Students need *time* for writing beginning in kindergarten, and they need to know the schedule so that they can come to the workshop prepared with topics and ideas. Legitimate activities for workshop time include looking at books for ideas, writing, and conferring.

TEACHING TIP

If it seems difficult to find enough time for instruction in all of the language arts, consider these possibilities (Graves, 1994b):

a. Teach spelling, grammar, and handwriting in mini-lessons.
b. Let students begin writing as soon as they come to class.
c. Although reading requires special instruction, combine writing and reading instruction when literature is used as a basis for writing.
d. Use literature as a basis for writing.

Students care more about their writing when they choose their own topics. Teachers, too, can expect more of students when students select subjects based on personal knowledge and experience. After all, they are the authorities on those topics! Here teachers can build self esteem by acknowledging students' expertise in special areas.

In addition to choosing topics, students make other choices as they write. They consider

- How to spend their workshop time.
- Continuing with their topics or abandoning them, at least for the moment, if they no longer seem viable.
- Accepting or rejecting recommendations from classmates.
- Alternate ways to structure their writing.
- Possibilities for publishing.

We teach through our *responses* to students' writing (Hansen, 1987). Simply correcting errors on finished papers doesn't teach students how to be better writers, but guiding them through the process does. We move among children as they write, listening to what they know and trying to catch what excites them about their writing. We affirm, question, and encourage them to tell us more in order to help them find their stories. Responses come not only from us, but also from classmates and others with whom children share and confer. By considering responses from others along with their own ideas, children construct their best possible pieces.

Workshops in Action

Ideally, teachers should have opportunities to visit classes where children are busily engaged in workshop activities. Since such visits are impossible for some teachers, the two following scenarios may help teachers understand what happens during workshops in two classes that I observed.

A Day in the Workshop Phase of Writing Workshop: Grade 2

As I walk into Arlee Freeman's second grade class, I see some children writing at their desks and others quietly conferring with each other. A few are standing at Arlee's desk, asking her to help with editing and for suggestions for improving their stories. Later, Arlee circulates among the children, stooping by each desk where a child needs her help. A tall swivel stool covered in colorful fabric stands near the chalkboard under the words "Author's Chair."

The room is well designed for a writing workshop. Desks are clustered in groups of four so that children can confer easily with each other, and on one table are several wallpaper-covered booklets with blank paper inserts. After Arlee has helped the children edit their drafts, each child may choose one of these booklets for making a published book. The children then place their books on shelves in the room so that they can read each others' books.

I notice a word bank on one wall with pocket charts holding brightly colored word cards with such words as *grumpy, leprechaun, rescued, trouble ahead, toboggan, rookery,* and *nuisance.* I ask Shauntay why those words are there. She explains that the children discuss words that they might need to use in their writing, and Mrs. Freeman puts them in the word bank so that they will know how to spell these words.

Mingling with the children, I notice that they are all at different stages of the writing process. Several are writing their own Cinderella stories after hearing several versions that Arlee has shared with them; others are writing stories about penguins, their current theme study; and some are writing stories on other topics. Ashley proudly volunteers to read her story about Scamper, the penguin, to me.

Arlee asks the children to help each other with their writing. She suggests that they use the author's chair if they want to share a published story or if they need some help from the whole class. She reminds them to listen as someone reads for the features that make a complete story:

- Who the characters are
- What the characters are doing
- The problem
- The solution to the problem
- A satisfying ending

David climbs into the author's chair, reads the beginning of his story to the class, and asks for suggestions about what the dragon should do (see Example 6.1). Three children volunteer endings, and David chooses one of these endings to use as he completes his story. (See Example 6.2 for the conclusion. Arlee helped David edit his story.)

David's Story:

The Transform of the Boy's Life

One day there was an eagle. He was a magical eagle. He spread the magic over a boy's head. The boy started to transform into a dragon. The dragon blew fire on the eagle, and the dragon started to transform back into a boy.

The Transform of the David A. Boy's Life

① One day there was an eagle. He was a magiccel leagle. ② He sprad the magic over a boy's haed. The boy stacted to transform iret a dragen. ③ The dragen blend fire on the eagle, and the dragen started to transform brck into a boy.

Example 6.1: Beginning of David's Story

The eagle gave the boy a magic necklace and whenever he wanted to transform he just touched the necklace.

④ The eagle gave the boy a magic necklace and when ever he wanted to transfrom he just tuch the necklace.

Example 6.2: Conclusion of David's Story

Although the author's chair isn't in constant use, children feel free to visit it whenever they wish to get advice or want the rest of the class to hear their finished books. Evan reads his Halloween story from the Author's Chair and asks the children to tell him if it is complete. He ends the story by having his parents check the candy to make sure it is safe to eat. The children suggest that he add that the candy is safe so then he can eat some of it and have a safe and happy Halloween. Arlee models responses for the children by saying what is good about the story: "The beginning sounds like a real book," and "Read the sentence that begins with *This* again. That's an especially strong sentence because it makes a picture in my mind."

In between children's visits to the author's chair, Arlee is helping a student who is assigned to special education classes for part of each day. He is practically a nonreader. He dictates a creative story to her and she enters it in the computer. Later he takes his place at the author's chair and reads his story, nearly perfectly, to the class.

Jaima has been working conscientiously on her story about a cat, a dog, and a hunter since I first entered the classroom. She is copying it from her draft into a blank book, but wants to make sure that the rest of the class agrees with her about the ending before she finishes publishing it. The class considers other endings, such as sending the cat and dog home with the hunter, but finally agrees that her ending is fine as it is. Jaima finishes copying her story into the booklet and places it on the shelf. (See Example 6.3 for a condensed version of her completed book.)

Two girls, collaborators on a Cinderella version, now claim the author's chair. Arlee points out that sometimes authors and illustrators work together to create a story, but this is often difficult to do because they don't always agree. Jordan confirms that she and Catherine did have different ideas at first, but they are now agreeing on the story. Jordan announces that she is the illustrator and shows her picture of Cinderella as a princess, which carries much of the meaning of the story. She also has ideas for ways to make Cinderella look ragged. Catherine explains that Cinderella is looking for her crown and that she trips over a pointed object in a mud puddle that turns out to be the crown. The girls are clearly pleased with their story and eager to share it, but they are more intent on developing their own ideas than getting ideas from their classmates.

One more student moves to the author's chair to share a published story. Miranda has used her classmates' names in her story entitled "Two Girls and a Boy," and she and her classmates giggle as her story unfolds. Arlee announces that it is now snack time, but most children continue writing voluntarily as they snack.

The Dog and Cat Are Frieds

Jaima Jan. 13, 1995

Once upon a time, There was a dog The dog was alone on the streets

One day he saw a cat. The cat Saw the dog They ran to each other and they became friends.

One day they went out to get food. The cat got lost and a hunter found the cat.

Then the dog found the cat with the hunter and he barked.

The cat jumped out of the hunter's hands and ran to the dog. And they lived happily ever after.

I can't do it

Example 6.3

Interview with the Teacher

ER: How long have you been doing the workshop and why did you start teaching writing this way?

AF: I've been doing it for about five years. I guess I started because I attended a workshop on creative writing and wanted to find a way to motivate my children to be more interested in writing.

ER: Do you do this kind of writing every day?

AF: No—usually just on Fridays, although we may occasionally do it more often. Sometimes the children get so involved in their writing that they want to spend nearly all day writing, so that's what we do. The children ask for more time because they are enjoying it so much.

ER: How do they get their ideas?

AF: Sometimes we brainstorm ideas around such general topics as colors or nature. Ideas come from the themes we are studying, and each child keeps a personal writing notebook. The children write down ideas as they think of them, then refer to them when they begin writing. Sometimes they start a piece and don't want to finish it, but they may return to it later and complete it. They also read books to get ideas.

ER: How do you make sure you are covering the skills that will be on the achievement test?

AF: I sometimes teach mini-lessons on such topics as pronoun referents, apostrophes, apposition, contractions, main ideas, and compound words. I also teach these skills one-on-one as I help them edit their drafts.

ER: I noticed that you seem to do all of the editing. Do the children ever do any of their own editing?

AF: At this time of year (January), I work with each child myself on editing. Later in the year the children will help each other edit.

ER: What do you do about nonstandard spelling and grammar?

AF: I don't correct their spelling if they have made the effort to work out spellings phonetically, but I do point out and help them with grammatical errors.

ER: What problems do you have with using the workshop approach? Has it been difficult to implement this type of writing with second graders?

AF: My only problem is that I can't help everyone at once. I hate to have a line of kids waiting for my help. Student teachers and practicum students are a big help, and the aide will make the booklets, but she doesn't feel comfortable helping the children with their stories. There's just not enough one-on-one time!

ER: I noticed that the children all seemed to be "on-task" and eager to write. Do you ever have discipline problems or trouble keeping their attention on their work?

AF: No—I really don't have any discipline problems. They all seem to enjoy the writing so much. Sometimes I suspect they may not be talking about their work when they are conferring, but most of the time they seem to be discussing their writing.

A Day in a Poetry Workshop: Grade 6

Holly Martin has been introducing a poetry unit and begins this lesson by reminding her students to practice their calligraphy so that they will be able to use it as they publish their poems. She asks them to recall the three guiding principles that help us understand and write poetry: story, relevance to personal life, and meaning (consisting of purpose, value, lesson, or theme—whichever seems most appropriate).

Because Holly has asked the students to bring in poetry books and rehearse poems to read to the class, most of the students have poetry selections that they are eager to share. Holly asks Scott to read, and he shares a poem entitled "Worlds I Know" by Myra Cohn Livingston. Scott leads the discussion that follows his poem, and someone comments that it was hard to tell from his reading when the poem was ending. The class decides that it is important to communicate well with your audience when you read poetry.

The next volunteer is Laura who reads "I Wish My Father Wouldn't Try to Fix Things Anymore" from a collection by Jack Prelutsky. At the conclusion of the poem, the children are bursting with ideas to tell about fathers and grandfathers who try to fix things. They think this poem is funny and observe that it tells a story.

Lillian reads Nikki Giovanni's "Rainbows" next. The children listen thoughtfully, and Holly asks Lillian to read it again. Laura says, "I really like that poem because I can see things going on in my head." Molly comments, "It makes you want to think about the things that are going on around you. It could go on forever." "It reminds me of my little brother," Beth says. "He talks about his rainbow boat that flies up into the sky." Molly adds, "It's a way of expressing feelings through visual images and details." Holly mentions that the poem makes her think of all the colors in the rainbow and how each color makes us feel a different way.

Holly reads a poem written by a tenth grader called "Heat Lightning" and asks the children to follow along with their own copies of the poem. She asks them to respond as a group, then to share their responses with the class. She hears them saying the poem is fearful, that it deals with family crises, that someone has been hurt. She tells them that she will soon ask them to write their own poems and that "the work you do is phenomenal; I'm impressed; you have talent!" Before they begin writing, Holly reminds them to use vivid words, "words that count," and to avoid writing long paragraphs. When they question her about using rhyming words, she tells them to use free verse.

As I watch the children begin to write their poems, I'm impressed with how quickly they begin. It seems they are already full of ideas and eager to put them down. Holly, too, is writing a poem. No one speaks. Some children are looking thoughtfully off in the distance, but everyone is concentrating.

While they are writing, I look around the room. The desks are arranged in clusters of four, six, or eight in the crowded room, and there is an author's chair with a high seat in front. Four milk crates hold class sets of file folders arranged in alphabetical order, one crate for each of the four writing classes Holly teaches. In an adjoining alcove there are sets of well-worn books that children refer to as they write their stories. Charts of the writing process and editor's proofreading marks are on the wall.

When it is time to stop writing, the children's hands fly up as they volunteer to read their poems. Colyn reads first, and as the others read their poems, she quickly adds a fourth stanza to her poem. A first draft of her poem appears in Example 6.4. Several others follow before it is time to change classes.

Interview with the Teacher

ER: How long have you been doing the workshop and why did you start teaching writing this way?

HM: I took some graduate courses about seven years ago, and I began using the writing workshop then.

ER: I noticed today that you did it differently than the last time I visited. When I saw you before, the children were writing nearly the whole time and you were conferring with them.

IN THE EYE (of a storm)

"Swoosh" say the trees as they float in the breeze
Crackle go the sticks as they twist and mix
As I watch the branches bend.
Will it ever end?
Will it ever end?

The woodpecker pecks no more.
The birds can no longer soar.
Everything that was is now no more.
No more.

Everything is gone.
It doesn't make any sense.
Why did it last for so long?
too long.

Is it starting over?
Is it happening all over again?
Was that just the eye?
Will it ever end?
Will it ever end?

— Colyn

Example 6.4

HM: That's what we usually do. Conferencing is a strong component, and we always have group share. But when I introduce a new unit, I spend a lot of time making sure they understand the theme before they really get into the writing. Today, for example, I wanted them to hear some poems and respond to them before they began writing their own.

ER: Have you had any difficulties implementing the workshop?

HM: One problem was with a parent who disagreed with my philosophy and wanted me to stress the mechanics of writing. It was hard to convince this parent of the value of process writing and to show that his child would learn mechanics during the proofreading and editing.

ER: Anything else?

HM: The School Board has told us that we must use worksheets at least some of the time, so I occasionally have my students complete worksheets on adverbs and adjectives. This district stresses skills teaching, and we are expected to give our students test-taking packets to prepare them for the achievement tests.

ER: Is there anything you wish you could change?

HM: I wish we were self-contained. I'd love to have a class all day and carry through themes in all of the subjects. Then I wouldn't have to rush so much to finish—an hour just isn't long enough sometimes.

ER: Do you teach reading too?

HM: I really want to do that because I believe so strongly in the reading-writing connection, and of course I do to some extent. Bonnie, who teaches social studies, also wants to teach these kids reading because she wants to relate reading to social studies, so we both tie in reading.

ER: Have you changed anything over the last few years?

HM: I'm changing my conferencing style. When I saw myself on a videotape holding conferences with the children, I found I was much too abrupt and direct with them. I'm trying to make myself more supportive.

ER: Have you noticed any other changes in yourself?

HM: At first I simply valued and affirmed their writing. I still value their writing, but now I declare myself the expert. I've had many more years of education and experience, and if I don't understand something they've written, I tell them so and ask them to clarify it. I say, "Make it clearer for me."

ER: I notice that you are discussing poetry now. Have you done other forms of writing this year?

HM: Yes, several. The students wrote autobiographies and we just finished spending several weeks on persuasive writing. You can see samples of their drafts in their folders.

ER: I was really impressed with the way the children began writing so quickly when you ask them to compose poems. Do they always do that?

HM: They really do get started easily. I think it's because they do so much writing and they always have ideas in their heads. We write every day and they are very comfortable with it.

ER: What do you think the best thing is about process writing?

HM: They enjoy writing more, they see the value of writing, and they are willing to take more risks with their writing.

Group Share

A sharing session concludes each workshop. Authors, often seating themselves in a designated author's chair, may begin by explaining why they need help with their writing and then read the passage in question. Nancie Atwell (1987, pp. 96–97) stresses that this is not just a time for students to perform, but an opportunity for them to get reactions from a wide audience. They may have the floor at the end of a writing workshop for a variety of reasons, such as these:

- To get different perspectives on a problem.
- To try out a new idea with the group.
- To share a new technique.
- To propose alternate solutions to a problem.
- To "celebrate" the completion of a piece.

The author's chair (Graves and Hansen, 1983) is a special place where authors, children and teachers, read to the class. It may be a rocking chair, a stool, or any *different chair,* which the students may decorate and label themselves. It is a place of importance, for authors use it to share significant pieces of writing and to direct the discussions that follow.

For his class's monthly newsletter to parents, Matthew Johnston contributed an article about the author's chair which reads as follows:

> Sometimes our teacher, Mrs. Ramsey reads us books. She always sits in her old rocking chair. She reads a few chapters out of a book every day. Some of the books she has read this year are: *James and the Giant Peach, The Doll in the Garden,* and *The Lion, the Witch, and the Wardrobe.* Sometimes we write stories and Mrs. Ramsey lets us sit in the author's chair to read our stories to the class. After we read, the class shares suggestions and comments about the story. We love the author's chair!

Children must listen carefully and critically as they respond to someone in the author's chair. Their purpose is to help the author with a problem or to give recognition for a piece of writing. Their comments should be specific and directed toward the author's purpose in sharing the piece. Vague comments, such as "I like your story," are not constructive. When little thought is put into the responses, the author gets little benefit. Teacher modeling and mini-lessons on ways to respond help children focus on specific comments that help the writer. Carol Avery (1993) suggests that responders begin with "I" instead of "you," saying "I wonder" or "I don't understand" so that the responder clearly is expressing a personal view and the author can accept or reject it. Figure 6.3 gives suggestions for topics that the audience might consider in responding to the author. Some of these topics are appropriate for mini-lessons.

Use of vivid descriptive and action words

Enticing leads that capture listener or
  reader interest

Well developed story line without gaps of
  information

Readily apparent conflict/resolution
  structure

Satisfying conclusion

Strong, consistent characters

Appropriate choice of words

Clear sensory images

Use of different genres or special features

Figure 6.3:   Topics for Group-Share Focus

For each of these topics, responders can find questions. For
example, when focusing on vivid descriptive and action words, the
responder might say: "I can't really picture what Ellen looks like when
you say she is pretty. Can you help me get a clearer picture of her?"

In some cases group share can take an entire class period. In a
year six class each child had just spent five weeks writing five short
stories to publish in books. On the day I visited, the children were
proudly reading their published stories. They began by sharing their
dedications, blurbs about their books, and their autobiographies.
Classmates responded with positive comments for the authors.

When you conduct a group-share session, a number of problems may arise. Here are some potential problems and possible
solutions (based on Graves, 1994b).

*Children don't understand how to conduct group-share
sessions.* At first, you need to provide a structure. Begin with a
small group of students, explain the procedures carefully, and
ask them to

- Listen carefully as Susan reads her piece.
- When she finishes reading, tell what you remember.
- Tell what strikes you about her piece and try to make
  connections to it from your personal experiences.
- Ask Susan questions to learn more about what she
  wrote.

Some children don't want to take the author's chair. Although
children may not choose to share for a variety of reasons, many
children are uncomfortable reading in front of a large group. Let
them choose two or three children as their audience until they feel
secure reading for a larger group.

Children give routine responses that don't help the author. Model higher-order, specific questions or comments that respond directly to the author's purpose for sharing. Conduct mini-lessons on valid types of responses.

The children show little or no growth in writing. "Nudge" your children into trying new forms of writing by asking them if anyone created a new character in fiction, tried a new genre, or used some interesting descriptive words. By encouraging students to experiment with different forms, you will broaden their writing skills. Sharing your own experiments with writing shows that you too are growing as a writer.

It's difficult to keep track of which children are sharing and responding. Devise a record-keeping form, a sign-up schedule, or some written observation so that you have records of which children actively participate in sharing and responding. This recorded information may also be helpful as you determine grades. You may want to find a way to identify the quality of the sharing and response, as well as the quantity.

There isn't enough time for all of the children to share. Time for sharing is limited because you want your students to spend most of the workshop time writing. If large numbers of students are eager to share, try the following:

- Divide the class into small groups and let students share within each group.
- Let students place their writing where others can read it, such as on bulletin boards and book shelves.
- Let students read their work to another class.

TEACHING TIP

To keep children within reasonable time limits when they read to an audience during group share, ask them to

a. Read just the part they need help with.
b. Focus on a specific problem, explain it, and ask for help.
c. Read just their favorite part from a published book.

Genres

Donald Graves (1994b) believes in nudging children to try new forms of writing. Too often, children pursue the same types of writing without showing much growth or progress, so they may need a nudge to try something different. He suggests that they keep records of the genres they write by recording the genre along with the title of each piece and its starting and completion dates.

Introducing children to different modes or genres of writing occurs naturally within the classroom as teachers present informational books as well as story books, various types of folk tales, brochures promoting healthy life styles, reports on the environment or endangered species, and so forth. Discussions of these genres help students understand distinctions among various forms of writing; for instance, the teacher reads a newspaper report and an editorial, then asks the students to contrast the two. When students realize that some types of writing are more suitable for specific audiences and purposes than others, they begin to consider writing in alternate forms. We will look briefly at some genres that young writers are likely to use.

Personal Narratives

The most natural form of writing for children is personal narrative, the recounting of an experience from beginning to end. Lucy Calkins (1986) refers to these as "bed-to-bed" stories. Even though a narrative may not begin with waking up and end with going to bed, the writer relates a complete account of an event—a family trip or a visit to the mall—without leaving anything out. The teacher can help the writer focus by asking such questions as "What was special to you about this experience?" and "Can you tell me more about the most important part of this event?" In Example 6.5 Jill, a student in Mary Martin's seventh grade class, focuses on her favorite place by describing the spot and her feelings when she is there.

Fiction

Of all the genres, fiction is usually the favorite and also the most demanding for young writers (Graves, 1994b). Instead of often focusing on violent, action-packed plots, children need to learn how to create fully developed characters whose behaviors determine the way the story unfolds. In writing believable fiction, children may also need help with settings, use of dialogue, and structure (e.g., lead sentences, problems and resolutions). Examples from good literary fiction can serve as models, and teachers can help by asking writers such questions as "Why is your character doing that?" and "How do you think your story should end?"

TEACHING TIP
If you want to encourage quality writing, place some topics off limits, such as a.   Video games. b.   Stories about popular superheroes. c.   Profanity. d.   Fictional blood-and-guts stories (Avery, 1993).

My Favorite Place

My favorite place is on the bank of one of our ponds. We have a twelve-acre farm with two ponds and several springs. One of the ponds is my favorite place because it is very peaceful and cool even on the hottest summer days. I go there often just to get away from my troubles. It is a good place for me to just sit and think, while I watch the fish splash in X the clear water. Small yellow flowers grow on the bank, and the shade trees make the soft grass cool. One can often X find me there thinking of problems or reading a book. Time passes quickly, and before I know it, my brother is standing in the yard whistling for me to come to the house. Unwillingly, I'll tuck away my X thoughts and head back to the house. Later, I will find time to slip away again back to my favorite place.

Example 6.5

Informational Materials

Although informational text is often neglected in elementary class-rooms, students will encounter much of it in later school years and during their careers. Informational writing extends into content areas and is functional and purposeful; it includes reports, procedures, and explanations. This type of writing is concise and accurate, without irrelevant details and personal bias (Wing Jan, 1991). Many reports begin with a general introductory statement and follow with supporting details or descriptions. Procedural texts, or "how to" texts, present instructions in logical sequence so that the reader can follow directions in order to do something. When writing explanations, the writer gives reasons or justifications for certain phenomena by stating how or why they exist. Young children can learn to write informational text and refine this style of writing as they proceed through the grades.

Numerous fascinating and brightly illustrated nonfiction books for young people serve as models for creating interest in writing reports on topics of special interest. In helping writers develop such materials, teachers might ask them to think about the clarity, organization, and completeness of their writing.

Persuasive Writing

Often considered a form of informational text, persuasive writing supports a position or makes a case for an issue that may be controversial. Class discussions and debates help children understand how to present or defend their positions with convincing arguments. Good topics for oral or written persuasion are "Should students be allowed to use candy and soft drink machines at school?" and "Should there be bike trails along the new access route?" Inspired by her mother's beliefs and encouraged by her teacher, Trudy wrote an editorial that gives reasons against constructing Palkway (see Example 6.6).

I am eight years old and I live on Milfred ave and I don't want palkway I and the outher people in my neighborhood do not want it eithe. I like to ride sofe but I cant if you put palkway. My Brother not beabol to go to Leos and he is cinda mad.

Trudy

Example 6.6

Poetry

Poetry begins with recalling images associated with strong feelings. It grows out of reflections on ordinary events that somehow become significant, perhaps because of their sensory impressions—the sounds, smells, touch, or visions. Poetry is compact, so each word counts. Poets often use figurative language to convey their feelings, and they use precise, concrete words to help readers envision their images. Rhythm is part of poetry, as are lines and stanzas. During a writing workshop in April Dix's sixth grade class, Kristen uses humor and imagination to create a bedroom jungle in her poem (see Example 6.7).

Children learn much about writing poetry by listening to good poems—those that enable them to visualize, appreciate the depth of feeling, recognize universal truths, and increase their sensitivity. When teaching children to begin writing their own poetry, make them aware of the elements that poets use by reading poems to them. Ask them, "How does the poet help you to share his feelings about dreams?" or "What words does the poet use to help you visualize the ocean at night?" Avoid using formulaic poems which tend to inhibit children's free exploration of poetry.

Kristen

My mother says my room's a jungle.
I really wish it was.
With snakes that wrap themselves in bundles,
And a loud mosquito's buzz.
With elephants that stomp around,
And birds that scream and sreech.
And some that do not make a sound.
And bullfrog's toungues that reach.
 I am sorry it's not exiting
To go to bed at night.
But I bet the tiger under
the bed will give my mom a fright.

Example 6.7

Alternatives

Variations of the writing process, alternate forms of workshops, and special writing projects abound as teachers seek ways to improve student writing. Here are three fresh approaches to writing.

Image-Making within the Writing Process

Believing that art and writing reinforce one another, Beth Olshansky (1994) created a method for integrating visual imagery throughout the writing process. Using a variety of media and techniques, children design fanciful, textured papers which they assemble into colorful collages, much like those of Eric Carle, Ezra Jack Keats, and Leo Lionni. From these images children create stories and discover rich, descriptive words to use in their writing. Some children create all of their images first, but others move back and forth between finding images and words.

Images are important at each stage of the writing process. Even as they work with their designs, children begin to discover stories. Using their imaginations, they find settings of dark clouds or beautiful sunsets, and characters such as dragons or strange creatures. Children rehearse by sharing what they see in their images, and they refer to them frequently as they compose their drafts. During revisions they once again consult their images, using them to enrich their language and find details to enhance their stories. Publication calls for children to match pictures with words as they prepare their final copies.

Beth has found her method to be particularly effective for children with diverse learning styles because of its manipulative and visual components. The colors, rhythms, and textures of the designs stimulate physical manipulation of the papers and oral discussions of what children see in their images.

Laws of Life

Believing that students need to consider thoughtfully their guiding principles, John Templeton (19) established an essay contest. By reading the "laws of life" espoused by respected individuals and by examining their own experiences, students write essays expressing their values and guideposts for living. Teachers help them brainstorm ideas, focus on themes, prepare drafts, and publish their essays in booklets.

As I interviewed students, teachers, and administrators involved with the Laws of Life program, I found them enthusiastic about its positive effects on students and the community. Writing essays expressing their beliefs appeared to make students more sensitive to others and more aware of the way people have influenced their lives. Excerpts from some winning junior high school entries follow.

My last law of life and probably the most important is to be true to yourself. If you abuse your body with drugs or alcohol, you are weakening your possibilities for a fruitful life.

Heather Hubbard

Play fair. Be honest and never cheat no matter what it is. Honesty is the best policy and cheating will not get you anywhere. For example, if you cheat on a test you really don't learn anything. What you're really cheating is yourself.

Jill Willis

Because life is uncertain, we should never take the people we love for granted and we should let them know that we love and appreciate them while we can.

Rusty Burt

Environmental Writing Workshop

Although she followed the advice of Atwell, Graves, and Calkins in establishing her writing workshop, Cheryl Kucera (1995) was less than enthusiastic about her results. She was swamped with papers, stick-on notes, and folders, and she despaired at the noise, confusion, and paperwork. Moreover, her students never spontaneously wrote persuasive or expository pieces, and their spelling and sentence variation had actually declined. Students eagerly wrote creatively, but used extremely poor English. The writing workshop was not working.

Looking for an alternative, Cheryl discovered the environmental writing workshop with more structure and stricter requirements than the typical workshop. Both workshops are similar in terms of conferencing, drafts, revisions, and publishing, but in the environmental workshop students are expected to use different forms of writing and to meet certain standards. Cheryl found herself teaching basic grammar and assigning specific types of writing. She organized conferencing groups of four students each and met with them to discuss problems. She set specific criteria for writing products, and she taught competencies that coincided with the performance-based state test.

Both Cheryl and her students liked this structured workshop. Cheryl felt more confident, and more of her students believed they could write, that it was easy to do so, and that they had something worth saying. Cheryl's experiences show us that teachers can construct workshops in a variety of ways. Some procedures work better than others, and teachers need to continually experiment with modifications in order to find the best procedures.

Summary

The writing workshop can take many forms, but it typically consists of a mini-lesson, a status-of-the-class report, time for writing, and a group-share session. During the sustained writing period, students often use the writing process, but can use any type of authentic writing. Group-share sessions conclude the workshop with students' sharing works in progress or published works with an audience. They often read from the author's chair.

Although it seems easy to break the writing workshop and writing process into series of steps, you should realize that you may have to explore variations in the basic procedures to find what works best for you and your students. The workshop allows a great deal of flexibility. Take your cues from your students; their responses should guide you in determining how you set up your workshop.

Reflections

Seriously consider the following questions. Some answers may be found by reflecting on the chapter; others may come from your own beliefs and experiences.

1. Considering the two examples given in this chapter on workshops in action, how would I set up my workshop? What would I want my students to be doing, and how would I interact with them? How could I best support their writing efforts?

2. How can I encourage students to use a variety of genres? Should I always let them choose the type of writing they do, or should I teach different genres and expect them to use them?

3. What alternatives have I observed that I might want to consider in my own workshop? Do I have some ideas for modifying the standard procedures in case they don't seem to be working for me? How long should I wait for the workshop to succeed before trying alternatives? Is there ever a time to give up and return to traditional teaching?

Bibliography

Atwell, N. (1990). *Coming to know.* Portsmouth, NH: Heinemann.
Atwell, N. (1987). *In the middle.* Portsmouth, NH: Heinemann.
Au, K. (1993). *Literacy instruction in multicultural settings.* Fort Worth: Holt, Rinehart and Winston.
Avery, C. (1993). . . . *And with a light touch.* Portsmouth, NH: Heinemann.
Calkins, L. M. (1986). *The art of teaching writing.* Portsmouth, NH: Heinemann.

Calkins, L. M. (1991). *Living between the lines*. Portsmouth, NH: Heinemann.

Calkins, L. M. (1994). *The art of teaching writing,* new edition. Portsmouth, NH: Heinemann.

Clark, R. P. (1987). *Free to write*. Portsmouth, NH: Heinemann.

Cunningham, P. M., & Allington, R. (1994). *Classrooms that work: They can all read & write*. NY: Harper Collins.

Emmitt, M., & Pollock, J. (1991). *Language and learning*. South Melbourne, Australia: Oxford University Press.

Fiderer, A. (1993). *Teaching writing: A workshop approach*. NY: Scholastic.

Graves, D. (1994a). Be a better writing teacher. *Instructor, 104* (4), 43–45, 71.

Graves, D. (1994b). *A fresh look at writing*. Portsmouth, NH: Heinemann.

Graves, D., & Hansen, J. (1983). The author's chair. *Language Arts, 60* (2), 176–183.

Graves, D., & Stuart, V. (1985). *Write from the start*. NY: E.P. Dutton.

Hansen, J., Newkirk, T., & Graves, D., eds. (1985). *Breaking ground*. Portsmouth, NH: Heinemann.

Hansen, J. (1987). *When writers read*. Portsmouth, NH: Heinemann.

Harwayne, S. (1992). *Lasting impressions: Weaving literature into the writing workshop*. Portsmouth, NH: Heinemann.

Hill, B. C., & Ruptic, C. (1994). *Practical aspects of authentic assessment: Putting the pieces together.* Norwood, MA: Christopher-Gordon.

Jackson, N., & Pillow, P. (1992). *The reading-writing workshop: Getting started*. New York: Scholastic.

Karelitz, E. B. (1993). *The author's chair and beyond*. Portsmouth, NH: Heinemann.

Kucera, C. (1995). Detours and destinations: One teacher's journey into an environmental writing workshop. *Language Arts, 72* (3), 179–187.

McCarthy, S. J. (1994). Opportunities and risks of writing from personal experience. *Language Arts, 71* (3), 182–191.

Olshansky, B. (1994). Making writing a work of art: Image-making within the writing process. *Language Arts, 71* (5), 350–356.

Pike, K., Compain, R., & Mumper, J. (1994). *Connections: An integrated approach to literacy*. NY: HarperCollins.

Puhr, K., & Workman, G. (1992). Monitoring student progress through a conferenced writing program. *English Journal, 81* (2), 49–50.

Rief, L. (1992). *Seeking diversity*. Portsmouth, NH: Heinemann.

Rief, L. (1994). Writing for life: Language arts in the middle. *Language Arts, 71* (2), 92–100.

Routman, R. (1991). *Invitations.* Portsmouth, NH: Heinemann.

Simic, M. (1993). Publishing children's writing. *Eric Digest,* Clearinghouse on Reading, English, and Communication. EDO-CS-93-08.

Sudol, D., & Sudol, P. (1991). Another story: Putting Graves, Calkins, and Atwell into practice and perspective. *Language Arts, 68* (4), 292–300.

Sudol, D., & Sudol, P. (1995). Yet another story: Writers' workshop revisited. *Language Arts, 72,* (3), 171–178.

Tchudi, S. (1994). *Integrated language arts in the elementary school.* Belmont, CA: Wadsworth.

Templeton, J. M. (1994). *Discovering the laws of life.* New York: Continuum.

Wing Jan, L. (1991). *Write ways.* Melbourne, Australia: Oxford University Press.

Yellin, D., & Blake, M. (1994). *Integrating language arts.* NY: HarperCollins.

CHAPTER 7

MINI-LESSONS FOR WRITING WORKSHOP

January 26

Looking in on Amy one afternoon after school, Kevin sees her brooding at her desk, chin cupped in her hands and eyes staring into space.

Kevin: What's the matter, Amy? You look as if you've lost your best friend.

Amy: I've had it. I'm giving up on workshops. I'll still give my kids time to read—they enjoy that so much. But the writing part just isn't working.

Kevin: What went wrong? You were so enthusiastic earlier.

Amy: I'm really afraid they're not learning anything about writing. Sure, they write drafts, but they don't want to revise, and the drafts are rambling and pointless. When I ask them to tell me more, they can't think of anything else to say.

Kevin: Some children never think they have anything important enough to write about. I've tried modeling my writing sometimes, and I purposely choose little things, but things that made an impression on me. One time I wrote about tripping over the trash can when I entered the room on the first day of school. I was so embarrassed and the students all laughed at me!

Amy: You probably did look pretty silly! But seriously, I'm not sure my class is learning anything. The other second grade teachers are talking about skill mastery and the achievement tests coming up this spring. They're still using skill sheets and spelling books. I don't want to do that—I don't believe there's much transfer from doing skills to actual writing—but I'm panicking because I'm not covering the skills systematically like they are.

Kevin: Here's an idea. Look at your children's writing. See what they need to learn. Then plan mini-lessons to help them learn what they need to know to be better writers.

Amy: That makes sense, but I don't know if I can do that. I guess I'm losing confidence in my ability to cover the material as completely as I should.

Kevin: Why don't you cut back on workshops then until you feel more secure, but don't give them up altogether. Maybe you moved into them too quickly. Just do the workshop two or three days a week and do more structured activities the rest of the time. But do let your kids write—that's the only way they'll ever really learn *how* to write. You can help them by conferencing with them too.

Amy: I'll try what you suggest and see how it goes. It's hard being the only second grade teacher who doesn't go by the book.

Kevin: I believe my students are learning far more about writing by actually doing it than if we were using the spelling and grammar books. Hang in there!

Introduction

Most writing workshops begin with mini-lessons which focus on single concepts or skills. Teachers observe the way students write and then plan mini-lessons to help them improve their writing strategies. For your convenience, I've divided the mini-lessons in this chapter into the following categories: workshop procedures, literary techniques, and writing skills. I've also labeled them (L) for lower grades (mostly K–1), (U) for upper grades, and (A) for all grades, but some lower-grade children may be ready for activities labeled (U).

Mini-lessons

Teachers present important writing procedures, concepts, and strategies through mini-lessons. Some consist primarily of giving instruction, but others may be interactive with students brainstorming and contributing ideas. During the first few weeks they use them to teach procedures that students must understand for participating in workshops. During the rest of the year teachers use mini-lessons to present various aspects of the writing process, introduce a variety of genres, help students develop their writing techniques, and teach writing conventions. Figure 7.1 lists topics for writing mini-lessons, but you will undoubtedly find others as needs arise.

Most writing mini-lessons last only five to ten minutes so that students can spend most of the class period writing. In order to add breadth and depth to her lessons, however, Shelley Harwayne (1992) finds that she sometimes spends twenty minutes or longer on them. Holly Martin, whose workshop is described in Chapter 6, also spends more time on mini-lessons when she introduces a new concept or genre. Although one brief introductory lesson is often too little time for all students to learn a skill, awareness of the skill or strategy will spread as children confer with each other.

Mini-lessons vary not only in length of time, but also in when to teach them. Some mini-lessons occur during the writing time if a number of students are struggling with a similar problem, and they may also re-emerge during group-share time if students point out specific techniques they have used. Shelley Harwayne (1992) suggests that some students may want to remain after the mini-lesson to work on the skill they have just learned, either by sharing ideas with classmates or examining the way a well-known author has used the technique.

Literary Techniques	Writing Skills
topic choice	capitalization
showing, not just telling	quotation marks
revisions	ending punctuation
strong verbs	invented spelling
descriptive words and phrases	spelling strategies
dialogue	possessives
story structure	proofreading
first versus third person	commas in a series
settings	inflectional endings
leads	paragraphing
letter writing	sentence combining
focus	run-on sentences
report writing	subject-verb agreement
persuasive writing	spacing between words
poetry	dictionary skills
character development	syllabication
voice	grammar

Figure 7.1:   Topics for Writing Mini-lessons

Students can take an active part in mini-lessons. After you model a variety of techniques, students proficient in a particular strategy or genre may lead mini-lessons by sharing their expertise with the class. You may also wish to involve them in helping you present a mini-lesson; these assistants can then teach others. Nancie Atwell (1987) finds role playing by students effective for helping students conduct peer conferences, and transparencies of students' writing are excellent sources for discussing various writing techniques. You might want to file these transparencies with the skills or strategies they illustrate so that you can use them again.

TEACHING TIP

To collect samples of students' work to use as class examples, delete names and make photocopies from pieces completed in . . .

a.   This year's class to use in later years.
b.   Another class where students are unlikely to know each other.
c.   Your own class to use now with student permission. Also, you can compose your own samples to teach specific skills.

Is there ever a time to use worksheets? Some teachers might say never, but I'm hearing a lot of teachers say they use them for special purposes. As in Amy's case, teachers are concerned that students are not learning the skills they need, whether for writing proficiency or achievement tests. Some teachers find that worksheets help students understand skills by providing additional practice for students who didn't grasp them fully during mini-lessons. Some teachers use them about once a week to check children's knowledge of skills, and some use them because of school district mandates. One teacher told me she is required to have her students complete their workbooks, so one day a week they sit together on the floor, quickly do about ten pages, and then get on with their writing.

TEACHING TIP

To maintain a mini-lesson file, organize lessons by categories and include

a.   Samples and transparencies of students' work.
b.   Appropriate worksheets for additional practice.
c.   A list of relevant children's literature.
d.   New ideas for teaching the lesson.

Procedural Mini-lessons

Children's familiarity with procedures is crucial for the successful operation of workshops. You may feel that you want to get on with teaching writing instead of spending time with class management, but the students will benefit in the long run if they completely understand what you expect them to do. Time spent teaching procedures initially will be saved later. You may need to repeat some of these lessons that don't sink in the first time around, and you may discover additional procedures that you need to address at a later time. Figure 7.2 gives some topics that you might want to use for procedural mini-lessons.

Workshop procedures
Use of materials
Availability of computers
Peer conferences
Evaluation
Use of writing folders
Storage of materials
Schedules
Publishing

Figure 7.2:   Topics for Procedural
Mini-lessons

Procedural Lesson
Mini-lessons

Kevin: Yesterday we talked about writing workshops, and today I'd like to explain more about mini-lessons. We'll begin each workshop with a mini-lesson, a short lesson about a specific writing skill. Because it is very short, you will need to pay attention carefully so that you don't miss anything. You may want to take notes and put them in your writing folders so that you can refer to them later.

The reason that the mini-lesson is so short is that I want you to spend most of our class time writing. If you need more time to understand the lesson, I'll meet with you individually or in a small group, or one of the other students can help you.

I'll choose topics for the mini-lessons as I observe your writing and see what you need to learn to be better writers. For example, if I see a lot of you are trying to write dialogue, we may have some mini-lessons on writing dialogue. You may ask me to teach you something you want to learn, and I can do that. I want you to see how you can use what I teach you to improve your writing.

Sometimes I may ask you to help me with a mini-lesson. I may want to use a sample of your work, or I may ask you to explain a technique that you use very well. When you are ready to learn something new, I may ask a few of you to help me plan a mini-lesson.

Dana: Will we have to take tests over the mini-lessons?

Kevin: Not really, but the writing you do will show me if you learned what was in the mini-lessons.

Cassandra: Will we be using our English and spelling books too?

Kevin: Not if we continue with the workshops. You should be able to learn the same skills through the mini-lessons and be much better writers because you will have time to write. Now this mini-lesson is over, so we'll do status of the class. Be ready to tell me what you plan to do.

Procedural Lesson
Use of Writing Folders

Amy, passing out file folders to the children seated around her: Boys and girls, today I'm giving each of you a new folder and I want you to take good care of it. You will keep your writing in it. I want you to save everything that you write, even the ideas that you get that you may never use.

When you go back to your seats, the first thing I want you to do with your folder is to put your name on the tab, the part that sticks up. Point to the tab on your folder. (The children do this.) Write your first name and your last name very neatly because I expect you to keep these folders for a long time.

Each day when I tell you that workshop time is almost over, I want you to put your writing inside your folder. Then take your folder and put it in this plastic crate, but I want you to put your folder in alphabetical order. Raise your hand if you remember how to put things in alphabetical order.

Seeing lots of hands go up, Amy asks Caleb to explain it to the rest of the class.

Caleb: It means we have to look at the last name and find the letter it starts with. Then we can look at the alphabet strip and see what letters come before our name and after it. We put it in between who comes before us and who comes after us.

Amy: Right—good explanation, Caleb. I'll help you the first time and after that try to remember who comes before you and who comes after you so that you will always get your folder in the right place. Why do we use alphabetical order?

Sherri: Because it's easier to find things.

Amy: That's exactly right. You can just look for your folder where it should be and not look through all of the folders to find it. Sometime before our writing workshop each day, I want you to get your folder so you will be able to begin writing as soon as the mini-lesson is over. Do you have any questions?

Jason: Can we decorate our covers?

Amy: That's a good idea. You may decorate them, but be sure that you don't cover up your names. Now take your folders, print your names carefully on the tabs, and continue with your writing.

Procedural Lesson
Publishing

Kevin: Some of you have been revising and editing your pieces so that you are nearly ready to publish. Today we will talk about some of the procedures for publishing. As you can see, I've sectioned off part of the room where there is a computer and a work table. This will be your publishing center, so I'd like you to think about what you could do to make it convenient and attractive. Also, think about the materials you'll need. For now we have the basics: typing paper, tape, some writing tools, a stapler, and construction paper.

Before you go to the publishing center, I must approve your work. That means I need to edit it and agree that the piece is ready to publish. You will need to copy it one more time after my editing, either by hand or with the computer.

We'll keep the publishing simple for now until we get more materials and learn some ways to put books together, but later you may select special writing projects to publish in a more permanent form. By the end of the year, you should each have several sturdy, attractively bound books. Any questions?

Tabitha: What about the computer lab? Can we do our publishing there?

Kevin: You may sign up to use the computer lab. I'll check to see when the open hours are and post a schedule.

Sara: How many of us can work at the publishing center at the same time? It's not very big.

Kevin: Oh, probably five or six, if you don't get in each other's way. Some of you may need to take the materials back to your desks to work on them if it gets too crowded. You won't all be publishing at the same time.

Stuart: Is it okay if I bring in some publishing materials from home—like my calligraphy set and and some matting board?

Kevin: I don't see any problem with that. Maybe some others would like to do the same thing. We'll talk more about publishing as we see how it works. I'll be doing status of the class now, and then you can continue with your writing.

Mini-lessons for Literary Techniques

The best source of information for developing literary techniques is literature. One time when I visited Holly Martin's sixth grade writing workshop, I found nearly as many students reading as writing. Students search through books to find ways authors construct leads, describe settings, develop characters, use dialogue, create and solve problems, and reach conclusions. They look at different types of material to become familiar with various genres so that they can use them in their own writing. Literary techniques are numerous, but we will consider only a few in this chapter.

(L) Literary Techniques Mini-lesson
Parts of a Story

After reading Leo Lionni's *Swimmy* to the class, discuss how the story began. (Swimmy was left alone after a tuna fish swallowed all of the other fish in Swimmy's school.) Point out that in the beginning Leo Lionni makes us wonder how Swimmy will survive without his family and friends.

Ask the children what problem develops in the middle of the story. (Swimmy meets a school of little fish who are very afraid of a big fish.) Then ask them how Swimmy solves the problem at the end of the story. (The fish swim together so that they look like one giant fish and scare the big fish away.) Write on the board or a chart:

Beginning: Swimmy is alone.

Middle: Swimmy meets some fish who fear a big fish.

End: Swimmy and the other fish swim together and scare the big fish.

Point out that most stories have a beginning, a middle (the problem), and an end (the solution). Tell the students to watch for these when they read books, and to think of ways to create problems and solutions when they write stories.

Source: Leo Lionni. *Swimmy*. Pantheon, 1963.

(A) Literary Techniques Mini-lesson
Strong Verbs

Tell the students that you've noticed many of them are using the same, well-worn verbs in their writing. Using the word *walked* as an example, ask them to brainstorm synonyms that would give more precise pictures of how a person actually moved. The children come up with the following list:

shuffled	strode	hobbled	ambled	marched
hiked	sauntered	wandered	waddled	stomped
strolled	tramped	trudged	limped	crept

As the children say these words, record them on a chart to post on the wall. Ask a few volunteers to act out some of the words. Then ask how precise verbs give stronger images than vague words. Tell the students to think as they write if they have used the best verb to convey their exact meaning. Ask them to look back through their recent writing to see where they could replace some general verbs with specific ones.

(A) Literary Techniques Mini-lesson
Adjectives

Read a few selected pages from *Many Luscious Lollipops*, a colorfully illustrated book of adjectives. Focus on specific descriptive words that Ruth Heller uses. For lower grades, use "twelve large, blue, gorgeous butterflies" or "a wet and soggy, drizzly day, rainy, wintery and gray." For upper grades use "a mesmerizing, colorful and glittering display" or "mysterious, star-spangled, asteroidal outer space." Point out how these adjectives help us visualize what the author describes.

Ask the students to think of sensory words for popcorn—words that help us smell, taste, feel, see, and hear it. Record the words as they dictate them; then suggest that they use rich, descriptive words to help readers visualize what is happening.

Source: Heller, Ruth. *Many Luscious Lollipops.* Scholastic, 1989.

(Note: Teachers can also use this book for mini-lessons on writing skills about adjectives because it deals with proper adjectives, predicate adjectives, comparatives and superlatives, possessives, and demonstratives.)

(A) Literary Techniques Mini-lesson
Creating Settings

Tell the students you want them to listen for the way Wilson Rawls creates his setting in *Where the Red Fern Grows*. They should listen for the sensory words he uses and the way he helps the reader experience the environment.

> When I left the camp ground of the fishermen, it was late. . . . The beautiful silence that follows the setting sun had settled over the river bottoms. The coolness of the rich, black soil felt good to my bare feet.
>
> It was the time of day when all furried things come to life. A big swamp rabbit hopped out on the trail, sat on his haunches, stared at me, and then scampered away. A mother gray squirrel ran out on the limb of a burr oak tree. She barked a warning to the four furry balls behind her. They melted from sight in the thick green. A silent gray shadow drifted down from the top of a tall sycamore. There was a squeal and a beating of wings.

Ask the children to tell you the words and phrases that make them feel (for example, coolness of the rich, black soil), hear (for example, barked a warning), and see (for example, a big swamp rabbit hopped out on the trail). Point out that authors use details that appeal to our senses to help us get the full flavor of their settings. You might want to put this passage on a transparency to show on an overhead projector. Then ask volunteers to underline with a non-permanent marker the words and phrases that help them visualize the setting.

Source: Wilson Rawls. *Where the Red Fern Grows*. Bantam, 1981, pp. 18–19.

(A) Literary Techniques Mini-lesson
Showing, Not Telling

Tell the children that writers often let us know what happens by giving specific examples, not just by telling us. They show us by describing little things that happen, by letting characters talk and act. As an example, tell them that Sheila Burnford could have simply said that the cat was afraid to cross the river in *The Incredible Journey*, but instead she writes the following:

> The poor cat now showed the first signs of fear since leaving on his journey; he was alone, and the only way to rejoin his friends lay in swimming across the terrible stretch of water. He ran up and down the bank, all the time keeping up his unearthly Siamese wailing. . . .The cat was beside himself with terror and it was a long long time before he finally made up his mind. When he did it was with a sudden blind desperate rush at the water, completely uncatlike. His expression of horror and distaste was almost comical as he started swimming towards the young dog who waited for him a few yards out.

Ask the students how the author conveyed the feelings of fear through the cat's actions.

Sheila: The cat ran up and down the bank.

Olin: The cat kept yowling.

Seth: He made a sudden, desperate rush at the water.

Discuss how these actions help the reader understand the cat's fear more vividly than if the author had just said the cat was afraid. Ask the students to recall when they've been afraid. What did they see or do? How did they feel? Tell them that their writing will be more powerful if they provide actions and dialogue that *show* how a character feels instead of just telling the reader what the character is feeling.

Source: Sheila Burnford. *The Incredible Journey*. Bantam, 1988, p. 63.

(A) Literary Techniques Mini-lesson
Focus

Refer the students to the chart they made from their field trip to the aquarium. The chart looks like this:

We went to the aquarium. We saw lots of fish and some snakes too. It was kind of dark inside. There were trees and birds and streams with lizards. In one area we could see turtles swimming. There were sharks and barracuda in one of the big tanks. It was a saltwater tank.

After rereading the chart with the children, ask them if they would like to say more about one part of their visit. Tell them that you want them to focus on something that was important to them and describe it in detail, rather than tell a little about so many things. The children mention some possibilities: sharks, swimming turtles, and snakes. They finally agree to describe the area with the turtles. You start another chart, this time focusing on one area of the aquarium. The children eagerly dictate sentences about turtles paddling through the water, the sounds of the tree frogs, the feel of the moist air, and the view of plants and tiny animals in the surrounding marshes. When they read their new chart, they quickly agree that the story about the turtle area is more fun to read. Ask them to remember to focus on a special part of their experiences instead of trying to tell everything so that readers will enjoy their stories.

(U) Literary Techniques Mini-lessons
Use of First Person

Tell the students that you've noticed that they write quite naturally in first person when they do personal narratives, but they write all of their fiction in third person. Tell them that they can also use first person when writing fiction, as many authors do. Read them a passage from *A Taste of Blackberries*:

I wanted my mother to come back. I wanted her to take care of me. I wished I hadn't pretended to be asleep; then she would have stayed to talk, or just to sit quietly on the side of the bed. I wished I was little and could sit on her lap and be rocked.

The tears kept coming until I had them smeared all over my face. My face was tight where the tears had dried. I was snuffling and fumbling around in the dark for a tissue.

Point out that in this book Doris Buchanan Smith chose to use first person, although the character she describes is a young boy. Ask the students why they think she uses first person, *I* and *me*, instead of third person, *he* and *him*.

Charlene: To see inside the character's mind, to know what he's thinking.
Roger: First person helps me identify with the character. I think this is how I might feel. It's more personal.
Carol: It makes the story more true to life, like it's an experience a real person is living through.

Tell them that these are all good answers, but point out that the writer must make a major decision at the beginning of the story. The author must decide which character will carry the story through his or her actions and feelings. This character will have the most influence on how the story develops, and the reader won't know what the other characters are thinking except through the eyes of the main character. Suggest that the children look through some books to see how authors use first person and that they then try using first person themselves the next time they write fiction.

Source: Doris Buchanan Smith. *A Taste of Blackberries.* Apple, 1973, p. 47.

(U) Literary Techniques Mini-lesson
Note Taking for Research Reports

Commend the students on the very fine stories they've been writing during workshop time, and tell them that you want to introduce them to another genre, or type of writing. Mention that the class theme is the Holocaust, and remind them that you've been reading aloud Johanna Reiss's *The Upstairs Room,* a fictional version of the author's own experiences during the Holocaust. Observe that some of them have become quite interested in this theme, so they might want to conduct research on it.

Tell the students that you have asked the librarian to help them locate informational books and reference materials when they go to the library this week. Ask them to identify several sources of information, either to check out or to use as references at the library. Explain that research reports must be based on facts and that they must find these facts in nonfiction materials.

Notetaking, you tell them, is one of the first skills they need to know. Explain procedures for taking notes as follows:

- Take several note cards and use a different one for each source you use.
- First, write the complete bibliographic information:
- author (last name first), title, publisher, date and place of publication, and page numbers.
- Read through the section you want to use. Then summarize key points on your note cards.
- If you want to use the author's exact words, put quotation marks around what the author says and write the page number.

Tell them that you will explain more about procedures for writing research reports in other mini-lessons.

(Note: Conduct related mini-lessons on locating information, organizing material, outlining, using references, recording bibliographic information, and so forth.)

Mini-lessons for Writing Skills

Writing skills are not important for first drafts, but they most definitely are for published pieces. Through mini-lessons you can teach students the writing skills they need for revising and editing their work. Language arts and spelling books offer writing skills in a predetermined, sequential way, but mini-lessons enable you to teach students what they need to know when they need to know it. Help students realize that the purpose for learning writing skills is to communicate clearly and effectively with readers. Here are some sample mini-lesson plans for teaching writing skills.

(L) Writing Skills Mini-lesson
Verbs Ending in *ing*

After reading the big book *Eeny, Meeny, Miney Mouse* to the children, go back through it with them to find what the mouse is doing on each page. As they find the words and dictate them, write them on a chart: *creeping, munching, hiding, living, talking.* Help the children discover that each word ends in *ing*, and call on them to underline these letters. Then ask them to suggest other "doing" words for you to put on the chart. Point out that when they want to use doing words in the stories they write, they need to add *i, n, g.*

Source: Gwen Pascoe. *Eeny, Meeny, Miney Mouse.* Newbridge, 1991.

(Note: Any book that uses several words ending in *ing* would be appropriate for this activity.)

(L) Writing Skills Mini-lesson
Invented Spelling

Greet the children, who are sitting on the floor in front of you, and tell them that it is time to write the morning news. Ask who would like to tell you a sentence to write on the chart.

Tina: I went to my grandma's house.

Tell Tina that you will put her sentence on the chart and you want everyone to help you write it. The children tell you to make a big letter *l*, which you write. Then you write *went,* and the children tell you how to spell *to* and *my* because some children already know how to spell these words.

When you come to *grandma's,* tell them to stretch it out and say it slowly so that they can hear all the sounds. (Say *grandma's* slowly together.) Then ask them to listen for the first sound and think what letter makes that sound. They tell you *g,* which you write. Then you say the sounds that *g* and *r* make together and ask them what to put next. Many of them know that *r* goes after the *g,* so you write it. Now say, "Let's think about the next part: *grand.* I think some of you know how to spell the little word we hear next," and the children say *and—a, n, d.* You write these letters and say, "I'll read what we have so far: *grand.* What letter do we need next for grand*ma*?" The children hear the *m* sound and tell you to write it next. You add the *a* yourself, then ask, "If it's the house belonging to grandma, what do we need to put next?" The children chorus "apostrophe!" You add one, and then say, "We have almost the whole word. What letter do we need to end it? Listen one more time: grandma'*s.*" The children tell you *s,* so you write it and ask them to read the whole word with you. Write house for them to finish the sentence.

(A) Writing Skills Mini-lesson
Commas in a Series

Using a big book, point out how authors often use commas to help readers understand meanings. A good example is *A Pocket for Corduroy,* which contains the following sentence: "Before he knew it, Corduroy was being tossed, together with all the sheets, shirts, shorts, and slacks . . ." Ask the children why commas separate *sheets, shirts, shorts,* and *slacks,* and get them to tell you it's easier to read with commas to slow you down between different types of clothes. Explain that good writers use commas to separate things or ideas in a series.

Write the following sentence on the board: "Tony went to the store to get some ice cream coffee cake and milk." Ask the students how many things Tony got, and they'll probably get confused. Ask a volunteer to put commas where they belong, first to show that Tony bought three things, then four things, then five things. As the volunteer adds commas, help the children see how commas make a difference in meaning. Remind them to use commas when they want to separate items in a series.

Source: Don Freeman. *A Pocket for Corduroy*. Scholastic, 1978, unpaged.

(A) Writing Skills Mini-lesson
Run-on Sentences

Show a writing sample with run-on sentences on an overhead projector. It might look like this:

Jerry went to get some ice cream and on the way he met Bill so he and Bill went to the store together and Jerry got a chocolate cone and Bill got strawberry and then they went back to Jerry's house and played ball.

Ask the children what they think about this story. The children may comment positively at first, noting that Jerry and Bill are friends and that it would be fun to get ice cream together. They will soon notice, however, that this is one long run-on sentence with too many connectives.

Ask the children how they might change the story. They begin suggesting ways to delete *and*s and add periods and capital letters to create new sentences. As you make the changes they recommend, the children see you modeling the use of proofreading marks. When the children are finished making changes, ask them to read the revised story with you to see if it sounds better. It might now read as follows:

On his way to get ice cream, Jerry met Bill, who went to the store with him. Jerry got a chocolate cone and Bill got strawberry. Then the boys went to Jerry's house to play ball.

(Note: Many other variations are possible.)

Suggest that they look at their own writing to see if they need to make similar changes.

(Note: You can use the same type of lesson in reverse for teaching students to combine short, choppy sentences.)

(U) Writing Skills Mini-lessons
Proofreading

Tell the students that you notice several of them have nearly finished their revisions and are ready to proofread before they write their final copies. Tell them that proofreaders have given us some shortcuts to use, and that you will share some of these ideas with them in today's mini-lesson.

Explain that it will be helpful for them to use symbols instead of words to edit their work, but first they need to know what the symbols mean. Tell the students that you have asked Tim and Natalie to help you with this mini-lesson because they are already using some proofreading marks. When you ask Tim to share a mark that he uses, he tells the class about a caret, an upside down v, that means you want to insert a word. Natalie says that she underlines a letter three times when she wants to capitalize it. Ask other children for marks they use and record these marks on a chart as they give you answers. (When completed, the chart might resemble the proofreading chart in Chapter 5.) The children may only give you a few marks during this lesson, but you or they may introduce others as they find uses for them.

(U) Writing Skills Mini-lesson
Quotation Marks

Praise the children for the way many of them are beginning to use dialogue in their stories. Point out that when authors use dialogue they put special marks around what people say to help readers understand who is talking and what is being said. Using an overhead projector, show a conversational passage from a book and read it for the children, pointing out what the characters are saying. A passage from Beverly Cleary's *Ellen Tebbits* is a good example to use.

"Please, Mother," begged Austine. "Ellen's mother says we may."

"But Austine," protested her mother, "I always buy your dresses ready-made. You know what my sewing is like."

"We'd pick out a real easy pattern," promised Austine. "Please, Mother, couldn't you make me a dress just once?"

Ask the children to tell you what they notice about ways to use quotation marks and write their observations on a chart. The chart might look like the one on page 156.

Quotation Marks

Put them around what people are saying.
Punctuation marks go inside the ending quotation marks.
Use a comma to separate what somebody says
from the rest of the sentence.

Tell the children that these are good rules and you
will put the chart up in class for them to look at when
they write. First, however, tell them that you want to see
if they can use these rules. Put up another transparency
of a conversational passage, but this time use one that
has all the punctuation marks deleted. (Delete the
marks on the copy before making the transparency.)
Ask the students where you should put the quotation
marks and other punctuation on this copy so that it will
be the same as in the book. By thinking of the example
(show it again if the children want to see it) and referring to their rules, the children tell you where to put the
marks. When you finish, ask the children to compare
their marks with those in the book to see if they agree
with the author.

Source: Beverly Cleary. *Ellen Tebbits.* Dell, 1979, p. 108.

(U) Writing Skills Mini-lesson
Spelling Strategies

Tell the children that they must know how to spell words
accurately so that readers understand exactly what
they mean. Point out that it's okay to make approxima-
tions during drafts, but they must be able to spell words
correctly when they write for an audience.

Remind the students that they already know a lot
about spelling; for example, they can double the final
consonant before adding *ing* and they know the rule
about "*i* before *e* except after *c*." Now tell them that
you are going to help them use the knowledge they
already have to spell a long word with you. The word is
experiment, a word they need to know when they write
science reports.

Help the students work through the word, pointing
out each sound and guiding them to think what letter
or letter combinations make that sound. Model the
procedure for spelling *experiment* by saying the following:

Let me think how this word begins. I hear *x*, but I
know that a consonant can't make a syllable by itself.
It must have a vowel with it. I've seen other words that
begin with the *x* sound that have an *e* in front of the *x*,
so I'll write *ex*.

Now I think of the next syllable. It's *per.* I know how to spell *person,* and this syllable may be the same as the first syllable in *person.* Now I have *exper.* What comes next? Oh yes, a little *uh* sound. Any letter can make that sound. I'll just have to guess and check it later. I'll write *expera.*

I only have one syllable left and it's *ment.* That should be easy because I can hear each sound and I've seen that ending on lots of words. I'll put the sounds together now and I have *experament.* Will someone look it up for me, either in your science book or dictionary?

The children check the word and discover that the *a* should be an *i.* Point out to them that many times they can work through a word by the sounds they hear, but there are some parts they may still need to check in a dictionary to make sure they spell it exactly right.

Summary

In writing workshops teachers use mini-lessons to teach literary techniques and writing skills young people need to know in order to become more proficient writers. There is no hierarchy or order, nor is there one complete list. Keen observation of students' needs enables teachers to select topics for mini-lessons. There is no need to teach what students can already do—or to teach what they are not yet ready to learn.

Some students may find it difficult to adjust to the workshop format, so be sure that your first mini-lessons stress procedures. Students must understand what you expect of them in order for the workshop to succeed. The short time span of the mini-lesson may not be sufficient for all students to learn the techniques and skills, so they may need reinforcement through conferences, the topic of our next chapter.

Reflections

Seriously consider the following questions. Some answers may be found by reflecting on the chapter; others may come from your own beliefs and experiences.

1. How should I organize my mini-lessons for future reference? Will I be able to use the same plans each year, or will I need to change them for each class? What kinds of ideas and materials should I save?
2. Do I want to use skill sheets? How might they help, or hinder, the students? What purposes would they serve? What kinds of worksheets might be helpful and where would I find them?

3. Should I involve students in the mini-lessons, or is this the time that I should provide directed instruction? If I involve them, will the interaction take too much of the brief time we have for mini-lessons? What are some ways I might want to involve them? How are the students likely to learn best?

Bibliography

Atwell, N. (1987). *In the middle*. Portsmouth, NH: Heinemann.

Calkins, L. M. (1986). *The art of teaching writing*. Portsmouth, NH: Heinemann.

Calkins, L. M. (1994). *The art of teaching writing*, new edition. Portsmouth, NH: Heinemann.

Graves, D. (1994). *A fresh look at writing*. Portsmouth, NH: Heinemann.

Harwayne, S. (1992). *Lasting impressions*. Portsmouth, NH: Heinemann.

Pike, K., Compain, R., & Mumper, J. (1994). *Connections: An integrated approach to literacy*. New York: HarperCollins.

Tchudi, S. (1994). *Integrated language arts*. Belmont, CA: Wadsworth.

Yellin, D., & Blake, M. (1994). *Integrating language arts*. New York: HarperCollins.

CHAPTER 8

CONFERENCES

February 14

Amy: Thanks for the card, Kevin. "Will you po-lice be mine?" Now that's original! I'll bet you got lots of cards from your students—they adore you.

Kevin: I got quite a few, and you probably did too. By the way, how's it going with the writing workshop?

Amy: I feel much better about the workshop since I've cut it back to Mondays, Wednesdays, and Fridays. That's the way I started out, and I guess I moved into all five days too fast. On Tuesdays and Thursdays I do more structured lessons, but sometimes I let the children write then, too.

Kevin: My students are in a pretty comfortable routine. They understand the procedures and most of them get busy right away. I have a few who don't ever seem to finish anything though, and I'm planning to conference with them about that. I probably need to do a mini-lesson on completing work and set a quota for published pieces each six-weeks period. The students can give me some input.

Amy: Speaking of conferences, I can't believe how well my second graders are doing with them! I wasn't sure how conferences would work, but we role played some conferencing techniques and they really caught on. It really tickles me to hear them saying exactly the same things I've modeled for them.

Kevin: What do you mean?

Amy: Well, Sandy was asking Joey how to spell *nation*, and Joey said exactly what I would have said. He told Sandy to think of the sounds in the first part of the word, and she came up with **na**. Then he said, "You remember how to spell **shun**—we learned that it's usually spelled the same way even though it's not the sounds we hear." Sandy said, "That's right—**t, i, o, n** spells **shun**.

Kevin: That's great! They're really learning when they can teach each other.

Amy: Yes, and the best part of it was that I was helping Kate at the same time Joey was helping Sandy. It's like having a lot of little teachers in there with me.

Introduction

As both Kevin and Amy realize, conferences are a way to keep the workshop operating smoothly. Some say conferences are the heart of the workshop, that through conferences teachers and students communicate and learn by sharing ideas about reading and writing. Some also say that conferences are their biggest headache, that there is never enough time for all they need to do.

Teacher conferences let us help students with individual problems and evaluate their progress. We come to understand our students as readers and writers—their interests, their struggles, their strategies—as we confer with them. Through peer conferences students help each other learn, thus offering a three-fold advantage: one participant reinforces and expands personal knowledge of reading and writing by helping someone else; the other participant receives help on an immediate need; and the teacher's load is reduced because children are teaching each other. In this chapter we'll consider some appropriate topics for conferences, alternative structures for them, procedures for conducting them, and ways to organize and manage them.

Reading and Writing Conferences: An Overview

Let's look at why conferences are an important part of workshops. Through conferences teachers and students get to know each other; conferences are oral versions of dialogue journals. As we ask students to relate their reading and writing to their experiences, we are more likely to understand why they think and behave as they do. When we comment on our own literary experiences in response to their remarks, students realize that we are readers and writers, too. Donald Graves (1994) points out that conferences enable students to teach us about what they know as readers and writers so that we can help them more effectively. During conferences teachers act as coaches by commenting on, refining, and supporting what a student is already doing (Calkins, 1991). Specifically, through conferences we can help students grow in their abilities to read and write by

- listening and responding to what they say.
- asking questions that expand their thinking.
- helping them to draw on their own experiences.
- pointing out what they know and can do.
- helping them discover ways to solve their problems.

When I've conferred with college students who are stuck with their writing, I find that they seem to get fresh insights and new perspectives simply by talking through their ideas. They leave our conferences with a sense of expectancy, eager to return to their writing.

In addition, we assess progress in reading and writing through conferences. As we listen to students read, we note miscues (unexpected responses), decoding strategies, and fluency. As students discuss their books with us, we observe the depth of their understanding. And as they talk to us about their writing, we become aware of their strengths and needs as writers. Quickly jotting down observations, we use them for helping us to arrive at grades, and we refer to them as sources for giving individual help or teaching small group or class mini-lessons.

Obviously, reading conferences are part of reading workshops, and writing conferences occur during writing workshops. A great deal of overlap exists, however, because reading conferences may actually take the form of written dialogue journals about books, and writing conferences may allude to literature. From the teacher's view, the purposes and focus are quite similar, as Figure 8.1 shows.

Reading Conferences	Writing Conferences
Guide students' book selection	Help students discover topics
Help students reflect on their reading	Listen to what students say about their writing
Extend reading abilities by questioning	Extend writing strategies through responding
Identify strengths and weaknesses in reading to plan instruction	Identify strengths and weaknesses in writing to plan instruction
Share students' pleasure in reading good books	Celebrate their successes in publishing their work
Evaluate progress in reading	Evaluate progress in writing

Figure 8.1:   Purposes of Reading and Writing Conferences

Topics for Conferences

Topics for conferences vary according to children's stages of development, reading/writing purposes and goals, and problems that students may be encountering.

Reading Conferences

Reading conferences generally consist of listening to a student read aloud a self-selected passage from a book and discussing the book. On occasion, you may want to teach a needed skill on a one-to-one or small group basis. Begin the discussion by asking such generic, open-ended questions as "What can you tell me about your book?" or "How do you like this book?" Then, listening carefully, take your cues for further questioning from the student's comments. Your purpose here is to probe: to encourage the student to think more profoundly about the book in order to arrive at greater depths of understanding and appreciation. The questions you ask may relate to such topics as these:

- emotional reactions (What were your feelings as you read?)
- vocabulary (What new words did you learn?)
- author (What did you like/dislike about this author?)
- comparisons (Have you read similar books?)
- personal experiences (Can you identify with the characters or situation? How?)
- problem/solution (What was the main problem and how was it resolved?)
- setting (How did the setting affect the plot development?)
- confusion (What part, if any, confused you?)
- new knowledge/appreciation (What is something new that you discovered from reading this book?)

TEACHING TIP

If you haven't read the book that a student is reading,

a.   Admit that you haven't read it and ask the student to tell you why he or she would or would not recommend it.
b.   Being careful to listen to what the student says in response to your generic question, flip through the book to get a general idea of what it contains.
c.   Let the student take the lead in the discussion.
d.   Ask the student to read you a favorite part and to explain its significance.

In the following example, students in Joy McCaleb's seventh grade reading class have just observed student presentations of an Anansi story and Aesop's "The Fox and the Grapes." Joy has asked them to write responses to the presentations. When they finish writing, they may confer with each other about what they wrote. She, too, is available for conferences.

Example of Teacher-Student Reading Conferences

After students had completed their writing in Joy's class, I glanced around the room and observed students quietly beginning to confer with each other. Students remained in their seats, simply turning to one another to form groups of two, three, or four as they discussed their responses to the student presentations. If any students appeared to get off task, as few did, Joy moved to that part of the room to confer briefly with those students.

As students who needed help caught her eye, Joy pulled her stool over and talked directly to them about their writing, although those seated nearby were obviously listening in. She began by asking, "What did you read that you want to share?", thereby inviting students to discuss any journal entry of their choosing, not just their response to the presentation.

Speaking with Christa about her response to Robert O'Brien's *Z for Zachariah*, a novel the whole class had read, Joy nudged her to think what else she could tell—perhaps add details that relate to what she knows about the story, use the language of gardening, compare her life to Ann's life and where she lives to where Ann lives, and tell where she gets seeds to plant her garden. Joy says, "I really want to know."

Noticing Kristin's request for help with her response to "The Fox and the Grapes," Joy asked her to read it aloud. At one point, Joy interjected the questions, "What does this sentence have to do with the one before it? How can you make the transition clear to the reader? What can you add to help me see the connection?", as she helped Kristin find the words to make a smooth transition. As Kristin continued reading, she asked Joy, "Is there something wrong here? Oh, I see. I used a double negative. That can be confusing." Making a quick correction, Kristin continued reading, and soon Joy commented, "I really, really like the sentence about living on the wild side. Can you tell me more about that?" (Kristin's response to the fable appears in Chapter 3.)

Moving on, Joy listened to Misty reading her response to a book she had read. Joy complimented Misty on the way she made a transition by saying, "You showed me how one thought led into the next." Joy asked Misty to tell her what she has done so far and then what she is going to do next. Misty explained that she would probably have to stop, fit the rest of the information into the last paragraph she just wrote, and then go on with the rest of the story. Misty observed that something was wrong, that she had gone from talking about the book into the presentation of it without making the separation clear. She asked if she needed to make transitions between journal entries, but Joy replied that she didn't need to do this, that journal topics don't necessarily relate to each other.

Writing Conferences

Any subject dealing with writing skills and techniques is fair game for writing conferences, but here we will look at five topics: prewriting, content, process, editing, and evaluation.

Prewriting conferences help students get ideas, overcome writer's block, and focus on a topic.

During *content conferences* students discuss their developing subjects and seek help in narrowing or expanding the topic, including significant details, and clarifying information for readers. Content conferences often lead into process conferences.

Through *process conferences* students become aware of *how* they go about writing: ways of finding topics and rehearsing what they will write, the overlapping processes of drafting and revising as they organize their thoughts, and decisions about editing and publishing.

Editing conferences help students check their work to see if they need to make corrections in spelling or mechanics before they publish. This is not the time to change content, for they did that as they wrote their drafts and revised. Despite careful editing, most published pieces still contain some errors. Don't worry! A perfect product is not the goal—the process of learning how to write is what counts.

Evaluation conferences focus on what the *student* thinks of the writing. Questions concern such issues as deciding whether or not to publish this piece, selecting the best part, identifying strengths in the writing, and comparing this piece to others written during the year.

In the following examples, Amy and Kevin are helping their students during writing conferences.

Writing Conference
Helping a Student Focus
Amy is conducting conferences during writing workshop, and she stops by Calvin's desk. As she listens to Calvin tell his story, she realizes he has too much to put into one piece, so she helps him focus on the most interesting part to develop into a story. **Amy:** How are you doing? **Calvin:** Okay, I guess. **Amy:** Tell me about what you're writing. **Calvin:** I've decided to write about wasps. Yesterday we had wasps all over. My mom killed one on the window sill with a fly swatter, and there was one in our car that we shooed out. There were wasps flying around our

back door, too. Once I got stung by a wasp and it really hurt! Then last night we were in the kitchen and it was real quiet and we heard this buzzing noise. Another wasp! And he was buzzing around the light and he crawled up under the glass part and buzzed real loud and then stopped. My mom said he was a fried wasp 'cause the light was so hot. Then another wasp came and tried to get into the light but couldn't—we think he's still in the kitchen.

Amy: You certainly have a lot to say about wasps. What will you write about?

Calvin: That's what I don't know. It's too much to write all that.

Amy: What was the most interesting part?

Calvin: Hmmm, I guess about the fried wasp.

Amy: That sounds like a good part to me. Why don't you think of all the details about how the wasp buzzed and how you watched him crawl into the light? That should make a good story.

As Amy moves on to another student, Calvin picks up his pencil and begins writing.

Writing Conference
Helping a Student Find Her Topic

After helping Chuck find a more compelling lead for his story, Kevin approaches Amanda's desk. He notices that she has a blank page in front of her.

Kevin: Are you having a hard time getting started today?

Amanda: I can't think of anything to write about.

Kevin: That happens sometimes. Let's talk and maybe you'll think of something.

Amanda: Nothing ever happens to me. I don't have anything to say.

Kevin: What do you usually do after school?

Amanda: Watch TV.

Kevin: Do you ever do anything else?

Amanda: Yeah. Sometimes I walk the dog.

Kevin: Tell me about your dog.

Amanda: He's just a mongrel.

Kevin: There must be more to say than that. What do you like about him? Does he ever do anything you don't expect?

Amanda: I guess I like him okay. One day when I was walking him he started to chase a squirrel. I wasn't paying much attention and he pulled so hard he got away from me. Then I had to chase him and I thought I'd never catch him. He went through the briars and down past the creek and . . . .

> **Kevin:** Could you make a story out of that?
> **Amanda:** Well, I guess I could. It was pretty awful.
> **Kevin:** Give it a try, and I'll check back later to see how
>   your story is coming.

Conferring with students who had opposite problems, both Amy and Kevin listened to their students and asked questions that helped them discover what they wanted to say. Before leaving them, both teachers made sure that their students were now ready to begin writing.

Conference Structure

You can structure your conferences in different ways according to who participates in them and what your purposes are. Here are some options.

Teacher-Student Conferences

Teacher-student conferences are valuable for informing teachers about what students know, how they think and reason, and the progress they are making. They are important to students also because students value the teacher's attention and respect the teacher's judgment. Holly Martin, a sixth grade teacher, says her attitude toward conferences has shifted. In the early years, she valued the children's writing and said little to cause students to change anything. Now, although she still respects their writing, she considers herself the expert as a result of her years of experience and education. Her conferences are more structured, and she expects her writers to clarify anything she doesn't understand.

Teachers can meet individually with children, or with groups of children who have similar needs. During individual conferences the teacher and student usually confer informally about the book the student is reading or the piece that the student is writing at the present time. Using a slightly different tack with her upper grade students, Georganne Harmon (1994) asks a student to select a piece of writing to read from her or his portfolio. Together they discuss the piece in terms of the main goal for that period, what the student does well and should continue doing, and one goal to set that she and the student agree is most important.

Often when a teacher meets with an individual, children seated nearby eavesdrop and pick up ideas they can use themselves. In the reading conferences that Ellen Blackburn Karelitz (1993) holds with her children, she says that one child occasionally joins another, sharing comments about books they have both read and teaming to read books orally in a "friendly collaboration."

During group conferences children benefit from hearing different points of view. Group members, including the teacher, may discuss a book all have read during a reading conference, and students and teacher listen attentively to help the writer decide what to do in writing conferences. Some such meetings are informal with students coming and going, but others are formal events. Georganne Harmon (1994) schedules group writing conferences at a conference table with three students at a time, and she reads each student's paper aloud as the students in the group read along silently from their own copies. After rereading a paper silently and making notes, each student completes a critique sheet that identifies two strengths and makes two suggestions for each author. Since it's impossible to cover everything in a single conference, each of Georganne's conferences has a specific focus which deals with content (focus, amount of detail), organization (good beginnings and endings, orderly progression), or style (sentence combining, elimination of unnecessary words). Georganne discourages any discussion of mechanics and spelling unless they interfere with comprehension; such matters can be taught with mini-lessons.

When conferring with students, keep in mind these widely accepted practices:

- Begin by asking, "How can I help you?"
- Listen carefully to what the student has to say.
- Help the student find as many answers as possible on his or her own to enable the student to become an independent learner.
- Offer suggestions, but don't impose your views.
- Focus on one issue.
- Try to offer suggestions that can apply to future pieces of writing, not just the one being discussed.
- At the end, be sure the student knows what to do next.

Experienced workshop teachers recommend letting students do most of the talking during conferences. In fact, Donald Graves (1994) suggests that students should do as much as eighty percent of the talking. Giving students so much talking time is one of the hardest things for teachers to do, however, because teachers are full of questions and suggestions. Some teachers who have tape recorded their conferences are amazed at how much talking they are doing and how little their students are saying. When teachers dominate the talking, they are taking control of conferences instead of giving students ownership of them. Actually, as a good listener, there is little that the teacher needs to say. Teachers can convey a great deal of meaning through nonverbal communication, such as an attentive expression that shows interest, a nod for understanding or appreciation, or a look of puzzlement for something that needs clarification.

TEACHING TIP

When a child asks for help during a conference, turn the responsibility back to the child by saying,

a.   How will you solve your problem?
b.   What do you plan to do about this? (Avery, 1993)

Peer Conferences

Peer conferences can be just as helpful as teacher-student conferences, and reactions from peers may sometimes be more meaningful than those from the teacher. Through peer conferences students learn to turn to each other for help instead of depending on the teacher. Also, when students are stuck or bored with their reading or writing, they may need to talk with someone about it, even though the teacher is busy elsewhere. Ruth Ann Freedman (1995) found that students' informal collaborations created a community of writers in her second/third grade classroom. The children influenced each other's writing through a variety of interactions, including peer conferences that helped them develop their stories.

During reading conferences students who have read the same books, books by the same author, books of a particular genre, or books on the same topic meet in pairs or small groups to discuss their books. They may discover commonalities or contrasts; differing perspectives; characteristics of authors' styles; the power of well-constructed settings, plots, and characters; and different ways that authors present ideas and information.

Classmates can pass along their knowledge of writing strategies through one-on-one conferences. When the teacher is in great demand, children can ask each other for advice, but you need to prepare your students well for participating in peer conferences. Figure 8.2 suggests some procedures to teach children how to participate in conferences.

Although you want to guide students in asking questions and making comments, guard against creating "canned dialogue" in which questions and answers become so routine that they are meaningless. I've heard students politely proceed through a series of comments that they could make about any piece of writing, remarks that are so general that they provide no help at all for the writer. Impress on your students the need to listen carefully, respond thoughtfully, and make remarks and questions that are specifically addressed to the piece under discussion.

Teachers and students should both remember that the piece of writing belongs to the author. Despite any ideas and new directions suggested during a conference, the writer makes the final decisions about what to say.

Help students establish social skills, such as not interrupting, taking turns talking, listening respectfully, considering the other person's feelings, and commenting on strengths.

Discuss how students should choose conference partners. They should consider who works well with them and who might be able to help.

Conduct procedural mini-lessons that focus on the roles of the participants, purposes of conferences, and procedures to follow.

Model appropriate questions and comments as you confer with students.

Hold group conferences so that you can guide children's interactions with each other.

Remind students to speak softly so as not to disturb others.

Discuss how long conferences should be; five to seven minutes is usually adequate.

Let students role play conferences, perhaps during mini-lessons, by asking volunteers to model ways to hold conferences and then inviting the class to discuss the role playing.

Invite experienced students from an upper grade to model a peer conference.

Ask another student to role play a conference with you.

Encourage students to begin conferences by listening to the writer and affirming what was said.

Make a transparency from a piece of writing and show it on the overhead projector. Ask students to make comments about it.

Read a piece of your own writing to the class and let students ask you questions to help you focus or clarify.

Make a chart of appropriate and inappropriate remarks or questions.

Appropriate questions might be
How are you doing?
How can I help?
Can you tell me more about . . . ?

Inappropriate comments include
I don't think your piece is any good.
That sounds really stupid.
You should say this.

Ask a volunteer to read a piece to the whole class. Then ask the students to tell what they heard and what they liked (Calkins, 1986).

Reteach procedures if you observe that students are not following them.

Figure 8.2:   Guidelines for Conducting Peer Writing Conferences

Conferences with Oneself

"When children ask questions of each other, they learn to ask questions of their own emerging texts" (Calkins, 1986, p. 129). As students gain experience in writing and peer conferencing, they anticipate questions about their work. Instead of waiting for a conference to jog them into thinking about ways to make their writing more acceptable to readers, they begin asking themselves questions. When they have responded to predictable peer or teacher conference comments through their revisions, they are ready to ask for a conference to see if they need to make further revisions. Some questions that authors might ask themselves as they read over their pieces are these (based on Atwell, 1987):

- Have I given enough information, or did I leave gaps?
- Have I repeated myself?
- Can I find a way to make the most important part more exciting or interesting?
- Is any part confusing?
- Have I focused on my topic, or do I ramble?
- Will my lead catch the reader's attention?
- Have I developed my piece logically so that it is easy to follow?
- Is my style of writing appropriate for this piece?
- Have I presented a satisfying conclusion?

Learning to examine one's writing critically and evaluate it calls for higher order thinking. Once students develop this ability, they can use it as they advance through school and then become active members of their communities.

Procedures for Conferences

Nothing seems to cause more consternation about workshops than how to conduct conferences. In this section are some practical suggestions, but you will have to find what works best for you by adapting the procedures and guidelines to your own situation.

Short and In-depth Teacher-Student Conferences

Many conferences only last a minute or two and take place as the teacher zigzags across the room, quickly touching base with as many students as possible. In this short time the teacher asks general questions, listens to what children say about their work, and helps them discover for themselves how to move on. Sometimes the teacher may suggest a peer conference to help a child work through a specific problem. Through these roving conferences, teachers get a general idea of each student's progress.

Although quick, "touch-base" conferences of a minute or two are often sufficient, many teachers agree that longer, in-depth conferences are sometimes necessary in order to make a difference in a student's reading or writing. Some teachers, therefore, schedule one or two long (fifteen minutes or more) conferences along with a few short conferences each day. These teachers try to have at least one in-depth conference with each student during a six-week period.

In-depth conferences are prearranged and scheduled with definite agendas. In reading, they may involve student responses to books, and in writing they may concern revising drafts or editing pieces for publication. Because Joanne Hindley (Calkins, 1991) believed she needed time for thoughtful conferences, she stopped trying to conduct twenty short daily conferences and held about six short conferences and three longer ones during each workshop. She felt that the additional time made a significant difference by letting her listen carefully, reflect, learn about the child, and monitor the child's continuing progress with greater insight. Diane Snowball recommends spending quality time with just one student a day to really get to know and understand that student.

Guidelines for Implementing Conferences

Since some teachers have been holding conferences for many years, they have found some procedures to be more effective than others. Here we will look at some of the conferencing strategies they use that you might wish to adopt for yourself. Figure 8.3 presents some guidelines for conference procedures (Atwell, 1987; Calkins, 1986, 1991; Rief, 1992).

You may feel overwhelmed by so many guidelines and think that you will never remember all of these during conferences. Few teachers do! It's difficult to think on your feet, deal with the unexpected, and react appropriately in every situation. If your basic intent is to help students think about their own writing and then to offer sincere, helpful suggestions, you'll do fine.

A frequent concern about conferring is that there isn't enough time to attend to each student's needs. Also, when teachers have a line of students waiting for help, the students tend to become noisy and disruptive. The following teaching tip may be helpful.

TEACHING TIP
To speed up conferencing procedures, • Don't pick up the student's paper. Let the student tell you what help is needed. • If a child says "fine" when you ask how it's going, move on to the next student. • Limit yourself to discussing the one most pressing need. • Use peer conferences to supplement your own. • With the students, make a chart of things to do if they are stuck (Fiderer, 1993).

When meeting with students at their desks, carry a small stool with you or kneel or crouch so that you will be able to talk with them at eye level instead of hovering over them.

Speak quietly so as not to disturb those working nearby.

Begin by asking "How can I help you?" so that students will assess their needs in advance and focus on the most critical ones.

Encourage students to make their own decisions; offer suggestions only when they have clearly done all they can do to help themselves.

Don't write on their pieces; doing this tends to take ownership away from the author.

Ask open-ended questions that cause writers to reflect on their writing instead of specific questions with one word answers.

Become involved in the writing by asking questions about it instead of simply saying "good" or "nice work."

Avoid evaluating work in progress by saying "This part is good" or "The ending is weak." Let students be the critical readers by asking them how they feel about their pieces.

Don't always ask for *more*. Perhaps there is enough already. Length isn't the goal; selective, quality writing is.

Figure 8.3:   Guidelines for Conference Procedures

Many teachers who are trying conferences for the first time find that the noise and confusion in class is a problem. First of all, be aware of the difference between constructive and disruptive noise and between purposeful and pointless movement. Low voices conferring about reading and writing are acceptable, but loud, out-of-control noise is not. Students moving to get books or writing materials is acceptable, but students wandering around aimlessly is not. You need to establish procedures for acceptable behavior through generating rules with the class, modeling acceptable behaviors, and teaching procedural mini-lessons. Establishing appropriate noise levels and movements may take considerable time, because many students may have never experienced such freedom and can't handle it well. Time spent at the beginning on making guidelines clear will pay off later when students have internalized appropriate ways to behave. There will be more noise and movement than in traditional classrooms, but remember that students are *learning* as a result.

When you begin having students do peer conferences, you may want to limit the number of partners conferring at one time until you are sure they can handle conferences well. Patricia Hagerty (1992) suggests placing four conference cards with procedures and starter questions on the chalk tray. When wanting a conference, a student gets a card and finds a partner. The student returns the card at the end of the conference so that someone else may use it. In this way no more than four pairs of students are conferring at one time.

During workshop time, an ideal classroom looks like this. The teacher is conferring with one student or with a small group of students. With partners, students are quietly conferring about their reading or writing at tables or in designated corners of the room. Most of the class is working independently, either reading books or writing. There is a low hum as students and teacher talk, and there is quiet movement as partners regroup or students find materials. All are engaged in purposeful activities.

Organizing and Managing Conferences

In the classrooms where I have observed conferences, I have seen them running smoothly, much as in the ideal classroom just described. But such efficient operations don't just happen; they require skillful organization and management. How do teachers enable students to move from traditional classrooms where they are expected to sit quietly in their seats to classrooms where quiet talk and movement are part of the routine? In this section we'll look at some physical arrangements, scheduling, and record keeping that contribute to operating conferences effectively.

Physical Arrangements

There seem to be almost as many ways to arrange classrooms for conferencing as there are teachers conducting conferences! Many teachers use conference tables with several chairs around them for group or individual conferences. The teacher and students assemble at this table to discuss reading and writing. When the teacher is not using the table, students may hold peer conferences there.

Sometimes teachers designate special areas of the room where students can confer with peers. These may be on cushions in corners of the room away from where students are concentrating on their reading or writing. In one classroom a teacher conducts her conferences on an old sofa, and I observed her and a child going over a piece of work while a second child hung over the back of the sofa listening in. In some classrooms students remain at their desks for peer conferences and simply turn toward someone when help is needed. This is particularly true for crowded classrooms where there is no room for special tables or corners.

Since you want conferences to cause as little disruption as possible, you want to consider smooth traffic flow to conference areas and comfortable seating arrangements where students meet. If you expect students to use different colored pencils during editing conferences, you should have them readily available. You might also place clipboards in conference areas because they offer firm support for papers that students mark.

TEACHING TIP
When setting up conferences,
a. Avoid having students come to your desk. Sometimes it's difficult to get them to leave so that you can have time to help others.
b. Post copies of rules for behavior (such as speak softly and don't interrupt) in conference areas.

Scheduling Conferences

Teachers handle conference schedules in a variety of ways. They need to be responsive to students' needs, so they may ask students to sign up for conferences. On the wall in one classroom I saw a list of student names on a piece of tagboard. Students attach clothespins beside their names if they want a teacher conference, and they remove the clothespins after the conference. Some children, however, might never schedule conferences, so you would need to invite them to join you to be sure that you meet with everyone. Conferences that are scheduled in advance allow both teachers and students to prepare by considering special needs and collecting relevant materials.

Donald Graves (1994) says that when conferences are working smoothly, teachers can delegate the responsibility of scheduling to one student each week. This student surveys the class to find who needs help and then works out a weekly schedule for the teacher, subject to the teacher's approval.

TEACHING TIP
To make sure you see each child every week,
a. Post a sign-up sheet and require each child to select a time for a conference sometime during the week.
b. Post a sheet on which you have assigned each child to a specific time.
c. Hint: Leave some slots open for children who may need to see you more than once.

Whereas most peer conferences seem to happen spontaneously and informally, some teachers believe they should approve student partners. Suspecting that some students won't accomplish anything when together, Ruth Nathan and her colleagues (1989) want students to sign up in advance for peer conferences. Then, if a working relationship doesn't seem viable, they can suggest another partner before approving the conference. It's risky to attempt group peer conferences since the temptation to get off task becomes greater as more students get together.

The length of conferences determines how many students teachers can see in a day. When students and teachers schedule conferences in advance, they are likely to last approximately five minutes each, with some taking more and others less time.

Teachers schedule group conferences in a variety of ways. Some call students together who are reading and discussing the same book, or who are at a similar stage in the writing process to discuss their work and the next steps to take. Sometimes groups are stable with the same members meeting together, and in other cases students move freely in and out of group conferences, taking or vacating the chairs around the table according to their needs.

Ellen Blackburn Karelitz (1993) analyzes her students' learning styles for about a month, then forms mixed-ability conference groups based on those who can work well together. Although she called her groups together randomly at first, she found that students preferred a regular schedule so that they could prepare. Ellen gathers five or six children at the conference table, but meets individually with each child as the others work quietly, waiting their turns. Students set the agenda, deciding what to share or what help to request, and other group members often benefit from listening to the exchange.

Although most conferences are scheduled during workshop time, some teachers believe that any time of day when opportunities arise is appropriate—before or after school, during breaks in the daily schedule, or when students are doing independent work. Similarly, teachers may want to hold whole-class conferences occasionally (Fiderer, 1993). These conferences deal with questions many students are asking and address widespread concerns that will benefit most of the class.

Record Keeping

Both teachers and students can keep records of conferences, and records can take many forms and serve a variety of purposes. Some teacher records are quick notes or reminders, and others are more formal documents that serve as references for what you have taught and for students' responses. Student records may be jottings in their writing notebooks or co-signed contracts. We'll look first at student record keeping.

Student Records. Students can keep lists of the dates and topics for scheduled conferences in their notebooks or portfolios. During conferences, they can make notes of new ideas they discover for themselves, suggestions from the teacher, and what to do next. As preparation for the next conference, they can write questions and purposes for conferring.

Because students often have trouble keeping track of informal notes, some teachers ask students to use record keeping forms and file them in special folders. Linda Rief (1992) uses conference sheet forms that include the date, how the teacher can help, questions, one suggestion, and what to do next. Students can also use peer conference diaries in which they record name, date, title of the project, conference partner, and a summary of the conference (Jackson and Pillow, 1993).

Although most student record keeping is of an informal nature, students may occasionally enter into a contract with the teacher. In this case, the student agrees to read and respond to a certain number of books or publish a certain number of pieces within a prescribed time frame. Such contracts may motivate students who have trouble completing their work. A sample contract, which is renewable, appears in Figure 8.4.

WRITING CONTRACT

Initial and date each responsibility when you complete it.

I agree to do the following:

a. Schedule a teacher conference at least once a week.   _____

b. Arrange a peer conference three times a week.   _____

c. Publish a piece at least once every two weeks.   _____

Duration of contract: two weeks

Beginning date: _____   Concluding date: _____

Student's signature: _____

Teacher's signature: _____

Figure 8.4:   Sample Student-Teacher Contract

Teacher Records. Even the best of us have trouble remembering everything we say and do, so written records of how often we hold conferences, with whom we meet, and what we discuss are essential. These records need not be complicated, but they should tell us when we met with each student and remind us of what we did. Although we don't evaluate student performance during conferences, we can use what we learn from conferences to influence our evaluations of students.

You will need to find a system for recording this information. Nancie Atwell (1987) keeps her conference journals in notebooks, using a separate notebook for each of her eighth grade sections and allotting six to eight pages for each student. She arranges names in alphabetical order and records skills she teaches in editing conferences, as well as anecdotal information about what happens during conferences. Using a similar method, Norma Jackson and Paula Pillow (1992) fill out a conference summary sheet to record brief notes about each conference. They keep these summary sheets in students' portfolios and find them particularly helpful when explaining to parents how they are meeting students' individual needs.

If you schedule conferences as suggested earlier, you may already have a summary sheet of sorts which may be used for either reading or writing conferences. Simply make an extra copy of each week's completed sign-up sheet and write brief comments at the end of each line. Using either ruled notebook paper or a ruled form, record essential information as shown in Figure 8.5. This form is partially completed to show typical information to record.

You can use an even shorter form to simply record general impressions from quick conferences. On this form, adapted from

CONFERENCE SCHEDULE			
Day	Time	Name	Comments
Monday	9:30	Jeff W.	Writing dialogue, using quotes
	9:35	Brent	Style for writing technical reports
	9:40	Lois	Writing personal narratives
	9:45	Ames	Editing, particularly end punctuation
	9:50	Julia	Working on creating an interesting lead

Figure 8.5:   Conference Notes

Avery (1993), use a set of symbols to represent your reactions. For example, + means doing fine, = means seems to be coming along all right, – means not doing as well as expected, and ? means not sure about how this student is doing. Later, when you review your checklist, you may observe that certain students need in-depth or more frequent conferences, but others are making adequate progress. Such records can also help you determine grades if you need to give them. Figure 8.6 gives a partial class list.

A quick glance at this form tells you that Jeremy may be slipping; Lisa seems to be gaining confidence; Cody needs help; and

Name	3/5	3/6	3/7	3/8	3/9	3/12	3/13	3/14	3/15	3/16
Jeremy	+	+	=	=	?	=	?			=
Lisa	–	–	=	=		+	=		+	=
Cody	?	?	–	–	?	–	=	–	–	–
Samantha	+		+	+		+		+		+

Figure 8.6:   Checklist for Quick Conferences

Samantha is doing very well.

For in-depth conferences, you will want to give a more detailed account of what occurred, including specific observations, student comments, progress since the last meeting, strengths, perceived needs, and guidance for future activities. You may want to write these observations on a full page and place the record in the student's portfolio.

Since it is important for you to have an open and trusting relationship with your students, conference notes should be available for students to see; they are not secret. In fact, you may want to ask students for their suggestions about what to record. They may have strong feelings about their strengths, their needs, and what they want to try next, so their ideas can help you decide what to write.

Summary

Clearly, the purpose of conferences is for us as teachers to learn from our students what they need to know and then help them discover within themselves how to advance their reading and writing strategies. Along the way, we can offer suggestions to guide them, and we can directly teach skills they need to know.

In this chapter we have seen how there is no clear distinction between reading and writing conferences because of the interactive nature of the language arts. Topics for conferences vary widely, and types of conferences include teacher-student conferences, peer conferences, and conferences with oneself. Although conferences vary widely, teachers generally follow some widely accepted guidelines. Managing conferences is not easy, but good organization and management are essential for their success.

You probably feel that "anything goes" with conferences because of the wide array of topics, types, procedures, and management styles. In a sense this is so, because teachers vary their methods of conferencing to suit their teaching styles and the needs of their children. If you keep in mind the purposes for holding conferences, you can work out your own strategies for helping students learn as they confer.

Reflections

Seriously consider the following questions. Some answers may be found by reflecting on the chapter; others may come from your own beliefs and experiences.

1. Could I hold a workshop without conferences? If so, how? What would be lacking if conferences were not part of my workshop?

2. How much noise and movement can I tolerate? What strategies can I use to keep noise and movement under control? How can I be sure students are conferring about their work if I am conferring at the same time with other students?

3. What records should I keep? What can help me in planning instruction? How can I use records for evaluating progress and informing parents?

4. How will I begin holding conferences? How can I prepare students to work independently while I confer with one student? Should the students and I construct some guidelines for conference procedures? If so, what should we be sure to include?

Bibliography

Atwell, N. (1987). *In the middle*. Portsmouth, NH: Heinemann.

Avery, C. (1993). *. . . And with a light touch*. Portsmouth, NH: Heinemann.

Calkins, L. M. (1986). *The art of teaching writing*. Portsmouth, NH: Heinemann.

Calkins, L. M. (1991). *Living between the lines*. Portsmouth, NH: Heinemann.

Clark, R. P. (1987). *Free to write*. Portsmouth, NH: Heinemann.

Fiderer, A. (1993). *Teaching writing: A workshop approach*. New York: Scholastic.

Freedman, R. (1995). The Mr. and Mrs. Club: The value of collaboration in writers' workshop. *Language Arts, 72* (2), 97–104.

Graves, D. (1994). *A fresh look at writing.* Portsmouth, NH: Heinemann.

Hagerty, P. (1992). *Readers' workshop.* Richmond Hill, Ontario, Canada: Scholastic Canada.

Harmon, G. (1994). Portfolios as tools for development: Teachers and students in collaboration in senior high English and writing classrooms. Presentation at the Tennessee Council of Teachers of English, Nashville, TN.

Harwayne, S. (1992). *Lasting impressions.* Portsmouth, NH: Heinemann.

Jackson, N. with Pillow, P. (1992). *The reading-writing workshop: Getting started.* New York: Scholastic.

Karelitz, E. B. (1993). *The author's chair and beyond.* Portsmouth, NH: Heinemann.

Nathan, R., Temple, F., Juntunen, K., & Temple, C. (1989). *Classroom strategies that work.* Portsmouth, NH: Heinemann.

Parsons, L. (1990). *Response journals.* Markham, Ontario, Canada: Pembroke.

Pike, K., Compain, R., & Mumper, J. (1994). *Connections: An integrated approach to literacy.* New York: HarperCollins.

Rief, L. (1992). *Seeking diversity.* Portsmouth, NH: Heinemann.

Sissel, P. & Nelson, M. (1994). Enhancing reading performance through reader's workshop. Presentation at the National Council of Teachers of English, Orlando, FL.

Sperling, M. (1992). In-class writing conferences: Fine-tuned duets in the classroom ensemble. *English Journal, 81* (4), 65–71.

Sudol, D., & Sudol, P. Yet another story: Writer's workshop revisited. *Language Arts, 72* (3), 171–178.

Weaver, C. (1990). *Understanding whole language.* Portsmouth, NH: Heinemann.

CHAPTER 9

MANAGEMENT AND ORGANIZATION

Amy, calling to Kevin: Kevin, do you have time for a soft drink? There's something I'd really like to talk to you about. I've had what I consider to be a brilliant idea! See what you think.

Kevin: Sure, I can spare a few minutes, and I'd like to hear your great idea.

Amy: Let's go to my room where we won't be disturbed. My children are on the playground.

Kevin: Fine. My class is at the library and won't be coming back for awhile. Let's hear your idea—shoot!

Amy: Why don't we do a cross-grade exchange? My class could learn so much from your big guys—in fact, they'd be awed! And think how important your students would feel as they shared their worldly knowledge with my little ones.

Kevin: That does have possibilities. Have you thought how we might work it out?

Amy: Not entirely, but I do have some ideas. We could try it every Friday. We could do mini-lessons and status of the class in our own rooms, then combine for the workshop and sharing part.

Kevin: That just might work. Whose room would we use?

Amy: I'm not sure. That could be a problem because our seats are too small for your big ones, and yours would be too big for mine. What do you think?

Kevin: We could alternate for awhile and see which room works better. Lots of times kids prefer to sit on the floor anyway—it might not make much difference. Will we do reading or writing workshops?

Amy: I think reading would work better. Writing requires so much equipment and a solid place to write. With reading they'll just need books.

Kevin: Okay, we'll do reading. I have 29 students. How many do you have?

Amy: I only have 24, so we won't be able to do a one-to-one match. Some of mine can have two big partners. I just think they'll learn so much with conferences and sharing time.

Kevin: This will take quite a bit of organizing and preparation. But it might be just the thing to inspire some of my less motivated students. I've got to get back to my class in just a minute. Can we talk more later?

Amy: You bet. Let me know when it suits you, and we'll make some plans.

Introduction

In all of these chapters, management and organization have played a part in the effective operation of the workshop. We have considered scheduling, record keeping, procedures, physical arrangements, and time frames. In this chapter, however, our *focus* is on management and organization: essential components for making a workshop run smoothly. Lack of skill in these areas can cause frustration, disappointing results, and even total breakdown. Lucy Calkins (1986, p. 183) is convinced that "the single biggest reason why many writing classrooms flounder is that the workshop context requires new sorts of expectations, rules, and rituals."

How can you set up a classroom that facilitates workshop activities? This chapter suggests ways to establish an inviting room environment, procedures for organizing and scheduling activities, and ways to select and obtain resources. As you read, think about how you can apply these ideas to your own classroom.

Classroom Environment

A viable workshop environment has many aspects: respect for students who become immersed in their own private worlds of reading and writing; a sense of being in a community with other readers and writers; a print-rich room that stimulates thinking about literacy; and a classroom that is physically arranged to enhance the kinds of activities that occur during a workshop.

Affective Environment

Within each classroom there is a feeling, a sort of emotional climate, which students experience in school. I've been in classrooms where I can feel the tension and sense the apprehension of students as the teacher moves toward their desks. In other classrooms I've felt the lethargy as students sit passively, waiting for class to end, because school offers them nothing stimulating and relevant to their lives. And I've visited classrooms where I observe an air of excitement and anticipation about learning, as well as a comfortable rapport among students and teacher. The first two types of classrooms thwart the workshop; it cannot survive when students feel tight and fearful of expressing themselves, or when they are dull and lifeless because they see no reason to learn. In the third type of classroom, with its zest for learning and sense of mutual respect, the workshop thrives.

Establishing the type of affective climate needed for workshops begins on the first day of school. Lucy Calkins (1991) believes in starting the year by getting to know each other—sharing photo albums, creating a class museum from students' collections, posting student-selected items on bulletin boards, reading aloud favorite poems or selections, and contributing family stories. Seated in a circle on the floor or talking in groups of two or three, students share what's important to them. Building such openness and trust enables students to feel comfortable about themselves and to join with classmates as members of a community of learners.

When beginning the school year, Nancie Atwell (1987) thinks how she can prepare her classroom so that it invites and supports writing in order for students to have what they need to be writers. She organizes for both affective and physical needs and points out the importance of reflecting on and revising teaching during the year in order to meet students' changing needs.

As you set up your workshop, consider ways to build rapport by getting to know and trust each other, and at the same time to provide the secure environment students need for carrying on their work. Try to establish a balance between enjoying the pleasure of each other's company and observing guidelines that make productive reading and writing possible.

Physical Environment

The workshops I've visited are nothing like the classrooms I used to know. A workshop is a busy place! Not only is the emotional climate more receptive, but the room arrangement permits many kinds of groupings and activities. Creative teachers arrange furniture and use supplies for many purposes:

- personal spaces for private reading and writing
- reading lofts or large cardboard carton "castles" for reading
- space for presentations or dramatizations
- centers for reading, writing, and publishing
- computer areas
- a group conference table and conference corners
- storage areas for portfolios and supplies
- library shelves

Your challenge is to arrange your room so that you can include as many of these features as your students will use. Clustering desks together in groups of four to eight saves space and lets children work in groups. Bookcases jutting out from the wall double as library shelves and as dividers that create nooks and crannies. Publishing centers result from placing computers and writing centers in the same work area. If you're lucky enough to have a loft, the space underneath is useful for storage and for creating additional personal places for reading and writing. Filing cabinets are space savers for storing supplies and folders of student work in progress, and counter tops serve as areas for displaying books and keeping supplies readily available for students to use.

Your school probably won't provide all you'd like to have for your workshop, so begin looking for the essentials in discount stores, at garage sales, at flea markets, and from sympathetic family members. Be prepared to scrub and paint! For audiovisual equipment, I suggest tape recorders and an overhead projector, which is so useful for teaching mini-lessons.

TEACHING TIP

Before moving furniture in and rearranging what you have, make a cardboard or paper template of your room and its furnishings to scale. It's easier to move paper desks than real ones, and you can readily see which arrangements are viable.

For a well-stocked writing center you'll need a wide variety of supplies and materials. Figure 9.1 lists some of these.

You'll want your own classroom library. Students need to be able to get their hands on books—lots of them! They need to look through them and select those they want to read during the workshop, not wait until it's library day and then be able to select only one book—as is the case in some school libraries I know. Although I like the idea of a library center, most teachers recommend placing books at different locations so that students can find them without getting in a traffic jam. Place a few that you don't want young

---

Writing utensils (pens, pencils, markers, colored pencils, calligraphy pens, crayons)

Paper (lined and unlined paper, index cards, poster board, scrap paper, colored paper, computer paper, and construction paper)

Rubber stamps and ink pads for stamping such things as the date and *Draft Copy*

Erasers and correction fluid

Tape and scissors for cutting and pasting and for publishing

Special materials for creating published books, such as staples, wallpaper, matting board, needles, dental floss, cardboard, rulers, brads, tape, and glue

Reference materials, including dictionaries, thesauri, usage handbooks, encyclopedias and other reference books, and magazines that publish student writing

Folders or portfolios of student writing

Access to library shelves for referring to ways authors write and illustrate books

Trays for completed student work

Directions posted on the wall for using materials at the center, constructing books, and using the computer

---

Figure 9.1:　Supplies for Writing and Publishing Centers

children to handle on a small shelf near your desk to share on special occasions. These include pop-up books that might get torn, miniature books that could be lost, and picture books from your private collection.

You should display picture books so that children can see their covers, perhaps in baskets that they can look through or lined up along the chalk tray. You can place junior novels in revolving racks or shelve them wherever there is space. Joy McCaleb wheels in a cart of 200 paperbacks for her seventh and eighth grade English classes for their book selection, and Melanie Childress places categories of books in plastic containers for her third graders. One of Melanie's children showed me a carton full of Robert Munsch books, proudly saying that he was their favorite author.

If you want to enhance your print-rich environment with materials that celebrate book week, illustrators, authors, and themes, you can order them from The Children's Book Council (568 Broadway, Suite 404, New York: NY 10012). The Council has attractive literature-related friezes, posters, streamers, and post cards.

TEACHING TIP
With young children who can read several small books during one workshop, put several books in a reclosable freezer storage bag and let them take the entire bag so that they don't continually search and select. With middle grade students, create a check-out system with a library card for each book. Students can check out their own books and file the cards.

With a writing/publishing center and several areas designated for library books, you are well on your way to creating a print-rich environment. Your room should reflect interest in books and authors and show the results of workshop activities. Figure 9.2 shows some possibilities.

Writing/publishing center
Library areas (lofts, cushions, carpeted areas, book nooks)
Commercial posters, displays, bookmarks
Bulletin boards of students' writing
Shelves with student-made books
Center for author study (containing several of the author's
    books, a related display, a poster featuring the latest book)
Theme-related books (display of a variety of books related to
    the current theme study)
Set of reference books
Rack of magazines and newspapers (including student-made)
Student-dictated charts
A map showing locations of settings from books students have read
A time line marked with time periods for books students have read

Figure 9.2:   Evidence of a Print-Rich Environment

Organizing the Classroom

The overall workshop format is simply this: mini-lesson, status of the class, reading/writing/conferring time, and group share. How you organize these activities and the routines you establish, however, are up to you and your students.

Careful planning and organization are essential for success, and you'll need to spend considerable time thinking through the procedures that you believe will work best. You shouldn't need to make up rules on the spot, because you may regret them later. Internalize guidelines so well that you can spend workshop time focusing on the students, not thinking about what to do next. Of course, you should build in some flexibility and realize that you may need to modify procedures as the year progresses.

The Realities of Scheduling

Teachers sometimes complain that it is difficult to spend an hour or more on workshops with all the other demands on their time. It's not a matter of *adding on*, but *substituting* workshop time for separate classes in spelling, grammar, literature, writing skills, and vocabulary study. The integration of these skills that occurs during workshops makes the learning more meaningful to students than isolated lessons.

In upper grades where students change classes and your time may be limited to forty or fifty minutes, try to coordinate with another teacher who shares your beliefs in workshops. Holly Martin, a language arts teacher, collaborated with the social studies teacher so that students pursued similar goals in both classes. Social studies can be part of the content of the writing workshop, and language arts can be an integral part of social studies.

My daughter-in-law Stacy Ross, a kindergarten teacher, found a system that works well for her. Before school starts each morning she puts the children's colored folders on tables at various places, keeping in mind who works well with whom. As her children gather on the rug, she asks them to share their news. This discussion time opens possibilities for the writing and drawing that occur later. She dismisses them by group color; for instance, she asks the yellow group to find their places at the tables and so on. As the children begin drawing and writing, they confer with her and with each other about their work. When some finish, Stacy takes a seat at a desk and calls two or three at a time to come share their pictures and their writing. She listens attentively to each one, asking questions for clarification and making supportive comments. After they explain their pictures, they read what they have written. Then each chooses a book and returns to his or her place to read until Stacy finishes conferring with the others.

TEACHING TIP

To help students locate their writing folders quickly and easily,

a. Use colored folders so that they first look for the color, then the name.
b. Have several containers for folders placed near different work areas so that children only have to look through a few folders in their container.
c. When you have several sections of English classes, use one file cabinet drawer for each section and arrange the folders alphabetically within each drawer.

Major obstacles to organizing the workshop are the interruptions that teachers constantly face. Special classes (for example, physical education, library, and music), pull-out programs which cause children constantly to be leaving or returning, special programs (for example, fund-raising and assemblies), and even announcements over the P.A. system interfere with the smooth operation of workshops. It is difficult to find an hour or more of unbroken time! Do what you can about these interruptions (perhaps ask the office to lump all announcements at the beginning or the end of the day), and adapt as best you can to other interruptions. Some days you simply have to schedule the workshop a half hour later, shorten the time, or allow for the interruption and return to work afterwards.

Expectations for Students

From the beginning of the year, students need to know what is expected of them and how to accomplish their tasks. They need the security of familiar routines, consistent time frames for activities, and suitable locations for working on different types of activities. At the same time, they need to know what freedom they have for choosing partners, selecting reading materials and writing topics, and completing projects, such as finishing books and publishing writing. Although specific guidelines for both reading and writing workshops appear in earlier chapters, Figure 9.3 shows some rules that apply to both.

An option to presenting a list of procedures such as those in Figure 9.3 is to start with a blank sheet of chart paper and record the procedures as you and the students decide you need them. For instance, if Curtis complains that Bobby is always bothering him while he is trying to write, perhaps the students will come up with something like this: *Do not disturb other students while they are working*. If Susan finds that she can never find a clipboard when she needs one, students may dictate: *Return all supplies to their correct places when you finish using them*. In this way, students see the need for the rules and thus are more likely to observe them.

Be prepared before the workshop begins (sharpen pencils, select book, sign up for conference or publishing center, pull your writing folder if you need it, etc.).

When it is time for the workshop, find a place to sit and listen.

Listen attentively during the mini-lesson and try to use what you learn.

Decide what you want to do during the workshop and respond quickly to the status-of-the-class check.

Get busy without wasting time.

Speak softly when you need to talk, and avoid disturbing others who are working.

If you need to leave your place, go directly to your destination and return as soon as possible.

Follow agreed-upon procedures for conferences.

When using supplies, return them as soon as possible to their proper places.

When I give the five-minute warning, begin completing your work so that you will be finished within five minutes.

Join the class for group sharing and be prepared to share, if you are to do so.

Listen respectfully and respond with appropriate questions and comments for the presenter.

Figure 9.3:   Guidelines for Workshops

Of course, you run the risk that some rules will be unreasonable, but the students will probably realize that themselves and change rules that don't work. Also, if the students see no need for rules of any kind, you may need to step in with a mini-lesson on ways to help the workshop run more smoothly.

Students who have never known anything but sitting at their desks and doing assigned work will need special guidance in adapting to such a free environment. You will need to move slowly and take the students step-by-step through the procedures for using space and materials. If noise is a problem, tell the students to speak in their "six-inch voices," which means that only those seated within six inches can hear them speak. Post rules that the class understands and agrees to for using centers, such as "No more than four people can be at this center at one time" and "Maximum length of time for selecting a book is five minutes." Role playing such situations as participating in conferences and using materials helps students understand your expectations, and you can deal with many procedural issues during mini-lessons. You may not be able to hold many conferences at first because you need to observe the students. If they are not using their time well, retreat and simplify, perhaps allowing no more than three or four students to be out of their seats at one time.

Figure 9.4 (adapted from Rief, 1992) offers expectations for students. In some of these, I've left blank spaces so that you, perhaps with input from your students, can decide what is reasonable. For instance, you may want your students to publish two pieces of writing each six weeks or write in their logs three times a week. You may begin with a shorter list, choose only those activities that are appropriate for your class, or add some procedures of your own. One danger in setting quotas is getting sloppy, poor quality work. For instance, one student may turn out several carelessly written pieces in a term, while another writes one excellent, carefully crafted piece. You may have to reassess your expectations after you see how your students are meeting them.

If your students are to keep personal records as suggested in Figure 9.4, they will have to understand where to keep them. You may want them to place records of books they read and lists of spelling and vocabulary words in writing folders or notebooks, and keep selected items from their reading and writing in portfolios. Students may keep folders at their desks and file portfolios alphabetically on shelves or in large plastic containers.

Spend _____ minutes reading at home each night.

Keep an ongoing list of books read (title, author, publisher, date of publication, and comment).

Write in your reading log _____ times a week.

Read _____ different genres each _____ weeks.

Record the context and definition for _____ new vocabulary words each week.

Keep a list of words you frequently misspell.

Complete _____ pieces of writing each _____ weeks.

Write _____ different genres each _____ weeks.

Confer with your teacher _____ time(s) each week.

Confer with your classmates _____ time(s) each week.

Select items for your portfolio _____ time(s) each _____ week(s).

Review your goals for yourself each _____ week(s).

Evaluate your own progress each _____ week(s).

Make entries in your writing notebook _____ time(s) each _____ week(s).

Figure 9.4:   Expectations for Reading/Writing Workshops

Ideally, when students understand what you expect of them, you won't have many behavioral problems. You may need to re-teach certain procedures and remind some students of them, and it may take a long time to achieve the kind of self-disciplined work-shop that you want. For the most part, students who are motivated to read and write cause few problems in the classroom. Occasion-ally, however, some students fail to live up to expectations and violate class rules. Here are some suggestions for assessing situations and helping these students regain their status in the class community:

- Gather as a group to discuss the problem and what should be done. Encourage students to make constructive sug-gestions.
- Reassess expectations and decide if they are fair and rea-sonable. Consider alternatives.
- Ask the student whose behavior is in question to explain to the class what happened and why.
- Ask this student to write an explanation of what occurred (or failed to occur) and how to avoid the problem in the future.
- If you feel that punishment is necessary, find a penalty that fits the situation. For instance, if a student misbe-haves in the reading loft, ban the student from using the loft for one week.

TEACHING TIP

If some students have difficulty working without the structure of a traditional classroom,

a.   encourage them to focus on short-term goals.
b.   pair them with responsible partners.
c.   ask them to sign contracts in which they agree to com-plete work and/or behave appropriately.

Correlation with the Curriculum

Another matter to keep in mind when organizing your workshop is the curriculum guide, if you are required to follow one. Although it would be nice to teach only what students need to know at the moment, some states expect students to master certain skills at specific grade levels. Many state-mandated achievement tests measure skill mastery, and both teachers and students may be judged primarily by the scores on these tests. Also, the new Standards for the English Language Arts may affect expectations for students and cause teachers to become aware of additional guidelines. Because of state and national objec-tives, teachers should consider ways to incorporate required skills into their workshops. Most teachers introduce and reinforce skills during mini-lessons, but children also learn them informally during confer-ences and by using them in authentic reading and writing situations.

In Tennessee, where we have a statewide curriculum guide K–8, many teachers devise a system for recording the skills they teach. Using a condensed two-page list of grade-level skills, some teachers mark skills they've covered with highlighter pens. When both pages are covered with yellow highlighter, they know that they have directly taught all of the required skills. Whenever they reteach a skill, they simply place a check beside it. In this way teachers keep track of what they've taught in terms of curriculum requirements.

Interclass Organizational Patterns

Cross-grade and interclass arrangements offer the potential for establishing new relationships, building self-concepts, and providing opportunities for expanding knowledge of reading and writing. Often, older children gain confidence and a sense of responsibility from partnering with younger ones, and young children feel reassured by having buddies to guide them through the intricacies of reading and writing.

Many schools in Australia have been deliberately placing students of different grade levels in the same class for years, and in the States multiage classrooms are quickly catching on. Broadly based themes and shared goals make such combinations workable. Chris McClendon's fourth, fifth, and sixth year grouping seemed only to enhance students' reading and writing, and I was fascinated as I watched students in a combination preps (kindergarten)-year one class work together. Whenever a preps child wasn't sure what to write, a year one child would patiently point out what letters make certain sounds.

Such organizational patterns are already established by administrators so you may have little to say about permanent cross-grade plans, but you may want to work out your own exchange as Amy and Kevin plan to do. Jay Friedman and Janis Koeppel (1990) arranged an exchange between first graders and pre-K children. They decided to form a writing workshop for both classes by combining the pre-K children's knowledge of language with the first graders' experiences in writing. After preparing the children through modeling and role playing, the teachers arranged for the first graders to go to the pre-K classroom for two fifteen-minute workshops each week. Children from both classes benefited, with pre-K children gaining a sense of self-worth as first graders wrote down their ideas, and first graders becoming aware of their capabilities by helping their younger partners.

Managing Resources

You will need different types of resources for workshops than for traditional classrooms with their typical basal readers, workbooks,

TEACHING TIP

To provide a wider audience for student work, make arrangements with another class at the same grade level to

a.   Exchange student-made books.
b.   Get together to read or recite original poetry.
c.   Get together to give book talks about class favorites.

spelling books, and so forth. You may want to begin by assessing what you already have that you can use and deciding what essentials you will need to begin a workshop. Then, considering your needs and available funds, draw up a shopping list and look for some good buys at discount stores, school supply centers, and office supply stores. Figure 9.1 lists supplies for a writing/publishing center, and your other primary need is likely to be a large supply of trade books.

Organizing Materials

Once you know what you have and what you can get, you are ready to think about ways to organize supplies in order to facilitate students' use of them. Place writing supplies in containers in a central, readily accessible area. Containers are helpful for saving space and making sure that children don't strew materials everywhere. You can use trays for different kinds of paper, folders for completed written work, pencil holders for different writing tools, and sturdy boxes for such miscellaneous supplies as staplers, glue, scissors, and correction fluid.

If you have a reasonably good supply of books, you will have to consider ways to organize them. Here are some possibilities:

- by author if there are many books by a popular author
- by topic, especially during theme studies
- by genre (nonfiction, fiction, poetry, or biography)
- by difficulty level

Arranging books by difficulty level can be tricky. First of all, it's hard to tell which books are difficult for readers. Their interest, prior knowledge, and determination to read certain books often motivates them to read books that would seem to be above their levels. Also, some children are embarrassed to choose only books labeled easy if they cannot read other books successfully. Not all picture books are easy to read; some contain difficult words and advanced concepts. Usually, predictability, pattern, and repetition are what makes books easy to read. Despite the problem of determining how to evaluate difficulty levels, a number of teachers prefer to arrange books in this way, sometimes calling them *easy, just right*, or *challenging*. One teacher suggests placing colored dot stickers on the backs of books to designate their difficulty, for example, green for easy, yellow for just right, and red for challenging. Again, turn to your students for solutions. What arrangements do they prefer?

Instead of trying to organize your library on your own, ask for help. With a little training, parents, teachers' assistants, and student volunteers can relieve you of much of the responsibility. Here are some things they can do:

- set up a check-out/check-in system.
- place library pockets and cards in books.
- display books attractively.
- help you identify new books to order.
- fill out order forms.
- repair books as needed.
- keep track of books checked out from the school library.
- record bibliographic information and comments about new books on cards and file the cards for reference.

TEACHING TIP

If you want your class to stay interested in the books you have available for the classroom library, don't put out all of the books at once. Bring out "new" books from time to time and rotate the selection so that children discover different ones throughout the year.

Selecting and Acquiring Books

Since funds and space are limited, you will have to choose books wisely. In your class are students with a wide range of reading interests and ability levels. Of course, you want to find books that everyone will enjoy. With thousands of books to select from, how do you know which ones to choose? Figure 9.5 offers some suggestions, and Appendix I, which lists books cited in these chapters, is a source of recommended books.

High-interest books based on the results of an interest inventory
Books from professionally compiled lists, such as Children's Choices
Award winners, particularly Caldecott (picture books) and Newbery
    (for older students)
Recommendations from students and other teachers
Popular classics
Socially significant and culturally diverse books
Books that span an appropriate range of readability levels for
    your students
Choices from a variety of genres
Discounted books to save money, providing they're of good quality
Recommendations from selection aids and library journals
Books related to themes you plan to teach
Books reviewed in professional journals and publishers' catalogs
Reading Rainbow books

Figure 9.5:   Sources for Selecting Books

When selecting books for your classroom library, it's wise to consult professional book lists and look through some books yourself. Read reviews of children's literature that appear in *Language Arts* and *The Reading Teacher*; visit book stores and peruse the selection, especially award winners such as Newbery, Caldecott, and Reading Rainbow books; study publishers' catalogs for featured books that meet your needs; choose from lists of Teacher's Choices, Children's Choices, and Young Adult Choices, published annually by the Children's Book Council and the International Reading Association; and browse through books at professional conferences and eavesdrop on what other teachers are saying about their favorite books. And, of course, consider your students' wish lists!

A primary criterion for selecting children's books is their interests. I believe you can learn much about their interests by listening to them, or by having them write their three favorite topics on a slip of paper. If you would like more specific information, however, you can give the Survey of Literary Interests in Figure 4.3.

Your librarian can help you select books on special topics or for general use in your classroom library. Ask the librarian to check out large numbers of books to you for extended periods of time. The school libraries I've visited in Australia have been small, and teachers check out many books, including multiple copies of the same book, to keep in their classrooms.

Although it's tempting to build your classroom library with whatever books are available to you, it's better to have fewer books than to shelve inferior books. Avoid those that convey negative stereotypes of members of multiethnic groups, series books that have no redeeming literary qualities, books with comic book style violence, and trashy romance novels. You may find others that are simply in poor taste for one reason or another.

Picture books are good for all ages. Of course, some are intended for young children, but others find their way into our hearts at any age. Once middle school students realize that it is not shameful to read picture books, they appreciate the powerful themes and the striking art work. There is nothing childish about Lynne Cherry's historical presentation of the creeping pollution and eventual reclamation of the Nashua River in *A River Ran Wild*, or in Patricia Polacco's *Pink and Say*, a true story of two young boys caught up in the Civil War. David Macauley's detailed line drawings in such nonfiction picture books as *Cathedral* and *Pyramid* offer information and inspiration for anyone. Jean Dickinson (1995), a fifth/sixth grade teacher, introduces her class to picture books in order to get them to think, share ideas, and tell personal stories. Her students were deeply moved when she read them Tsuchiya's *Faithful Elephants*, a World War II story. Also, seeing you read picture books with the class justifies their acceptance in the eyes of poorer readers who cannot yet read entire chapter books on their own.

You'll also need to help students make wise selections. One way to do this is to model ways to choose books during a mini-lesson by looking through them and making comments about their difficulty, the illustrations and format, your interest in the topic, and so forth. You can introduce students to class library books by showing them and giving brief talks about them, so that students will know what books might interest them. When you read a book aloud to the class, you can usually count on some students wanting to reread the book for themselves—or another one by the same author or on the same topic. Students also like to read what their friends recommend, so you might ask students to record on a chart or on file cards books that they enjoyed.

Acquiring so many books isn't as easy as selecting them, but I do know teachers who have built their classroom libraries to several hundred books in a few years. These teachers are persistent, determined, and imaginative in obtaining books, and they get them in a variety of ways, including those shown in Figure 9.6.

Money to purchase books can come from many sources. Several years ago we got a $500 grant at our university to buy multiple copies of books to use for literature response groups, and we're still using them. Check your central office or a nearby university for the availability of mini-grants. In some schools teachers use money intended for workbooks and part of their discretionary funds to buy trade books. Although book club orders are time consuming to complete, children love to get new books, and you can use the bonus points for ordering additional books.

Bonus points from book clubs (Scholastic, Troll, Trumpet)

School library

Community library

Books stored at the central office

Rejects from libraries that can be restored

PTO/PTA funds

Mini-grants

Garage sales, flea markets, used book sales (be selective!)

Discount book stores

Stories from old basal readers, cut apart and rebound into individual books

Contributions from friends and relatives

Gifts from parents (on child's birthday, for Christmas)

Figure 9.6: Inexpensive Ways to Acquire Books

TEACHING TIP
When acquiring books, consider your purposes:

a.   If you want students to read as partners and share journal responses, get two copies of some books.

b.   If you want to set up literature response groups, order six to eight copies of popular books.

c.   If you want to expand your classroom library, find as many single copies of quality books as you can.

d.   If you want to read aloud to students, select a few fine quality books that are beyond their reading levels.

Using Computers

Word processing offers an alternative to handwriting, which many children find tedious. Connie Kinnaird encourages her first graders to think like authors and write about their families or what's going on in class when they use the several computers in her room. At the beginning of the year, the children free write, but after Christmas she helps those who are ready with editing. Hannah told me that she enjoys using computers because she likes to use the keyboard. She has written several stories about moles, including the one in Example 9.1.

It reads like this: There once was a mole who was different than other moles and he wanted to know why he was so different than the others. They always said he was different in a way. He did not know why they always said he was so different from them. Then one day he found out the reason was he ate neat and he was more loving and caring.

Computers are particularly useful in writing workshops because they make editing easy and enable students to word process pieces they are ready to publish. They are also useful for creating class newspapers, posters, greeting cards, and other types of printed materials, and computer graphics give them a professional look. The list that follows gives information about a variety of programs useful for publishing (Ramondetta, 1993), but you will need to check current sources because publishers update programs and introduce new software fairly often.

Newsletters and Newspapers (*Children's Writing and Publishing Center*, Apple II series, IBM and compatibles; *The Writing Center*, Macintosh; *The Bilingual Writing Center, Spanish/English*, Macintosh, The Learning Company, grades 2–12). You may need to help young students enter news stories, but older students will enjoy working independently to publish class newsletters and newspapers. These programs can create multicolumn papers with or without headlines, and they include over 100 color graphics for illustrations.

There wats was a
mole who was
difrit thin othr
moles and he
wotid to no wy he
was so difrint thin
the othrs. Thy
allways sed he
was diffint in a
way. He didnot no
wy thy allways
sed he was so difit
from thim. Thin
one day he fand
alt the rysun was
he ate nete and
he was more
loveing and cering.
The End By
Hannah Leigh
Brown

Example 9.1

Fairy Tales and Tall Tales (*Big Book Maker: Favorite Tales and Nursery Rhymes; Big Book Maker: Tall Tales and American Folk Heroes*, Apple II Series, Toucan Software, grades K–6). Students can use these programs to make fairy tale and tall tale books, or they can create different stories by mixing characters from familiar stories and by changing dialogue and outcomes.

Big and Little Books (*Big and Little*, Apple II Series, IBM and compatibles; *SuperPrint!* and *SuperPrint II!*, Apple II Series, IBM and compatibles; *SuperPrint for the Macintosh*, Macintosh, Scholastic, Inc., grades K–12). These programs enable students to publish their stories as small (6 inches high) or big (22 or 33 inches high) books.

"Wide-screen" Books (*Banner Books: On the Street Where You Live, Banner Books: Writing Across America, Banner Books: Your School Day*, Apple II Series, Toucan Software, grades K–6). Using tractor-feed computer paper, these programs produce horizontal books that are twice as wide as regular books. Each program has several scenes that students can select as backgrounds for their stories, as well as hundreds of graphics to illustrate scenes.

Group Writing (*Muppet Slate*, Apple II Series, Wings for Learning/Sunburst, Grades K–2; *Monsters & Make Believe*, Apple II Series, Macintosh, IBM and compatibles, Toucan Software, grades K–6). With a large-print word processor such as *Muppet Slate*, letters appear on the screen four times as large as usual so that you can use your screen as an electronic chalkboard for group reading and writing activities. Gathering your students around your computer, teach mini-lessons by demonstrating writing skills and showing children how to edit.

Summary

For your workshop to be truly effective, you need to spend time planning ways to create an emotionally supportive and a print-rich environment. You want your students to feel comfortable and secure, willing to take risks and at ease within your classroom community. The physical arrangement of the room, evidence of books and writing materials, and inviting displays all contribute to motivating students to read and write.

Organization, scheduling, and correlation with your curricular framework are also important considerations. Selecting and acquiring quality literature for students is a high priority, but adequate funding can be a problem here! Be sure to use whatever computers are available to you, for they can make editing and publishing much more rewarding for your students than traditional paper and pencil copies.

Reflections

Seriously consider the following questions. Some answers may be found by reflecting on the chapter; others may come from your own beliefs and experiences.

1. If I must fill out a lesson plan book, how will I show what I plan to cover in language arts? If I teach in response to my students' needs, how will I know in advance what I'll be teaching? Should I make some plans anyway, and then change them if I need to?
2. What type of interclass groupings could I try? Is there another teacher who shares my views? Would I want to partner with the same grade level or a different one? What benefits would there be for my students?
3. How can I work more closely with the school librarian to support the workshop? Do we share the same goals? Can the librarian help me locate materials, lend me books for periods of time, introduce my students and me to new offerings, or cooperate in other ways?
4. How can I help my students make responsible choices and decisions? They need to feel a sense of empowerment for their learning, but they may not have the maturity they need to make wise decisions.
5. Where can I get books for my classroom library? What do I already have that I can use? Do I need to add certain genres to have a balanced collection? What discretionary funds are available for buying books?

Bibliography

Atwell, N. (1987). *In the middle.* Portsmouth, NH: Heinemann.

Calkins, L. (1986). *The art of teaching writing.* Portsmouth, NH: Heinemann.

Calkins, L. (1991). *Living between the lines.* Portsmouth, NH: Heinemann.

Dickinson, J. (1995). Talk and picture books in intermediate classrooms. *Primary Voices K–6, 3* (1), 8–14.

Eisele, B. (1991). *Managing the whole language classroom.* Cypress, CA: Creative Teaching Press.

Fiderer, A. (1993). *Teaching writing: A workshop approach.* New York: Scholastic.

Friedman, J., & Koeppel, J. (1990). Pre-K and first grade children: Partners in a writing workshop. *Young Children, 45* (4), 66–67.

Graves, D. (1994). *A fresh look at writing.* Portsmouth, NH: Heinemann.

Hagerty, P. (1992). *Readers' workshop.* Richmond Hill, Ontario: Scholastic Canada.

Hansen, J. (1987). *When writers read.* Portsmouth, NH: Heinemann.

Harwayne, S. (1992). *Lasting impressions.* Portsmouth, NH: Heinemann.

Hoff, L. (1994). From omnipotent teacher-in-charge to co-conspirator in the classroom: Developing lifelong readers and writers. *English Journal, 83* (6), 42–50.

Jackson, N., & Pillow, P. (1992). *The reading-writing workshop: Getting started.* New York: Scholastic.

Pike, K., Compain, R., & Mumper, J. (1994). *Connections.* New York: HarperCollins.

Ramondetta, J. (1993). Whole language computing. *Learning93, 22* (3), 22–25.

Rief, L. (1992). *Seeking diversity.* Portsmouth, NH: Heinemann.

Strickland, D. (1994/1995). Reinventing our literacy programs: Books, basics, balance. *The Reading Teacher, 48* (4), 294–302.

CHAPTER 10

EVALUATION

Amy, speaking to Kevin as she puts on a light jacket and gathers her books: I'm glad our faculty meeting ended early. I can use the time, with report cards coming out Thursday.

Kevin: Yes, I've really had a tough time putting grades on them this year. None of the easy grade averaging with spelling and grammar tests. With workshops, it seems so subjective.

Amy: And no basal reader tests to go by at the end of each unit either.

Kevin: How have you been getting your grades, Amy?

Amy: I have to give one grade for reading and one for writing, as you know, and we have to give them in percentages, even in the lower grades.

Kevin: That's so incompatible with what we do!

Amy: I've been considering a variety of sources. I look at my conference notes, anecdotal records, checklists, and any notes I've made when I observe. Then I look through the children's portfolios and see what progress they've made during this six weeks. Somehow I put all that together, analyze it, and reach a ballpark estimate. I feel like I'm shooting in the dark sometimes, but I convert my estimate into a percentage that comes as close as I can to what I think each student is doing.

Kevin: I've experimented a lot this year with grading, and I'm not sure I've got it right yet. I do more or less what you do, but my kids and I developed a rubric for writing. That helps a lot in arriving at a grade. I also use their literature response group evaluations.

Amy: I know you've tried self-evaluation. How is that working?

Kevin: Self-evaluation is definitely part of their grades. The students are getting better at understanding their own strengths—and at recognizing some areas that need improvement. At first, I had to meet with quite a few individually to discuss how they should evaluate their work. I ended up having a couple of mini-lessons on self-evaluation.

Amy: I've worked with my children on that, too, but some of them really don't get it. Some don't realize that they need to do better, and others aren't aware of how well they are doing.

Kevin: Well, nobody ever said it would be easy.

Amy: That's true, but I have so much evidence of what they've actually accomplished this year in their portfolios. When I show the portfolios to parents on conference days, I believe they understand what their children can do better this year than ever before.

Kevin: Report card grades really don't matter as much when we have samples of students' work to back them up.

Amy: It's always good to talk with you, Kevin, and know that I'm not alone with this grading dilemma. See you tomorrow.

Introduction

Many teachers agree with Amy and Kevin that evaluation is one of the most perplexing problems for workshops; traditional grading procedures simply do not mesh with workshop practices. Yet, evaluation is essential because it provides students with feedback, informs instruction, and satisfies demands for accountability.

Someone said that an achievement test score is simply a snapshot, but evaluation of student growth calls for an entire photo album. In this chapter we'll consider supplements or alternatives to standardized and traditional teacher-made tests, and we'll look at ways teachers can integrate instruction with assessment as they observe students and confer with them. Teachers learn much about student progress as they respond to literature logs, complete rubrics, and examine portfolios, and students learn to reflect on their own progress through self-evaluation. Reporting this progress effectively to parents is critical, for parents must understand what their children can do in order to provide support.

Overview

Assessment is the gathering of data from various sources, and *evaluation* is the interpretation of these data. In workshops, assessment occurs as teachers record information while observing, conferring, completing checklists and rubrics, and examining portfolios. Teachers evaluate progress by summarizing this information, reflecting on its significance, and making professional judgments about it. Barclay and Breheny (1994, p. 215) define evaluation as "a periodic, more comprehensive review and subsequent judgment regarding each child's current knowledge, skills and attitudes with respect to curricular goals and objectives." Here are some principles for assessment and evaluation in workshops.

Assessment is authentic. Assessment is meaningful and occurs as part of regular workshop activities. Tests that measure mastery of a skill in isolation are not authentic; records of observations about ways children respond to literature during the reading workshop are authentic. Authentic assessment deals with real-life situations, and your students can see its relevance to actual reading/writing situations.

Assessment and instruction are integrated. Consider the kinds of assessment procedures you can use for gathering information during workshops that will guide you in providing the instruction that students need. For example, you notice that many students consistently use weak verbs, so you teach one or two mini-lessons on using strong, precise verbs to make their writing more effective. Then you observe which students apply this skill in their writing. Thus, you first assess by observing, then instruct, and then assess students' ability to apply the instruction.

Students participate in evaluation. Students grow in their understanding of their strengths, needs, and progress by assuming some responsibility for evaluating their work. They may select items for inclusion in portfolios, complete self-evaluation checklists, and contribute to the construction of rubrics.

Assessment is continuous. Instead of averaging test scores at the end of a term to determine student achievement, teachers observe students on a day-by-day basis. By doing so, teachers are sensitive to student growth, aware of what they need to teach, and prepared to communicate regularly with parents.

Teachers emphasize students' strengths. Instead of focusing on students' weaknesses, look first at what they *can* do. Developing their strengths helps students gain confidence and transfer their strengths to other areas. If a student fails to demonstrate certain competencies, wait for these competencies to develop naturally at a later time or adjust your instruction to make the student aware of them.

Teachers use a variety of assessment strategies. Workshops provide many opportunities to assess students' growth in literacy. By considering a number of factors, teachers get a fuller picture of the whole child. Figure 10.1 gives some evidence teachers can use to assess students during workshops. You may think of additional sources of information.

Assessment strategies for special learners and Limited English Proficient (LEP) students are essentially the same as those for other students. For both groups, traditional tests are often inappropriate because they fail to measure what the child knows and can do. Special education teachers may want to team with regular classroom teachers in collecting data, particularly portfolio inclusions. Advantages of using workshops for teachers of special

> Reading response journals
>
> Group share
>
> Author's chair
>
> Conferences
>
> Portfolios
>
> Student self evaluations
>
> Participation in the writing process
>
> Published pieces
>
> Portfolios
>
> Literature logs

Figure 10.1: Sources for Authentic Assessment during Workshops

learners are (1) additional time for gathering in-depth data while working with individual students or small groups and (2) getting to know certain students quite well from working with them over a period of years. Special education teachers must also consider local, state, and federal regulations related to assessment, which are often incompatible with authentic assessment.

Teachers of both groups should make special adaptations for these learners by accommodating their special needs and learning styles. For example, a student who has great difficulty writing may dictate to a teacher instead of writing, and an LEP student may convey knowledge in her or his native language or through tactile or kinesthetic modes.

Components of Workshop Evaluation

As Figure 10.1 shows, workshops offer an abundance of opportunities to evaluate student progress without giving tests. These alternative sources of assessment will not be as quick and easy to use as test scores, however, and you will have to rely on your professional judgment to reach decisions about grading. Be sure to record and date observations in order to use them to evaluate student growth over periods of time. Form and structure are important for recording, because brief notes written randomly on scraps of paper and stuffed in desk drawers are of little use when it comes time to summarize data. Some teachers file this information in student portfolios, but others keep such evaluative records in individual file folders in their desks or filing cabinets. Here are some types of informal assessment, along with ways to record information.

Observation

No doubt the most common and useful form of evaluation is observation, often referred to as "kid watching." As teachers, we continually notice what our students are doing and how they are doing it. "Maria got right to work today," "Stu chose a book that is too hard for him—I wonder if he'll stick with it," or "Cathy's attention is wandering—there may be more trouble at home." These thoughts come quickly and may be forgotten unless we jot them down, date them, combine them with other data, and evaluate their significance for learning.

Teacher intuition is a major factor in kid watching, according to Bill Harp (1994). Intuition is based on professional knowledge of how children become literate and their developmental stages. What might seem insignificant to the untrained observer—scribbles for writing and oral reading riddled with errors—may show the skilled observer that a child is actually making advances toward literacy. The more we observe, the more we refine our intuition and understand how children learn.

> ## TEACHING TIP
> When recording brief observations, use a clipboard for support and
> a. Jot a comment on a sticky note, temporarily attach it to paper on the clipboard, and later place it in the student's file.
> b. Make a flip chart by taping large index cards to the clipboard, with each card slightly overlapping the previous one so that the bottom edge of each card is visible. Have one card for each student with the student's name at the bottom of the card. Jot down your observation. When a card is full, file it and replace it with a new card.
> c. Attach a ruled sheet of paper for each student, placing the student's name at the bottom. For an ongoing record, write each date and comment in order.

Anecdotal Records

Anecdotal records for workshops are brief accounts of meaningful literacy events that involve one or more students. Observations may be only a word or phrase, but anecdotal records give more of a scenario. By perusing them, you get a good idea of how students are doing and what you need to teach. These records may deal with such topics as the following:

- sustained attention on task
- social interactions during conferences
- interest in participating during group-share sessions
- enthusiasm for reading and writing
- use of different genres in reading and writing
- questioning strategies for classmate in author's chair
- use of portfolio (selection of samples, organization)

Ideally, the teacher should make anecdotal records about each student two or three times a week to get a representative sampling of performance in different contexts. The teacher may make notes on index cards to place in student folders or enter observations in notebooks.

> ## TEACHING TIP
> When using notebooks to record anecdotal records,
> a. Use looseleaf notebooks so that you can remove full sheets and place them in student folders, add more paper if needed, and easily reorganize for new students or students who withdraw.
> b. Use a tab for each student with a few pages after each tab. Tabs help you to find student records quickly.
> c. Organize notebooks for convenience. Alphabetical order may be easiest, but also consider organizing by groups of students who work together.

Evaluation Conferences/Interviews

Students reveal much about their interests, attitudes, reading and writing preferences, and goals as they talk with you. Some teachers periodically interview students to evaluate the effectiveness of their instruction and to learn what students think about reading, writing, and literature. They use interview sheets to record answers and then file these sheets. Yvonne Siu-Runyan (1994, p. 146) asks her students two questions which give useful information for teaching and assessment:

"What kinds of things do I do that help you as a writer?"

"What kinds of things do I do that help you as a reader?"

At first students give vague, useless answers, but they begin giving valuable suggestions when they realize she is sincere. Other useful questions relate to ways students select pieces for portfolios, genres they prefer to read or write, revision procedures, plans for future reading, and goals for strengthening their writing (Fiderer, 1993).

Nancie Atwell (1987) holds an evaluation conference during the last week of each grading period. She posts interview questions in advance and explains them during a mini-lesson so that students will be prepared to answer them. She records responses on a pre-printed form during conferences—a procedure she prefers to tape recording answers and transcribing them later, a time consuming process. At the end of each interview, she gives students one or two goals and asks them to identify at least one goal for themselves. She believes that this process helps students reflect on their learning and enables her to evaluate their progress.

Checklists

Checklists are a quick and easy way to record observations. You can design them for any purpose or grade level, and you know where a student stands simply by glancing over the list. When constructing checklists, keep in mind realistic expectations for your students and focus on those items that are crucial for your purposes. It's easy to get bogged down with too many criteria, actually more than you need for a quick summary of a student's status. You might want to ask students to contribute criteria that reflect their personal goals so that they understand what you are evaluating.

You can construct checklists fairly easily, and once you make them, you can copy them to use again and again. Checklists need a primary focus with related criteria, as well as a rating scale, such as + for *doing well*, 0 for *adequate*, and − for *needing improvement*. You may prefer to rate each criterion from 1 (lowest) to 10 (highest). In order to keep records of progress, allow space for periodic checks. The checklist in Figure 10.2 shows desirable behaviors for workshops that can be recorded on six different dates.

Student's Name _____							
Desirable Behaviors	**Observation Dates**						
Follows workshop procedures.							
Reads/writes in different genres.							
Keeps complete records.							
Pays attention to mini-lessons.							
Applies mini-lesson strategies.							
Shares during group share.							
Confers with other students.							
Comes to workshop prepared.							
Uses time wisely.							
Uses journal effectively.							

Key: + = good progress; 0 = acceptable; − = needs improvement

Figure 10.2:   Desirable Workshop Behaviors

Other appropriate topics for checklists are:

- Emergent literacy checklist for young children
- Home reading checklist for parents to fill out and return
- Checklist of reading competencies
- Checklist for use of writing conventions
- Checklist of attitudes toward workshop activities
- Self-evaluation checklist

Obviously, you don't want to spend a great deal of time giving checklists because the information on them is only superficial, but they enable you to observe and record what students do while engaged in authentic literacy tasks. You can file checklists along with other records of student achievement and use them as one source for reporting progress.

Response Journals

Journals and logs can take many forms, from the casual daily entry with no assessment to the more formal literature log in which students are expected to respond to what they are reading. Entries give information about their understanding of what they've read, as well as insight into their writing proficiency.

Students are apt to find journals less threatening than tests, so they are likely to take risks and show you their best thinking (Wollman-Bonilla, 1991). From journal entries, you can observe students'

- knowledge of literature.
- extent of involvement in what they are reading.
- awareness of literary techniques.
- depth of comprehension.
- ability to relate to personal experiences.
- reading strategies.

Although you can use anecdotal records and checklists to evaluate journal entries, you may find brief narrative summaries or critiques more useful. In many cases you will have already been responding on a regular basis to literature logs, so your collective comments should enable you to form judgments about students' reading skills, as well as their abilities to express ideas in writing.

Rubrics

Rubrics provide standards or guidelines for evaluating student achievement in any subject, usually on a three- to six-point scale. They are useful for letting students know the criteria on which they are being judged and for informing parents of what their children can do. At the lower end of the scale, students show almost no knowledge of a skill or competency, but at the highest level they demonstrate outstanding proficiency. At each level descriptive words and phrases identify levels of competency. In some schools rubrics are already in place, but in others the classroom teacher, with student input, constructs them. By helping to create rubrics, students understand expectations and know how the teacher evaluates them. Although some rubrics give much more detail, Figure 10.3 is a sample of a three-point rubric teachers can use to evaluate writing on the basis of ability to focus on a topic, use descriptive words, and vary sentence structure.

In scoring rubrics, teachers can match student work to the closest descriptors and mark them in some way. Students can use rubrics to evaluate their own work, and they can see their scores improve as they gain competence in writing. Together, teacher and students may modify or expand a simple rubric such as this as students gain knowledge of ways to assess writing.

Points	Focus	Descriptive Words	Sentence Structure
	Student's Name _____ Date _____		
3	Relates all ideas logically to topic	Uses descriptive words and phrases to create effects	Varies sentence patterns and lengths for impact
2	Refers to topic inconsistently	Uses ordinary words to express ideas	Uses some variation in sentences but without purpose
1	Mentions topic briefly, then goes off subject	Makes poor and inappropriate choices of words	Uses same sentence patterns repeatedly

Figure 10.3: Writing Rubric

Self-Evaluation

No type of evaluation is more beneficial for students than self-evaluation, which enables them to make decisions about their own work. Self-evaluations give students some control in judging the effectiveness of their work instead of simply turning it over to the teacher for grading.

Students need time and training, however, to become good self-evaluators. Having little insight into reading and writing processes at first, they may evaluate their reading in terms of how many books they read and evaluate their writing based on how many pages they filled or the quality of their handwriting. The teacher can guide students toward effective self-evaluation modeling ways to critique the teacher's own writing during mini-lessons, analyzing techniques authors use in trade books, and providing opportunities for students to analyze their work and that of their classmates during group teacher-student conferences. As a result of self-evaluation, many students set high goals for themselves which motivate them to do their best work (Hoff, 1994).

Students can evaluate themselves in a variety of ways. Questions that teachers ask during conferences may cause them to reflect on their reading or writing, and a checklist offers a framework for identifying strengths and areas that need improvement. Barbara Lee asks her fifth graders to evaluate themselves on a simple form at the end of the semester. (See Example 10.1 for Bailey's responses).

In Language Arts . . .

The grade I think I deserve is A because I am very croAtive, I am very involved with language Arts, and I am a natural learner

I think my strengths are Reading, Reading Skills, Spelling, Creativity, Computer and Journal

I need to work on My Languaage and Language Skills

- -

The best part about Language Arts is Journal - in the spiral notebook because

It makes me think and let's me get my creativity out.

The part I like least is the Language skills and Big Hairy Spelling Papers because I am awful at Lang.

I wish we would do more

Journal, and Reading Novles because

Journal let's every body get their creativity out and Reading Novles helps our Reading Skills.

Example 10.1

Evaluating Reading

Nothing is more important in school than learning to read and enjoying it. Workshops give students opportunities to choose books, time to read them, and ways to share them. Yet, teachers struggle with how to evaluate reading. Essentially, reading is a silent process that goes on within the mind of the reader, and it isn't easy for the teacher to know the reading strategies the student is using and what responses the reader is making.

You can use any of the strategies discussed in the previous section for evaluating reading, and you and your students may find other techniques as well. I'd like to offer a couple of cautions as you consider ways to evaluate reading.

(1) Don't stress the number of books read as a measure of reading achievement. Go for quality, not quantity. If students see that you grade by the number of books read instead of by the quality of the literature, they will look for easy books to simply increase their numbers. Emphasizing numbers discourages them from reading challenging, high-quality literature.

(2) Although it's important for students to keep records of their reading, don't let record keeping become a burden. Require a minimal amount of recording (for example, a complete list of books read and journal entries twice a week), and encourage students to do more if they wish. Of course, older students are capable of doing more detailed record keeping than younger ones.

Literature response groups, or literature circles, were discussed in Chapter 3, and here I'd like to suggest some ways to use them as part of your reading evaluation. As an evaluator, you may record your observations of student participation on a chart such as the one shown in Figure 10.4. Your own chart may differ according to your purposes and grade level. You may simply place a check by each criterion observed, or you may devise a scale to rate each item (i.e., 1 = not observed; 10 = highly evident).

When all of the students have finished their books, they should evaluate themselves. Their evaluation form might look like the one in Figure 10.5.

In order to assess students' progress in reading, you may also want to review periodically the status-of-the-class reports presented in Chapter 2. They can tell you much about students' book selections and patterns of reading. In Figure 10.6, based on such a report in a fourth grade class, I'll give some background information about each child, a week of entries, possible interpretations of those entries, and suggestions for students. Some entries are abbreviated due to time (for recording student responses) and space limitations; (f) means the student finished a book and (d) means the student dropped or abandoned the book. You may want to analyze the entries yourself before reading my suggestions.

Date: _____ Book: _____						
Criteria for Evaluation	**Student Names**					
	Beth	Stu	Jose	Juan	Tyler	Chris
Wrote in log.						
Shared log entry.						
Asked questions.						
Made thoughtful comments.						
Assumed leadership role.						
Appeared interested.						
Began reading.						

Figure 10.4: Evaluation of Literature Response Groups

Evaluating Writing

Writing lets teachers integrate instruction and assessment as they observe works in progress, confer with students, become aware of needs, and provide instruction to meet those needs. Teachers need to be able to assess students' progress as they move through various stages of the writing process, as well as their published pieces. Figure 10.7 is a checklist that considers both the writing process and the product.

Rate yourself from 1 (lowest) to 10 (highest) on the following statements.

1. I read all of the assigned chapters each time.   _____
2. I wrote in my literature log each time.   _____
3. I participated in group discussions each time.   _____
4. I always had my book and my log with me.   _____
5. I responded thoughtfully to what I read.   _____
6. I was respectful and courteous during group meetings.   _____

Total score: _____

Figure 10.5: Self-Evaluation for Literature Response Groups

Patrick: avid reader, bright, likes adventure stories

Lynette: low-achieving reader, eager to read, likes humor

Ricardo: poor reader, unmotivated, likes fantasy

Angela: capable reader, very social, likes realistic fiction

Doreen: average reader, unmotivated, likes historical fiction

Patrick	Scorpions -(f)	Light in Attic	Volcano	Volcano (f)	Island Dolphins
Lynette	One-Eyed Cat (d)	Egg Tree	Egg Tree (f)	Wasting Game (d)	Time of Wonder
Ricardo	Hobbit (d)	Cat in Hat (f)	King Arthur (d)	Chitty Chitty Bang Bang →	
Angela	Baby Sitter series (f)	Baby Sitter →			
Doreen	Sarah, P+T →				

Interpretations and Suggestions:

Patrick is doing a fine job of selecting material suitable for his reading and interest levels. He reads different genres—realistic fiction, poetry, and nonfiction.

Lynette tries to pick books that sound funny, but isn't very successful. She finds her choices too hard to read or not funny. Suggest books of children's limericks, poetry by Jack Prelutsky, and Judy Blume's *Freckle Juice* and *The Pain and the Great One.*

Ricardo has trouble selecting books. He drops many because he finds them too difficult. Help him find books he can read successfully. Since he likes fantasy, suggest that he read picture books by Hans Christian Andersen and simplified versions of Kipling's *Just So Stories.*

Angela finishes one of the Baby Sitter series books and starts another. She needs to move into better quality literature. Recommend realistic fiction books by Beverly Cleary, Judy Blume, and Katherine Paterson.

Doreen's choice is appropriate, but she has been reading the same fairly short book all week, much longer than she needs to complete it. Is she wasting her time? Help her create a plan to finish this book and move on to others.

Figure 10.6: Analysis of Status-of-the-Class Report: Reading

Criteria	Dates					
Writing Process						
Uses references/resources well.						
Stays on task; completes work.						
Makes constructive revisions.						
Participates in conferences.						
Takes risks; uses different genres.						
Knows/applies editing skills.						
Writing Product						
Selects topics wisely.						
Organizes material logically.						
Focuses on topic; develops it well.						
Chooses words to create effects.						
Grabs reader's attention.						
Uses writing conventions well.						

Evaluation Scale
N = Not evident   D = Developing
E = Emerging   P = Proficient

Figure 10.7: Writing Checklist: Process and Product

Students should play an active role in evaluating their own writing. They can help set criteria, share their ideas during conferences, and select the pieces to be evaluated. If the teacher or school system overemphasizes evaluation and imposes criteria without regard for the students, the students may be less willing to take risks and make choices in their writing. When students are part of the evaluation process, however, they learn to set goals, feel motivated to write, and take responsibility for their work (Hill and Ruptic, 1994).

Your status-of-the-class reports from writing workshops can also be useful in evaluating ways that students use the writing process. Figure 10.8 shows a sample of this report in which the teacher has recorded information students gave her about their proposed daily activities. As you can see, each student moves through the process at a different rate, with some beginning a new topic search as soon as they complete a piece. An analysis of student progress follows the report.

Tony	TS	TS	D1	TS	D1
Nick	D2	D3	ED	PB	TS, D1
Theresa	D1	D1	D1	D2	D2
Cemil	D1	PB	D1	D2, ED	PB
Kim	D3	ED	PB	PB	TS

Interpretations and Suggestions:

Tony has spent three days on topic search and attempted two first drafts, apparently abandoning the first. Ask how he might find a topic that he can stick with, and be prepared to suggest personal experiences and ideas from his writing notebook.

Nick seems to be moving along fine, having written three drafts, edited, published, and found a new topic. Let him tell you what he would like to discuss about his work.

Theresa seems to be taking a long time on her drafts. Find out if she is stuck for ideas, not using time wisely, or is simply taking her time to think through her writing. Ask how you can help.

Cemil is moving very rapidly through the writing process, perhaps too rapidly to reflect on his writing. Look at what he has published and ask him if he might have expanded or revised his piece before editing it. Suggest that he confer with other students before completing his next piece.

Kim appears to have carefully completed a piece after three revisions, editing it, and spending two days publishing it. She is searching for a new topic now. Ask her if she needs any help.

Figure 10.8: Analysis of Status-of-the-Class Report: Writing

A trend toward large-scale holistic scoring of writing is occurring, with students being judged by rubrics on their writing ability. Often, students write in response to prompts and are evaluated by predetermined criteria. In our state, disappointing scores on these tests are causing teachers to use the writing process and to let students begin writing early in their school careers. Mary Martin, an eighth grade English teacher, acknowledged that teachers were helping students learn to write five-paragraph essays that would appear on these tests. The writing workshop, with its mini-lessons and extended time for writing, provides an excellent framework for enabling students to become writers.

Portfolios

A portfolio is a container which holds carefully selected, organized samples of student work. Although both teacher and student can place items in portfolios, the selection process belongs primarily to the student, who must thoughtfully evaluate best pieces to place there. You may need to conduct one or two mini-lessons on criteria for selecting materials so that students will know how to make wise choices. Students have access to their portfolios and may add or remove materials as they see fit through the year. They should date all items and be sure that they include work from each grading period so that they can see growth throughout the year. Portfolios are useful because they

- cause students to reflect on their work as they make selections.
- show progress over the course of a year.
- help students set new goals for themselves.
- inform parents of what their children can do.
- provide evidence to support achievement when test scores are questionable.
- empower special learners by valuing their work.

TEACHING TIP

When planning the types of containers to use for portfolios, consider the following:

a. closed-ended expandable folders available at discount stores.
b. twelve-inch pizza boxes covered with contact paper and containing folders of theme studies.
c. loose-leaf, three-ring binders with cover letter to explain contents and organization, table of contents, and dividers in front of different types of materials.

Students produce many materials during workshops that are suitable for inclusion in portfolios. Since one purpose of portfolios is to show students' growth as readers and writers, they should include not only published pieces, but also preceding drafts to show progress from the initial topic choice through revisions to the final product. Example 10.2 shows how Anna, a second grader in Pam Petty's class, moved from a list of descriptive words related to her topic, through a rough draft, to her final copy. Anna's portfolio includes a sample from all three stages.

I   If I   was a nerse

Arthtis,   Anna

aslkep

help

office

people

nerse

hospitl

anthis

medeson

work

pashent

well

Example 10.2   Page 1

If I Was a Nurse
Anthtis

If I were a nrlce anthtis I would work at a hospitl. I would put people to asleep. I would help people get well. I would love my pashents. The people I help get well will thank me. I thank them for coming. I would have an ofice. I would give the people who come medoson that would help them get well. Then I would go back to my ofice and work in there. My ofice would have a computer.

Example 10.2   Page 2

If I Was a Nurse Anne Anesthesist

If I were a nurse anethetist

I would work at a hospital.

I would put people to sleep.

I would help people get well.

I would love my patients.

The people I help get well will

thank me. I thank them for coming.

I would have an office.

I would give the poeple medicine

that would help them get well.

Then I would go back to my

office and work in there. My

office would have a computer

Example 10.2   Page 3

A portfolio is not simply a collection of student work over the year, but it reflects a rigorous selection process. Narrowing items to be included serves a dual purpose: it requires students to evaluate their work critically, and it keeps portfolios from becoming too unwieldy. Figure 10.9 lists some types of workshop materials that might be included in portfolios.

Samples of writing from different genres

Graphic organizers

Evidence of writing process from drafts to finished copy

List of books read, possibly with critiques

Responses to literature, including different genres

At least one "best piece" with reasons for choice

Entries from literature log or dialogue journal

Self-evaluations

Figure 10.9:   Workshop Materials to Include in a Portfolio

In terms of evaluation, portfolios are much more useful for observing learning patterns, detecting growth, and knowing what needs to be taught or retaught than for giving grades. Understandably, teachers would find it challenging to convert evidence from portfolios into percentages on report cards! If you want to assess portfolios, Linda Vavrus (1990) suggests setting standards related to your goals in advance. Then evaluate portfolios in terms of these standards or on growth within individual portfolios. You may apply rating scales similar to rubrics to the contents of the portfolios in order to arrive at a grade. However, if students know that you are going to grade their portfolios, they are likely to stop taking risks, include only polished pieces, and feel a loss of ownership. The true value of portfolios for evaluation lies in the evidence of student performance and reflection, not in their potential for yielding grade scores.

Because of the vast amount of information currently available about portfolio assessment, I can only scratch the surface here. You will find helpful guidelines and strategies for implementing portfolio assessment in books devoted entirely to this subject, some of which are listed below. Although you may prefer to prepare your own materials, many of these books include reproducible record keeping forms, checklists, and letters to parents explaining portfolios.

Batzle, J. (1992). *Portfolio assessment and evaluation.* Cypress, CA: Creative Teaching Press.

DeFina, A. A. (1992). *Portfolio assessment.* New York: Scholastic.

Farr, R, & Tone, B. (1994). *Portfolio performance assessment.* Fort Worth: Harcourt Brace.

Frank, M. (1994). *Using writing portfolios.* Nashville, TN: Incentive.

Glazer, S. M., & Brown, C. S. (1993). *Portfolios and beyond.* Norwood, MA: Christopher Gordon.

Hewitt, G. (1995). *A Portfolio Primer.* Portsmouth, NH: Heinemann.

Hill, B. C., & Ruptic, C. (1994). *Practical aspects of authentic assessment: Putting the pieces together.* Norwood, MA: Christopher Gordon.

Jasmine, J. (1992). *Portfolio assessment for your whole language classroom.* Huntington Beach, CA: Teacher Created Materials.

Jasmine, J. (1993). *Portfolios and other assessments.* Huntington Beach, CA: Teacher Created Materials.

Porter, C., & Cleland, J. (1995). *The portfolio as a learning strategy.* Portsmouth, NH: Heinemann.

Student Portfolios. (1993). Westhaven, CT: NEA Professional Library.

Tierney, R. J., Carter, M.A., & Desai, L. E. (1991). *Portfolio assessment in the reading-writing classroom.* Norwood, MA: Christopher Gordon.

Reporting Student Achievement

Once you have applied assessment techniques and evaluated results, then what? You will need to find effective ways of communicating findings to those who are interested.

Audiences for Reporting

The primary audiences for reporting, of course, are the students and the teacher. From the various types of authentic assessments presented in this chapter, the teacher finds out what students know and still need to learn, and the students see what they are learning and what else they need to know. Through conferences and dialogue journals, teachers know how to plan future instruction that will enable students to advance their knowledge.

Parents also want to know how well their children are doing. Some teachers invite parents to attend meetings early in the year in order to explain expectations, procedures, and assessment policies so that parents can understand the program. Often, teachers send letters home which introduce concepts, such as workshops and authentic assessment, that may be new to parents. During the year, parents may come to conferences where teachers show them portfolios of their children's work, or teachers may send portfolios home periodically for parents to review. The better informed parents are, the more likely they are to support your efforts.

Other audiences are also interested in student achievement. The principal wants to know how effectively you are teaching; the school board may look at standardized test scores; and legislators are interested in accountability, usually as revealed by test scores. To make sure that your students perform as well as possible for outside audiences, become familiar with test formats and curriculum expectations. If you know that onomatopoeia is on the fifth grade achievement test, present it in a mini-lesson and encourage children to use it in their writing. If you know students will have to write a descriptive paragraph in response to a prompt on a statewide writing test, be sure they have opportunities to do this during writing workshops. Although it would be nice if evaluation were just among you, the students, and their parents, the real world tells us that we must also consider skills valued by those in authority.

Giving Grades

In light of current trends toward authentic assessment, many teachers and school systems are using descriptive narrative reports or redesigning report cards so that the criteria on them reflect instructional goals. Nevertheless, many parents and school systems still expect to see either letter or percentage grades on report cards that are sent home regularly. Converting authentic assessment into grades isn't easy, so let's look at some ways to do it.

Authentic assessment can take many forms, as we have seen in this chapter. Begin by changing assessment results into numerical values or letter grades; average them; consider portfolios, written comments, and student self-evaluations; and assign grades. For instance, as part of your reading grade, look at the numbers you gave students during literature response groups (Figure 10.4). Convert these numbers into grades as follows:

Mostly 9s and 10s = A
Mostly 7s and 8s = B
Mostly 5s and 6s = C

Likewise, scores on rubrics become grades by giving A to the highest level(s), B to the next highest, and so forth. It takes time to consider several sources, especially when many are subjective, but the result will show a child's capabilities better than an average of test scores.

Teachers have experimented with a variety of approaches, and here are some strategies they have used for arriving at grades. Perhaps you can adapt some of these ideas for your own assessment plan. For writing, Linda Rief (1992) considers a variety of sources and gives a process grade based on attitude and effort, a content grade based on quality of writing, and a mechanics grade for legibility, spelling, punctuation, and usage. Nancie Atwell (1987) suggests a weighted scale with several writing criteria that have been emphasized during that grading period, such as content, clarity, focus, and risk-taking. Each criterion is assigned points (i.e., 10, 15, or 20) to total 100, so teachers can reach a percentage grade by adding the number of points each student earns.

Marian Allender (*Grading and Evaluation,* 1992) considers effort and improvement for the writing workshop grade, amount of time spent reading and quality of responses for the reading workshop grade, and evaluative conferences based on work completed and progress toward meeting goals. During conferences, she and the student agree on grades for both workshops, and she reaches a final letter grade by averaging the two.

Beverly Mackie told me she gets a writing grade by developing a five-point rubric for five writing skills. (For instance, a student could make from one [lowest] to five [highest] on the skill of beginning a sentence with a capital letter.) By adding the scores for each of the five skills and multiplying the total by four, Beverly gets a percentage grade for that part of her language assessment.

Using a "choose your own grade" method, students in Lorraine Cella's class contract to complete certain requirements to receive an A, B, or C (*Grading and Evaluation,* 1992). Students must write ten one-page entries about their reading in logs. A *C* grade consists simply of summaries of what they have read; a *B* grade requires them to connect the plot to their experiences; and an *A* grade asks students to make connections and comment on the author's style.

In designing your personal evaluation strategies, be sure to consider your goals, give students your expectations at the beginning of the grading period, use a variety of techniques, and involve students as you develop a plan. Remember, too, that you may want to modify evaluation procedures and criteria as you grow in your understanding of how students learn.

Summary

New directions in teaching and learning have led us into new forms of assessment. No longer is it enough to average test scores, but now teachers must consider observations, anecdotal records, conferences and interviews, checklists, response journals, and student self-evaluations. This change in assessment tools causes problems for teachers who are tied to traditional methods of reporting, so it is important to discover new ways to report student progress or find ways to convert results of new assessment techniques into traditional grading systems.

The wonder of authentic assessment is that it enables teachers to assess student progress in the context of purposeful, real-world activities. It involves students by causing them to think critically about their work and evaluate their own progress. Portfolios, with

their carefully selected student work samples, open up many possibilities for students, teachers, and parents to review what a student
is learning over the course of a year. Workshops challenge teachers
to use forms of assessment that match workshop goals and to find
effective ways of reporting student progress.

Reflections

1. What types of evaluation are required by my school district?
   How can I use workshops to prepare my students for meeting
   expectations set by those outside my classroom?

2. Which of the assessment instruments presented in this chapter might
   I want to use? What problems are there in converting them into
   the kinds of grades we are expected to give?

3. How would I evaluate myself on reading and writing? What
   criteria would I use? Am I a good model for my students?

4. What place does student self-evaluation have in my classroom?
   How can I help students thoughtfully critique their own work
   and set reasonable goals for themselves? How can I use their
   evaluations as part of my overall evaluation?

5. Are there other teachers in my school who see a need to re-
   vamp our report cards? Could we get together and consider
   ways of reporting that correspond more closely with workshop
   activities and holistic learning?

Bibliography

Atwell, N. (1987). *In the middle.* Portsmouth, NH: Heinemann.

Barclay, K., & Breheny, C. *Hey, look me over!* Assess, evaluate
   and conference with confidence. *Childhood Education, 70,*
   215–220.

Calkins, L. M. (1991). *Living.* Portsmouth, NH: Heinemann.

Clark, R. P. (1987). *Free to write.* Portsmouth, NH: Heinemann.

Cockrum, W. A., & Castillo, M. (1994). Whole language assessment and evaluation strategies. In Harp, B. (Ed.), *Assessment and evaluation.* Norwood, MA: Christopher-Gordon.

Downing, S. (1995). Teaching writing for today's demands. *Language Arts, 72* (3), 200–205.

Dye, J., & Hawk, J. (1994). Portfolios & writing conferences: The
   "REAL" world of reading. Presentation at Southeast Regional
   IRA, Birmingham, Alabama.

Farr, R., & Tone, B. (1994). *Portfolio performance assessment.*
   Fort Worth: Harcourt Brace.

Fiderer, A. (1993). *Teaching writing: A workshop approach.* New
   York: Scholastic.

Gahagan, H. S. (1994). Whole language assessment and evaluation: A special education perspective. In Harp, B. (Ed.), *Assessment and evaluation*. Norwood, MA: Christopher-Gordon.

Grading and evaluation in the reading/writing workshop. (1992). *English Journal, 81* (6), 80–82.

Graves, D. H. (1994). *A fresh look at writing*. Portsmouth, NH: Heinemann.

Hagerty, P. (1992). *Readers' workshop*. Richmond Hill, Ontario, Canada: Scholastic Canada.

Hansen, J. (1987). *When writers read*. Portsmouth, NH: Heinemann.

Harmon, G. (1994). Portfolios as tools for development: Teachers and students in collaboration in senior high English and writing classrooms. Presentation at Tennessee Council of Teachers of English, Nashville, TN.

Harp, B. (1994). Principles of assessment and evaluation in whole language classrooms. In Harp, B. (Ed.), *Assessment and evaluation*. Norwood, MA: Christopher-Gordon.

Hill, B. C., & Ruptic, C. (1994). *Practical aspects of authentic assessment*. Norwood, MA: Christopher-Gordon.

Hoff, L. (1994). From omnipotent teacher-in-charge to co-conspirator in the classroom: Developing lifelong readers and writers. *English Journal, 83* (6), 42–50.

Jackson, N. R., with Pillow, P. L. (1992). *The reading-writing workshop: Getting started*. New York: Scholastic.

King, D. (1994). Assessment and evaluation in bilingual and multicultural classrooms. In Harp, B. (Ed.), *Assessment and evaluation*. Norwood, MA: Christopher-Gordon.

Nathan, R., Temple, F., Juntunen, K., & Temple, C. (1989). *Classroom strategies that work*. Portsmouth, NH: Heinemann.

Parsons, L. (1990). *Response journals*. Portsmouth, NH: Heinemann.

Peterson, R., & Eeds, M. (1990). *Grand conversations*. New York: Scholastic.

Rief, L. (1992). *Seeking diversity*. Portsmouth, NH: Heinemann.

Siu-Runyan, Y. (1994). Holistic assessment in intermediate classes: Techniques for informing our teaching. In Harp, B. (Ed.), *Assessment and evaluation*. Norwood, MA: Christopher-Gordon.

Vavrus, L. (1990). Put portfolios to the test. *Instructor, 100* (1), 48–51.

Wilder, A. (1995). Young adult literature: A high school reading workshop. Presentation at National Council of Teachers of English, New Orleans.

Winograd, P. (1994). Reading assessment. *The Reading Teacher, 47* (5), 420–423.

Wolf, S. A., & Gearhart, M. (1994). Writing what you read: Narrative assessment as a learning event. *Language Arts, 71* (6), 425–444.

Wollman-Bonilla, J. (1991). *Response journals*. New York: Scholastic.

POSTSCRIPT

Amy, walking slowly down a deserted hall with Kevin late one afternoon: Well, it's almost over.

Kevin: And it's been an interesting year. I think our experiment with the cross-grade exchange went really well. I'd like to try that again.

Amy, laughing: Yes, I remember when Casey looked up at Joe with his big eyes and said, "You are so smart!"

Kevin: And Joe, poor guy, was one of my weakest students. What a boost for his self esteem.

Amy: And I remember how patiently Crystal helped Linda with the lead for her penguin story. First, she helped her find a clever idea; then she guided her into finding the right words to express her idea.

Kevin: Yes, Crystal's a really good kid. She has four younger brothers and sisters so she's used to working with young children.

Amy: Are you going to try workshops again next year?

Kevin: I've given that a lot of thought, and I already have some ideas about how I can get my workshops off to a better start next year. Since I understand a lot more about how they operate, I hope to avoid some pitfalls. I want to involve the students in setting expectations early in the year, and we'll begin with the reading workshop, then move into writing. How about you?

Amy: I plan to try them again next year, but I know I'll have to spend **plenty** of time building social skills and practicing procedures before I can expect my children to be good independent workers. I want to find more books this summer at conferences, and I need to think through my evaluation process before we start next fall.

Kevin: I wonder if more teachers will be interested in doing workshops next year. I wish we could get others interested so we could share ideas—and perhaps do something about that report card that we've used for ages.

Amy: Several teachers have been asking me about what I've been doing this year. They poke their heads in from time to time and are impressed with how much reading my children are doing.

Kevin: Come to think of it, Kelly and Ruby have been asking me some questions, too.

Amy: I'll bet we could encourage them to join us. Maybe we could get an in-service on workshops that would help us all.

Kevin: That might work really well—let's see what we can come up with over the summer. By the way, Amy, I hear there's a new restaurant in town and it's supposed to be pretty good. Would you like to have dinner with me there Saturday night?

Amy: Sounds like a great idea!

Kevin: Good, I'll make reservations for us and give you a call.

As Amy and Kevin talk, they are already planning ways to improve their workshops and recruit teachers to work with them. If you want your workshop to succeed, you may want to consider their ideas, along with some others that teachers recommend.

Go slowly. If you move too fast, your program may founder and your students may not understand what you are trying to do. Take small steps. For instance, begin with writing folders and move gradually into portfolios; let students work with partners before they work in groups; and spend more time on mini-lessons at the beginning until students understand procedures.

Take time for students to understand procedures. It's tempting to begin teaching reading and writing strategies and assume that students will catch on to procedures. This is usually not the case. Rehearse, role play, model, and demonstrate procedures until you are sure students understand them completely. Even then, you may need to reteach some procedures, because many students have never had opportunities to direct their own learning.

Be flexible and patient. If your workshop isn't developing as you anticipated, stand back and look at what you are doing. Are there changes you could make? Are you sure the students understand? Can someone else give you advice? Be willing to change if there are alternatives. Don't give up. One teacher told me it took her until March before her students did as she expected them to do.

Accept a nontraditional classroom. Children need to talk, move, and form groups in workshops. Your classroom can be organized and orderly, but not in the traditional sense. Learn to tolerate purposeful movement and talk, but don't let either become disruptive.

Learn from your children. Listen to your children during conferences and think about what they are telling you through their journals. Plan your teaching strategies based on their goals, their points of confusion, and their needs and interests. Let your role be that of responder and facilitator, rather than director.

Recruit other teachers. Let your classroom be an example that other teachers want to follow. Invite them to your room, share materials that inform them about workshops, show them what your students are doing, and offer to help them get started. If other teachers adopt workshop procedures, children will find it easier to move from one grade to the next because they already understand what to do. Teachers also find it helpful to have schoolwide support.

Get parent support. From the beginning of the year, communicate with parents about your expectations, your workshop program, and your evaluation procedures. Invite parents to a meeting in your class, send home letters, share portfolios, hold conferences, and ask them to volunteer in your classroom to make blank books or serve as librarians. At first parents may be upset because you aren't sending home worksheets and red penciling every error in their children's work. Without exception, however, teachers have told me that when parents understand what you are trying to do through workshops, they enthusiastically support the program.

Convince your principal. In order for your program to succeed, your principal must understand what you are doing and why. Discuss your plans and explain why you want to implement workshops. Share professional sources—journals, books, reviews of presentations—to support your arguments. Otherwise, different rules, materials, structure, and assessment tools are likely to confuse an administrator who values quiet classes and traditional tests. If you can convince the principal, you have a valuable ally.

Involve other school personnel. The librarian can help you by locating books for your class and checking them out to you in large quantities for extended periods of time. You can also consult the librarian for advice on new books to order and request that some multiple copies of books be available for literature response groups. You should also collaborate with teachers of special learners in order to provide integrated learning experiences and combine materials for portfolios.

Continue professional development. As you implement any new program, you uncover problems and raise questions. College courses, workshops, publications, and professional organizations can help supply answers. Join the International Reading Association and the National Council of Teachers of English and their state and local affiliates. With membership come publications to offer information and invitations to conferences, and at conferences you will meet others who share your interests.

Participate in networks for holistic teaching. Whether within your school or on a large scale, support groups exist to help you work through your ideas. Teachers Applying Whole Language (TAWL) has local chapters where teachers can share experiences and learn new strategies, and the Whole Language Umbrella Conference meets annually to address issues that interest whole language teachers. When I attended the NCTE Convention in Orlando in 1994, I heard teachers from Florida trying to organize a network of teachers committed to using workshops.

By adopting the workshop concept, you are creating an environment that challenges your students to experiment with language and discover its power. No longer will students sit immobilized at their desks with never-ending worksheets, for now they can eagerly anticipate the pleasure of shared reading and writing.

APPENDIX I

TRADE BOOKS CITED IN TEXT

Ackerman, Karen. (1988). *Song and Dance Man*. Knopf.

Anno, Mitsumasa. (1978). *Anno's Journey*. Philomel.

Babbitt, Natalie. (1975). *Tuck Everlasting*. Straus & Giroux.

Base, Graeme. (1989). *The Eleventh Hour*. Abrams.

Baylor, Byrd. (1986). *I'm in Charge of Celebrations*. Scribner's.

Brett, Jan. (1989). *The Mitten*. Putnam.

Fox, Paula. (1984). *One-Eyed Cat*. Bradbury.

Hahn, Mary D. (1988). *December Stillness*. Clarion.

London, Jack. (1985). *White Fang*. Puffin.

Lowry, Lois. (1993). *The Giver*. Houghton Mifflin.

Lowry, Lois. (1989). *Number the Stars*. Houghton Mifflin.

Mathis, Sharon Bell. (1986). *The Hundred Penny Box*. Puffin.

McKissack, Patricia. (1992). *The Dark-Thirty: Southern Tales of the Supernatural*. Knopf.

Myers, Walter Dean. (1988). *Scorpions*. Harper & Row.

Naylor, Phyllis. (1991). *Shiloh*. Atheneum.

Norris, Louanne. (1989). *An Oak Tree Dies and a Journey Begins*. Houghton Mifflin.

O'Brien, Robert. (1974). *Z for Zachariah*. Atheneum.

Paterson, Katherine. (1977). *Bridge to Terabithia*. Crowell.

Paulsen, Gary. (1987). *Hatchet*. Bradbury.

Reiss, Johanna. (1972). *The Upstairs Room*. Crowell.

Ringgold, Faith. (1991). *Tar Beach*. Crown.

Rylant, Cynthia. (1982). *When I Was Young in the Mountains*. Dutton.

Sauer, Julia. (1986). *Fog Magic*. Troll Associates: Puffin.

Scieszka, Jon. (1989). *The True Story of the 3 Little Pigs!* Viking.

Spinelli, Jerry. (1990). *Maniac Magee*. Scholastic.

Taylor, Mildred. (1976). *Roll of Thunder, Hear My Cry*. Dial.

Taylor, Theodore. (1969). *The Cay*. Doubleday.

Van Allsburg, Chris. (1988). *Two Bad Ants*. Houghton Mifflin.

Voight, Cynthia. (1982). *Dicey's Song*. Atheneum.

White, T. H. (1987). *The Once and Future King*. Putnam.

Young, Ed. (1989). *Lon Po Po: A Red Riding Hood Tale from China*. Philomel.

MAGAZINES REGULARLY OR EXCLUSIVELY PUBLISHING STUDENTS' WORK

The Acorn. (grades K–12) 1530 Seventh Street, Rock Island, IL 61201. Phone: 309-788-3980.

Child Life. (ages 7–9) Children's Better Health Institute, P.O. Box 567, Indianapolis, IN 46206. Phone: 317-636-8881. FAX: 317-637-0126.

Creative Kids. (ages 8–14) Prufrock Press, P.O. Box 8813, Waco, TX 76714-8813. Phone: 800-998-2208. FAX: 817-772-4146.

Creative with Words Publications. (family) P.O. Box 223226, Carmel, CA 93922.

Kids Today Mini-Magazine. (ages 7–11) Today Publishing, 2724 College Park Ropad, Allison Park, PA 15101. Phone: 412-486-1564.

Merlyn's Pen: The National Magazine of Student Writing, Grades 7–10. (grades 7–10) Merlyn's Pen, Inc., 98 Main Street, P.O. Box 1058, East Greenwich, RI 02818. Phone: 401-885-5175 or 800-247-2027. FAX: 401-885-5222.

Skipping Stones: A Multicultural Children's Quarterly. (ages 7–14) P.O. Box 8939, Eugene, OR 97403. Phone: 503-342-4956.

The Stone Soup: The Magazine by Children. (ages 6–13) Children's Art Foundation, P.O. Box 83, Santa Cruz, CA 95063. Phone: 408-426-5557 or 800-447-4569. FAX: 408-426-1161.

Word Dance. (grades K–8) 435R Hartford Turnpike, Vernon, CT 06066. Phone: 203-870-8614.

Young Voices. (all ages) P.O. Box 2321, Olympia, WA 98507. Phone: 206-357-4683.

A

Ackerman, Karen, 93
Adjectives, 147
Affective environment of classroom, 182–183
Allender, Marian, 223
Anderson, Bruce, 38
Anderson, Richard, 5
Anecdotal records, 205
Angelotti, Sara, 42, 48
Anno's Journey (Anno), 48
Assessment, 202–204
Atwell, Nancie, xv, 5, 20, 41, 46, 64, 93, 127, 135, 141, 170, 177, 183, 206, 222
Authentic assessment, 202, 222
Author/illustrator study, 72
Author's chair, 127, 128
Avery, Carol, xvi, 127
Ayers, Nivia, 46

B

Barclay, K., 202
Basal readers, 39
Base, Graeme, 26
Baylor, Byrd, 93
Becoming a Nation of Readers (Anderson et al.), 5, 40
Big books, 63
Books, selecting and acquiring, 193–196
Breheny, C., 202
Brett, Jan, 48
Bridge to Terabithia (Paterson), 53
Bromley, Karen, 95

C

Calkins, Lucy, xvi, 21, 95, 98, 101, 130, 135, 170, 182
Cambourne, Brian, 4, 5
Carle, Eric, 134
Cathedral (Macauley), 194
Cause and effect, 78
Cay, The (Taylor), 37
Cella, Lorraine, 223
Characterization, 68
Checklists, 206–207
Cherry, Lynne, 194
Child-centered learning, 4–5
Children's Book Council, The, 185
Choice, students' freedom of, 3, 4–5, 116, 117
Chomsky, Carol, 6
Class population, and flexibility in workshops, 25–26
Classroom environment, 182–185
  affective environment, 182–183
  physical environment, 183–185
Classroom, organizing, 186–191
  correlation with the curriculum, 190–191
  expectations for students, 187–190
  interclass organizational patterns, 191
  realities of scheduling, 186–187
Cohen, D. A., 6

About the Author

Elinor Parry Ross is the author of 12 books and over 60 articles in such publications as *Phi Delta Kappan, The Reading Teacher, Language Arts,* and *Journal of Reading.* Dr. Ross received her Ed.D. in Curriculum and Instruction at Tennessee Technological University, Cookeville, Tennessee, she has also taught grades 1, 2, and 3.

Her research interests includes the teaching of thinking skills through literature, the language experience approach, and measuring attitudes toward reading. She is actively involved in presentations and workshops both in the United States and abroad.